Small Town Cops

Donald Gill

ISBN: 978-0-9961651-0-5

Dedication

I dedicate this book to my French Gal, Vicky my wife. After being together for 44 years, 36 years of them as a cop's wife, and hanging in there, you have proven that you are tougher and more forgiving than I. Thank you for your patience, love, and support.

To Steve Pigman, my best friend, thank you for having the guts to stand with me when others wouldn't, and for the wisdom to refuse me when you knew I was wrong or screwing up. Thank you for keeping me safe as I "did my thing". Most of all, thank you for being an "Amicus certus in re incerta", a faithful friend in uncertain times. This book is for you.

I dedicate this book to all those men in Sumner who taught me how to get along with difficult people, all the while building a position of respect that would allow me to go home after shift. A special thanks to all of you.

To the men in my family who followed me in this profession, I dedicate this book to all of you. Thank you for showing me that I made a positive influence in your life. I know you are a cop for all the right reasons.

I dedicate this book to my kids. You never hid the fact that your father was a policeman. I recall many times on Christmas day when you would patiently wait for me to get off shift, even if it were the afternoon, so we could open gifts together as a family. That is a tough call for little kids, but you two made the call and waited. You are grown and gone now and have become successful, responsible citizens and parents. Your mother and I are very proud of you.

Thank you!

Contents

Preface

I wrote this book to let people know that there is more going on behind the scenes than what Hollywood and the media portray or want you to believe about cops. Many nights, especially after a tough one, I would come home and slip quietly into my kids' rooms and look for covers to rise and fall, knowing that they were okay in spite of what I just experienced out there in the dark.

What people normally see and hear about cops are those big town cops. They are the ones featured in the newspapers, in televisions, and in the movies. Yet there is a big sector of cops who live in small towns. This is what I want the readers to see. I want them to know what really happens in small towns across America. I want them to see the real people behind these cop uniforms -- people who have feelings, fathers and mothers who have spouses and children, and people who have taken a big risk to save others.

This book is based on real life stories of small town cops and is therefore not fictional. Though some names and locations have been changed, the stories are still about real people that happened in actual places. The names of suspects that I and others arrested have been changed, as have most of the cop's names. Conversations and words from actual people have been reconstructed for the most part, but have retained its original message.

I wrote this book to shed a positive light of all first responders. Besides police, there are fire departments, dispatchers, and medical people who are first to arrive, not to mention those professionals who await us all in the emergency rooms across America. Thank you to all of you.

The main focus of this book is small town cops – cops who do work alone and learn that they must build relationships with people in their communities to simply survive, and in most cases just get a difficult job done. To those who have accomplished this challenging task, hats off to you.

Towards the end of writing this book, I returned to Sumner, the small town where I started as a cop. I simply walked the Main Street to see what still remains of that place – that same place where I walked wearing a police uniform.

I remember that there were eight bars that I did bar checks in during that time. Now there is but one and it does not even have the same name. The others have been turned into beautiful little family-owned gift shops, including a bar called Club Tavern that had been shut down years earlier.

The alleys had been turned into little areas where people could sit and visit or enjoy a coffee with a friend. I did find one little tavern that still had the same name in the eastern end of Sumner, The Waterhole Pub. I went in and introduced myself and the barkeep recognized my name and told me that "Marge" was still alive and at the age of 91 was quick witted and sharp as a tack. Marge is not her real name but I left a card hoping she might call. I want to thank her for keeping an eye on me. The barkeep called the owner and we had a brief conversation about the book. I asked permission to use the name of the bar and she had no problem with that. Thank you for allowing me to use the real name of your bar in my story.

I made it clear in this book that I disliked the DEA. This was true in the past when I worked for them and didn't care for them. It wasn't the agents I had problems with but their administration. These feelings have changed though over these last years. I realize that agents are just pawns caught in government politics since DEA is a member of the federal government.

Lastly, I want to acknowledge my three favorite police chiefs of those I have worked for during my career. First is the chief who hired me in Sumner, second is my last and current chief at Puyallup, and third is the chief who had the guts to promote me.

To the Puyallup Police Department, I am very proud of you. You are men and women who are very dedicated to the profession and the people you serve.

"Be careful out there."

D. L. Gill, Sergeant, retired, PPD/SIU

Prologue

Never Run Out of Apples

I was 16 and rummaging around my father's carpenter's shop when I came across an old wooden chest. I noticed that the lock had been removed. Curiosity took over and I quickly dragged it out from where it had been hidden for years. I opened it and recognized that the tools in it were those of my grandfather who died when I was four. It was what I found next that grabbed my soul. I lifted the top tray of the tool-laden shelf and there I saw something I immediately recognized: a gun belt complete with an old fashioned leather holster; Smith and Wesson 38 caliber revolver that broke down in the middle; a hand cuff case with handcuffs properly stored; and a tell-tale suicide strap that policemen of years gone by wore as part of their uniform. I dug deeper and found a lead-filled leather sap, an item of the old police times; a wrist chain used to get a fighting prisoner under control; and a soft felt bag. I hurriedly opened the bag and found a badge that had the words "Sumner Police" stamped on it. I was shocked. This is family information that I had no knowledge of and I wanted answers.

When I found my father I asked him directly "Was grandpa a policeman?" He hesitated and said, "Back in the old days when a mayor got elected he pretty much appointed his friends to positions in the city, and your grandfather was a policeman for a number of years for as long as the mayor was mayor."

He didn't want to talk much about it so I was full of questions that never got answered. I took the items I found and hid them. Someday they would be mine. I didn't know then that these would become some of the most valued treasures I would ever own.

I was busy with my life and had found a nice French girl with gorgeous legs at the bulb farm where I worked the summers. Dating was top of the list. Sports and high school antics were controlling my life, and like all teenagers life was blooming. I never got traditionally arrested but was summoned to the police chief's office on two separate occasions. The first one was for throwing snowballs at passing cars during class intermissions. I couldn't help myself, it was too much fun. Unfortunately, someone turned me in. The second time was more complicated. During home-coming week it was tradition to attack the school courtyard. Well, we did things right and all was going according to plan until some skinny armed sophomore failed to clear the roof of the school with a rhubarb root ball and it flew through a class room window setting off a silent alarm. We worked feverishly turning ill-gotten chickens loose in the school and we had managed to locate a farmer's pig and released it to roam the halls. Someone sprayed the name of a disliked teacher to the sides of the pig. We were a creative class but stupid. Soon the police arrived and my best friend and

I made a clean get away until we realized that most of the stuff that we had released into the school had been transported there via his van that was parked abandoned at the crime scene. When he and I figured that out, we knew our scheme would be opened and all that participated would be corralled and then we would be held accountable. As my friend left into the dark to face the police he told me to go home and that we would talk the next day. I practically low crawled all the way home and slipped into my bedroom unnoticed, until there was a knock at my door and mother came in.

"Where is my car?" she asked.

"Crap, I forgot about that, it's at my friend's house, forgot it there" was all I could come up with.

I got dressed and low crawled to my buddy's house to retrieve the car. I thought I was about to make yet another get away when I was cornered by my best friend's father wanting to know where his son was at. I came clean and told him we had a little run in with the local police.

"I suppose I'll be getting a call soon," he said as he turned and walked back to his house.

The next morning I found my friend and he said they got a lot of them and all the names including mine had been turned over to the police. All of us were to report to the chief's office at the end of the school day. My friend and I knew that we both had parents who owned businesses in town so we thought that they would probably be easy on us. But then that would mean that they would have to be easy on the remainder of the kids who were involved. It worked, but back in those days you were held accountable, something that seems to have no meaning anymore in our society today -- Parents were accountable to their kids, kids were accountable to their parents, media were accountable to facts and truth, and police were accountable to the people they serve.

We spent the remainder of the year every weekend cutting, chopping, stacking wood into cords that we sold until all people and the school we owed were paid back in full for our night of terrorism. We surely learned a valuable lesson. The tradition of "decorating" the courtyard of the high school on home-coming week came to an end.

Following my first year of college, the economy turned on its head and waiting in long lines for gas came to be the norm. Money dried up. I had two jobs, went to school, got married to the French girl, and then the kids came. Then I got a break and got a job working in a saw mill and had a steady income and attended college at night. Then unions showed up at work and there was a push to unionize. The company laid everyone off and I was back to life guarding, security work, and part time college. Life was chipping away at us.

I had been taking civil service exams and did well, but when veterans got an extra 10 point for serving in the Vietnam War my name slid off the top 10 list and after 11 attempts I needed to make drastic change if police work would be my calling. We joined the army and in 1975 I was a military policeman patrolling the streets of a little fort in Alaska, Fort Greely. My French girl gave me a son while I was in Alaska and soon she and the kids arrived for a different life that had a constant paycheck. We were grateful.

Fort Greely was a middle of nowhere place in the middle of Alaska and visiting infantry troops from the 82nd Airborne and 101st Airborne would visit our little post in the winter and spend it doing "Jack Frost" exercises. When they finished they would descend on our little village and all hell would break loose.

I remember them having heavy socks filled with marbles that were tied off, making a formable weapon to use against us, swinging them wildly above their head as they moved towards us. I learned how to be a street fighter, always outnumbered and always at night in the snow. Coming home with a fat lip, black eye, cuts, and scrapes was the norm.

In the winter of 1978 I sent my family home knowing that I would follow soon. Then I got an interesting letter in the mail. It was from the chief of police in Sumner Washington.

"I hear you are getting out soon, we have an opening and hope you will test, enclosed is an application, fill it out and we will wait till you get here then test."

This was the same chief that had chewed my sorry high school ass out when I was a teenager and he was now waiting for me to come home.

As soon as I landed in Seattle, I proceeded to Sumner and took the test. I always did well. Now I was armed with veteran's points that would surly get me in the top, and hopefully land a job. Unfortunately, it was a much different outcome. I finished 11th, the worse I ever did but I saw nothing of veteran's points added to my score. I visited the chief to ask why and he simply said, "We quit that program two years ago. All police departments no longer give veteran's preference."

It was crushing, not to mention that the struggles of income were back. I began working for a rental business then got a job with a construction company wiring new homes. And just when I was discussing with my brother about using my veteran benefits to start our own company, I was offered a job at the Sumner Police Department by the Chief of Police himself. It was February 1979 and the starting pay would be $1108/month. Thus was the beginning of my saga as a policeman.

My French gal and I live in a house next to the sea and little worries me now. I once went outside and five deer stood in my yard looking at me, I knew what they wanted, apples. They have become the usual beggars because they know I give them apples when they show up. Sometimes I do worry, and make sure I don't run out of apples.

I began writing this book because I thought it would help ease the anger I had developed following my forced retirement. It's not easy being hunkered down in the back of a van with body armor on and assault rifle ready to go into battle one day, and wearing a bath robe and watching sit-coms the next. I know what it is like going from "cock of the walk to raggedy man," a line used in the movie Thunder Dome.

Introduction

La Dolce Vita

I began writing this book because I thought it would help ease the anger I had developed following my forced retirement. It's not easy being hunkered down in the back of a van with body armor on and assault rifle ready to go into battle one day, and wearing a bath robe and watching sit-coms the next. I know what it is like going from "cock of the walk to raggedy man," a line used in the movie Thunder Dome.

In the middle of one of our lengthy and dangerous store front operations in which we actually set up a chop/hawk shop and bought stolen goods to include cars, the Chief told me that I and my unit were running at "red line," "pushing hard," but we always had. Pig and I had often questioned ourselves as to why we did this, why we chose the big case, difficult cases that came with the dangers of such investigations. We could have done as many others did and still do, just handle small easy to work cases and not lose any sleep over them. Neither of us could figure it out, but we just continued. Even as street cops we both were always up to our waist in alligators and thought it was perfectly normal.

It was in August 6, 2014 when I got an e-mail from my editor, Lisa Maki. Without ever being asked why we did what we did she answered it for us by saying, "I believe God has planted a sense of purpose in men's hearts and it's up to them to discover it. Some men have died trying to figure out their purpose; others have given up even before they could even get there. Few men find their purpose in their jobs. They go about their daily duties, dragging their feet to work. You, on the other hand, found your true purpose in your work, and that lives on even after your retirement. There is surely someone up there looking out for you and smiling and saying: I GOT YOUR BACK. YOU ARE GETTING IT. Your book will be your legacy that will live in the hearts and minds of its readers."

When I shared this writing with Pig he simply said "explains a lot." Then I asked Pig why he was still doing it, police work. Again a simple answer, "I'm afraid to quit." Pig and I had completely different upbringings. His' was in an urban setting in Florida and some of his movements had to be calculated and well thought out. He told me that white kids got out of school 15 minutes early to get home and off the street before the black kids got out of school. Pig made it clear that there would be a big price to pay if you got caught out and about by black kids. On the other hand, I came from a rural setting, thus a free range kid, and spent much of my spare time hunting and fishing; fun stuff. As a young boy I learned how to move silently through the forest stalking whatever prey I was after. An odd thing happened the day I became a cop, I never hunted a four legged animal again. It's not that humans are smarter, some clearly are not but I rather liked the idea of the season. The season was open 24 hours a day, 7 days a week, and lasted 365 days per year, with no bag limits.

As you read this book, you will see that I'm a little rough on college educated folks. Some realize an education doesn't necessarily make them a smarter, better person but that it's just a great step in the process. But many believe it's a rite of passage and if you do not have the degree you may not pass. These same people make sure you know who they are and expect complete submission. To those folks I like to point out that there were two groups of people trying to be the first to fly. One group of people was all college educated, the other group led by the Wright brothers, not one had a college degree. We all know how that turned out.

Men don't follow titles, they follow leaders and their beliefs, and leaders inspire others by their beliefs. I was always fortunate with the people I had around me, especially the last 10 years of my career.

Pig and I still get together although not as often as we had following my retirement, but we stay in touch and continue to remember stories of our early cop days and I continue to take notes and write. The stuff that happened in Sumner simply can't be made up, the village was as unique as some of the people that lived there, and luckily I was one, having been born and raised there.

Writing this book has erased my anger and I have been able to grasp my ending as the only way I was going to go out, suddenly. Writing this book has allowed me to retire satisfied and fulfilled. I'm now ready for "La Dolce Vita."

Endings & Beginnings

When one reaches the latter part of his life, the journey back to yesteryears can be a painful and rewarding process at the same time. It can be painful to look back when the memories are bad, which is not the case with me; or if you were not ready to give it up when it ended, which is the case with me. It can be rewarding when you now see how every piece of the puzzle connects together, something you will never be able to tell while it is happening.

This is where everything ended, and started, in my career as a cop.

Join me as I revisit my past.

On the long drive home I began to think of the last 36 years and how I had lived them in a police uniform or playing the role of a dirt bag as an undercover officer. The good times, sad times, violent times, and the people I had met — those I had done battle with, those I had saved and those whose lives I have changed. I had an unlimited list of stories, most involving Pig and I coming up with clever ways to fix, deter, arrest, and save people. Pig and I had more than once mentioned that we should keep track of these stories and put them into a book before age stole the memories, never to be shared with anyone. How many times after doing a job did we say "You just can't make this shit up" and "I can't believe they pay me to do this?" I didn't want to regret and say to myself someday "I wish" or "I could have, would have, should have done it," wrote that book.

Chapter 1

Beginning of the End

I noticed a drip of sweat land on the trigger housing of my assault rifle. Something is wrong with me, I thought. I felt claustrophobic in my own body. I held out my leather gloved trigger finger hand, trying to keep it concealed from the other four cops in the van. I am crouched to a knee, waiting to erupt in another police-initiated violent act that would bring down a car thief, and trafficking in stolen vehicles.

Shaking! Shaking like a man suffering from hypothermia. Another drop of sweat strikes the trigger housing.

"Get yourself under control, figure out what was going on later, and stay focused," I quietly commanded myself. My head was pounding and I could see my once stellar vision beginning to blur. What is wrong with me? Keep yourself together Gill, got a job to do and I'm the boss! I nervously checked and rechecked the safety on my rifle. It's safe, leave it alone I thought, and focus!

In my right ear was an ear speaker. My best friend Pig was talking, giving me updates. Pig's voice seemed to calm me a bit, he had been my angel looking over me for years as I did the undercover work by buying or selling, God knows what, to the hundreds of dealers, thieves, and tweakers that bought my line of bullshit. I flat refused to do a deal without Pig being my operator, but that was in the past.

He was my eyes to the action in the parking lot near the Tacoma Mall, near "the tree" as we called it. We had done many deals from our careers in the area – dope, cars, guns – anything that was illegal we had done right here in this spot. In my left ear I could hear the faint voices of UCs, undercover cops who are young, smart, and tough! They are fast on the feet where bullshit is fluently spoken. They usually tell funny jokes to each other or talk about crap going on in their lives. I did that too in my years working under cover. I found out, as they did, that acting normal prior to doing something extremely dangerous had a calming effect.

I glanced out the darkly tinted windows of the van and could see the UCs bullshitting in their undercover truck. There were four open parking spaces from our van, good spot I thought, another example of Pig's OCD planning. The position would almost guarantee that the suspect would park the stolen truck between us and the UCs, we'd be on him quick, and the shock of our sudden appearance would freeze him long enough for a physical take down and not give him time to reach any weapons he may have concealed.

The UCs announced the target was arriving, driving a stolen 2009 Ford Pickup that had just recently been given an extreme make over, complete with what would appear to be valid title. It was all a lie! The truck was stolen by some meth head tweaker, sold to Ricky, and prepared by other tweakers with new paint and vehicle identification numbers. The vehicles were then given stolen titles, forged by a source that only Ricky knew of within the State of Washington Department of Licensing. We want Ricky and his source to the titles. Another drop of sweat lands, this time on the magazine containing 20 rounds of 223 ammunitions.

Hot damn, dumbass parked right next to us! Game on!

I felt like I was in a compactor slowing, crushing, slowly making it tough to breathe, struggling to pay attention, struggling not to show it. A tap on my left shoulder by Rob told me I wasn't doing a good job in concealing it.

I met Rob 16 years earlier when I was his field training officer. I noticed then that this kid had talent. After the first year of his career I decided to take him with me once I take over and get promoted. I wanted to surround myself with the best people I could find.

Rob mouthed the words "you okay?" Rob had dark piercing eyes that made entry into my head. I growled back, "I'm fine!"

Pig's voice calmly said over the radio that Ricky was arriving in a different vehicle, a grey SUV. This was the first time he ever showed up for a deal. Usually he sent a tweaker that he had met off sight of his chop shop, and paid him to drive the stolen vehicle to the location where it would be sold. Ricky would watch the deal from a distance and then follow the tweaker to a remote spot, collect the money, and pay the drug addict enough to get re-upped with whatever his or her drug of choice happened to be.

I wanted to look but soon Pig put out the description: tall Hispanic male, well dressed and groomed. My thoughts of the pending assault soon disappeared as I wiped another drop of sweat off the trigger house of my Bushmaster rifle.

"What the hell is going on?" I thought. "Am I even going to be able to open the door of this minivan Trojan horse to allow the take down team out to engage the two suspects and keep them from turning on the undercovers once they realize this is a police bust and they're totally screwed?"

Breathe dumbass; just breathe, but the vision, all a blur. I checked the safety again.

As I listened to the speaker in my left ear I could make out the muffled voices of introductions. "So far so good," I thought.

A quick glance over my right shoulder showed three other cops. Young, sharp, all SWAT team members who have proven themselves many times. I had picked wisely! We were all dressed alike in jeans, heavy boots, and long sleeve black shirts with **POLICE** boldly written on each arm sleeve and covered in body armor with various police patches and badges. All of us had low slung semi-automatic pistols strapped to our thighs.

My boots were Harley Davidson, square-toed with bright large metal buckles. I wore them always! My armor differed slightly also, I bore the weight of chevrons. Their weight seemed ten-fold at this moment!

They did not know me as well as Rob did, he knew something was wrong and he had seen it but he kept quiet. Silence is golden I had told him a hundred times, silence is golden right now!

Pig, calm as always, said he doesn't think the deal is going as good as it appeared. He had better communications listening to the undercovers and there appeared to be a problem with trust. Ricky was a clever bastard and smarter than most. He suspected something and was turning the conversation away from the stolen truck to more questions to the undercovers' authenticity. The UC's were about to be tested; earn their money so to speak. This is where everybody (cops, bad guys, prosecutors, judges, your boss, your family, your friends) figures out if you are a good undercover cop – if you are in fact the best liar.

Ricky wasn't buying their line of bullshit! Pig's voice was a bit sharper than usual. Pig then began a conversation with perimeter units concealed in undercover vehicles peppering the area.

The subject of the conversation was basically this: if the deal doesn't go, do we want to take Ricky here, or let him walk to wait another day to go to prison? "Good question Pig," I thought.

Soon the decision was made by Randy, a task force operator and case agent on this operation. If the deal doesn't go, let Ricky walk.

Randy announced that surveillance units would follow the stolen truck from the area and then quickly stop the truck using a blocking method. Detectives would arrest the driver immediately to keep him from notifying Ricky by phone that the cops were onto him. It would buy us precious time to hunt for Ricky and only if Randy decided he had enough evidence to convict Ricky.

For once in my life I secretly wanted, needed Ricky to turn and walk so I'd be off the hook and I could figure out what the hell is wrong with me and more importantly, save my reputation. To fail in this arena would send a cloak over me. Walk Ricky, walk.

Pig was back on the radio, they're still talking, UCs working it, let it soak and just be ready. Pig's voice was calming but I was gripped in terror, I was falling apart and felt completely out of control. My mind raced! I was beginning to pant like a dog trying to cool off from a run on a hot day in some field. Not good!

I reached the mini van's sliding door handle with my left hand and positioned my thumb carefully over the button I would need to push to unlatch the door. This would allow me to whip it open and release all hell on Ricky and his drug fueled pawn that was showing signs of tweaking.

I noticed the shake of my hand, as I had moved it, and now tightly gripping the door handle, concealing my shakes. I glanced at Rob who was staring directly into my eyes. He had been watching my every move and I knew he was concerned. My head pounded with pain!

Come on Ricky, man up, take the money and run or just get the hell outta here! Seconds seemed like minutes. Glancing at my rifle I noticed three more drops of sweat on it.

Sometimes silence is deafening, nothing coming through my ear mics either. Oddly quiet. "What's going on?" I thought to myself. I didn't want to butt in right now, didn't want to be "one of those type supervisors" but I had an undying need to know what was happening. Come on Pig, talk to me! I reached for my radio mic, can't take this silence, hiding in the dark with no sight of the theater before me.

I pressed the talk button on the mic and said "sam5 to 246". I was Sam 5, meaning sergeant #5 and Pig's badge number was 246. We used our badge numbers to identify ourselves on the radio. Prior to my promotion I was 244, a good number!

Pig didn't answer, again, odd. The mic in my ear calmly awoke, "stand by Sam 5". Ok, I thought, he's watching something intently, let him do his job. He is probably the best I've worked with in this profession.

My head was pounding with pain, and I was sweating, shaking, and panting like a dog! Damn it! Hang in there, got to get through this.

Suddenly the mic in my right ear exploded with chatter from Pig and the surveillance units, Ricky had turned and walked, no money exchanged! As planned, two surveillance units broke off and followed Ricky as he quickly left the lot.

I threw the rifle strap off my shoulders as I lunged between the two bucket front seats, sliding my rifle muzzle down in the passenger floor. I wiggled my way into the driver's seat. "Hang on guys," I shouted. "No deal, we are moving, stay ready." Ricky walked and we are getting this stolen truck back.

Everyone knew the drill: stop the truck and do not get into a pursuit doing it. By now the tweaker driving the truck had backed out of the parking spot next to us. There was a controlled rush by detectives to try to box him in on whatever road he decided to leave the lot on. It was our job to box him in, light up our emergency equipment, and slowly bring him to a stop. No one gets hurt!

As I slipped the shifter selector into drive, I grabbed a small black cloth from between the seats and covered my exposed body armor, not quite ready to reveal myself or the presence of the police.

I maneuvered into position near the rear of the stolen truck as the driver carefully drove through the parking lot and turned left onto Tacoma Mall Boulevard.

Randy had made a quick swing behind an electronic box store and was already on Tacoma Mall Boulevard. He had just passed by the stolen truck as it pulled in behind him. I slid my van slowly up next to the stolen vehicle and quickly glanced over at the driver. He was a young, shaggy looking guy. He had stringy, greasy long hair. Typical, I thought. The radio was barking with information as other units pulled in line behind us as we still waited for the red light to turn green. This part of Randy's case would soon be history.

Lights green, I announced over the radio, "let's get him stopped before we get to 38th."

Checking my mirrors I could see unmarked police cars. To the average citizen that's all they saw, just regular everyday cars that everyday folks drive. Nothing stood out, all appeared normal. A surprise awaited the citizens around us.

"Ok, light him up," came over the radio and suddenly nothing seemed normal. Even my mini-van had hidden lights. Everything slowed down outside, everything sped up faster inside. I shouted at Rob, "Pop the door bud, get him! Directly in front of you when you open the door! Go!"

I bailed out of the front seat, grabbing my rifle as I went. Cops in plain clothes were everywhere. Rob and his small group of bad guy greeters got busy dragging the meth maggot from the seat of the stolen truck yelling "stop resisting, stop resisting" which I found a bit humorous. Kid didn't have a chance and was already screaming, "I didn't know it was stolen." We hadn't even had time to read him his rights and he was giving up Ricky. He knew what was about to happen to him; clearly he had been through this routine before.

The pounding in my head seemed to back off. My crushing feeling had also let up! "Adrenaline, can't we put that into pill form?" I thought. It will be short-lived, I reminded myself; something was wrong.

Randy quickly announced that he had all he needed. Find Ricky, arrest him, and seal down his house for a search warrant.

I took a moment to take in the sight before me – cops running around taking care of their assignments, citizens in cars slowly passing by, windows down, mouths open but not saying a word. I turned slowly around and realized that we had done this traffic stop directly in front of the windows of a popular sports bar restaurant. It looked like everyone in the restaurant had rushed to the windows to watch the unannounced dinner show!

I tapped Pig, "hey bud, check this out" I whispered. He turned and looked at the patrons in the restaurant. I asked him "have you ever watched Meer Kat Manor?"

"Couple of times, why, oh I get it," he replied.

They looked like a scene out of Meer Kat Manor, frozen, wide eyed and all wondering "what the fuck just happened?"

We have a job to do. We are not done, actually just beginning. Time to move guys, let's get going! A marked Tacoma Police Unit had arrived and were transporting the tweaker to county jail and impounding the confirmed stolen truck to an evidence lot. Detectives were dispersing to their assigned locations.

The two detectives following Ricky stated that they couldn't keep up with him and lost him near Fife, a small freeway town. As a high school kid growing up, I and my classmates called kids from Fife cabbage heads, because they used to grow lots of cabbage out there. It's a high school thing.

Ricky knew we were onto him and the game of cat and mouse began. He couldn't go home because we would be waiting, and he knew it. What he didn't know was that we had placed an electronic tracking device on his SUV weeks earlier and he could not hide from us. It was a classic case, you can run but you cannot hide, and he damn well knew it. The problem with that is how he wanted to end this: fight, run, or just give up. It was a dangerous scenario for the police and a dangerous spot for Ricky, especially if he wanted to fight.

A task force detective announced over the radio that Ricky's vehicle was hiding in a group of warehouses just North of Puyallup. Puyallup was my home department and I have sworn years ago to protect and serve the citizens there. How befitting that Ricky came back to me, in my backyard. I know that area like the back of my hand and so does Pig and Rob. Within minutes detectives had raced to the area and slowly unmarked cars without headlights weaved through the warehouses like sharks circling a prey. "Where are you at Ricky? Where are you?" I said to myself.

The radio came to life, "got him" Pig said. Ricky is directly north of the Puyallup Recreation Center backed into a loading bay. He was trapped and he knew it. Responding to the location, four detectives' vehicles slowly rolled in, headlights out and lined up directly in front of Ricky. "Your move buddy," I thought to myself. It reminded me of a scene out of National Geographic on the wolves of Yellowstone.

I remember watching a weary coyote exhausted from the pursuit of relentless wolves ... not willing to run more ... knowing it would be futile ... fully aware that once a wolf begins the pursuit of a trespassing coyote, the wolf will never quit. And the wolf, well he is a wolf. The big dogs of the woods will have their way with the coyote.

I noticed a small glow of a lit cigarette inside Ricky's SUV. He was smoking his last cigarette, I thought. The radio was silent, everyone just waited to see what was next. A small roll of cigarette smoke escaped a slight crack atop of Ricky's driver's door window. Ricky was pondering what his chances were with the liberal courts of the Washington State and with us.

The door to Ricky's SUV slowly opened as did ours. Both his hands appear as our firearms came to bear on his every move. Rob and his team moved in a static line towards Ricky and he did as he was told. Ricky was in custody and no one got hurt. Good day!

A marked Puyallup police car monitoring the action from a short distance responded to the scene and the delighted young kid cop was more than happy to take Ricky to jail.

Pig said he was heading to the "Hotel California." I agreed. "Let's go meet up there and wait till the warrant is signed by some judge in a bathrobe awakened by Randy needing the official document completed by the judge's signature."

Hotel California, I smiled. Ricky's home was now Hotel California. As the song goes, "We are programmed to receive; you can never leave." Ricky's home will be surrounded, as we had done hundreds of times before in a suburban neighborhood of the middle class America. No one would know we were there till we hit the front door. Once again, within hours, a second police-initiated violent act would occur.

While watching a house prior to warrant service, a car might arrive and the occupants of the vehicle would be allowed entrance as they did not know of our watchful eyes, but, they could never leave. A leaving vehicle would be stopped by police and the occupants detained. No evidence will escape now; we have worked too hard for this moment.

I grabbed Pig, "hey bud."

"Yeah," he said.

"I'm not going," I said.

"What?" He replied.

"Yeah something is seriously wrong with me; scared the shit out of me, didn't even know if I could make it to the parking lot near the mall." I told him I'd let the other sergeant know and Piper could handle it. "Damn Pig" I said, "you don't need me standing around getting in the way."

Pig's face was in shock, "what the hell?" he responded.

Rob, listening to the conversation said "Pig, something is wrong with him, I saw it, let it be!"

A moment of long silence and fleeting glances between the three of us. Pig soon raised his big right paw and gave me a hug, "got it, I'll take care of it, get out of here you dusty old guy."

I stepped back, "I know you will, I'll catch up later."

Pig and Rob turned and walked towards their vehicles. Rob took the keys to the van before leaving me. As Rob and Pig walked, he was talking, telling Pig what he had seen me going through in the back of the van. Pig looked confused and stunned and glanced back at me before disappearing into the night.

I climbed into a marked police car and told the kid staring back at me to take me to my war wagon. It's parked behind the Puyallup PD.

"Yes sir," he responded.

The next morning I awoke to the irritating buzz of my damn phone. It was a phone these days; years before it was the dreaded pager. I was shaking off the side effects of Ambien, Xanax, wine, and a pain pill I had saved from an injury suffered during a SWAT entry in 2004. It's 7:20 in the morning, it was Pig.

Calling him back, as I wasn't quick enough to get to the phone he asked "how you doing bud?"

"I'm alive," I responded. "How'd you do at Ricky's house last night?" I asked.

"Mother Load – bag of VIN numbers from previous stolen cars and trucks, Ricky and his tweakers had given a new identity, he's history," Pig said.

"Good, nobody hurt?" I asked.

"Smooth bud," Pig responded, "Just the paper work left to do."

Steve pried into what happened in the van with me the previous night. I explained that I didn't have a clue, never experienced something like that. But something was wrong; even now I knew something is seriously wrong.

Pig stated that I had surely scared the hell out of Rob, not something that is easy to do. I agreed.

"Get your ass to the doctor and get it sorted out," Pig said, "old or not, we need you."

"Fuck you and the old crap," I responded.

"Okay, I'll call and get an appointment and get back at you later, okay?"

Pig responded, "Get fixed, later."

I figured calling the doctor's office on a late notice asking for an appointment would not work out so well for me. Just show up, they'll see me, know there's a problem and get me in to see doc with no questions asked. They will see I'm messed up, my head still pounding, shaking like a leaf and know I wasn't fooling around.

Arriving at the doctor's office, my plan worked well. I couldn't sit and wait and I paced the waiting room like a caged animal. I couldn't stop moving. After about 45 minutes Nurse Sandy called my name. I love Nurse Sandy. She was a no nonsense woman and a straight shooter and she was in my opinion the ultimate nurse. She really cared for her patients.

"What's wrong with you, you're running 90 mph and jittery?"

I thought, "Yeah, good nurse." "I don't know" I responded, "but something is definitely wrong."

"Ok, get on the scale, let's weigh you in," she ordered.

"Hold it," I said. I needed to start a sudden weight loss program. I removed my personal wallet from my right rear pocket, badge wallet from left rear pocket, and tossed them on the counter. Next was my Beretta from my right hip holster and belt clipped gold badge. A flip knife from right front pocket, pistol from right Harley boot, and boot knife with sheath from left Harley boot -- all on the counter. "I'm ready," I said. Nurse Sandy was not impressed but it was a routine for me, and she had witnessed it many times before during other doctor appointments I've had.

"Get on the scale," she ordered.

210, not bad, I thought.

"Roll up your sleeve," she ordered as she got ready to take my blood pressure. I had not shut up since I got into the office, telling of the prior nights escapades.

"Quiet," she said.

She ran the blood pressure machine but when it was done the look on her face was clearly "concerned" and then she shook her head, "not right" she mumbled to herself and started over. Again when the machine displayed the reading she froze. Looking at me with that care and concern I've known her for, she said "sit here, don't move, I'm getting Ted, I'll be right back, don't move, okay?"

"Okay," I said back and she darted form the room calling for the doctor.

Moments later Doc walked in and shut the door. He retook my blood pressure and simply raised his eyebrows and asked "what happened last night?"

About half way through the story Doc stopped me.

"How long have you been a cop?" he asked.

"Almost 36 years" I responded. I knew what was coming, the usual talk about me thinking of retiring. We talk about it all the time, he's been a Doctor for about the same amount of time I have been a cop, and I usually turn the subject on him, something I'm good at.

"Your fucking blood pressure is 200 over 141!"

I was shocked at the number, and his language, I have always cussed around him, but he, never.

Then he asks, "Is your vision blurred?"

"Yep" I answered.

"You're shaking uncontrollably?"

"Obviously, yes" I said.

"You're sweating?"

"Obviously" I responded.

"You have migraine type headache?"

"Yes." He knew something.

"Okay, you're taking cholesterol meds and now your blood pressure, you should be in a hospital and frankly why you didn't have a stroke or heart attack last night is beyond me explaining!" the Doc said seriously.

A moment of silence came about the room and I just stared at him. Then he swung the chair around and sat down in front of me and looked deep into my eyes. His look, it was like no time before, not like two men playing word chess, matching smartass exchanges, skipping over the reality of the subject. This time he was serious.

"I'm giving you two options and my total honesty from all my years of being a doctor."

"Ok" I replied.

"One, I will give you directions and the drugs to get this under control, those drugs will change your life forever, but you must retire now and you will get at least 10 more years, hopefully, out of your life. Or two, I will give you those drugs, and you go back to work, but you'll be a dead man soon. Your head is full throttle and your body is breaking down. Enough is enough. Retire now or die soon! It's your choice."

I had no come back, he was not messing around and I believed him. I felt my eyes trying to water up and I fought it back. Somehow, someway, I knew he was right. Last night I was scared shitless, now I'm frightened beyond anything I had ever faced before. Pig couldn't save me, no body armor to stop this one, no ducking or hiding, this was a bullet with my badge number on it and there was nothing I could do to stop it! Nothing!

It was a quiet moment, and then he turned away and began writing notes onto my chart. Dead man walking, I figured.

I stared down at my feet, thinking. "Okay, I quietly responded, write me a three week pass for my boss that I'm off for duty-related illness. I'll take three weeks to give you the answer."

He said without looking up, "It's not me that needs the answer to this problem, I already know the answer, you need to answer this question; you need to be honest with yourself."

"Yes, you're right," I responded.

He quickly filled out the prescriptions and said, "Don't go home without this stuff and see you in three weeks."

"Doc", I said, looking at him while standing, trying desperately to keep the water out of my eyes, "thanks!"

"You know what you must do. Do it, you owe this community nothing more, and I thank you." With that, he turned and walked briskly out to his next patient.

As I walked from the building I struggled yet again with my vision, but this time not from the pounding pain in my head but with tears I was fighting back. Get to my truck, get there now. I need those tinted windows I could hide behind, not wanting any weakness to show.

Climbing into my truck I just sat and took in what had just occurred. A flash of my years as a cop played quickly through my head. The faces of all those people I had worked with – Pig, Rob, and many others. The faces of my family, wife, kids, and grand children, and the young males in my family that now wore a badge for the community they swore to protect and serve. We had become a family of cops, not just me.

I put my hands on the steering wheel of my truck, near the top, buried my face into my arms. I knew what I had to do; the time in my life I had dreaded cornered me, the time to retire. I was losing the battle to contain my tears but I had to deal with this and move on. There is kryptonite, I had just found it.

After picking up the meds my doctor said I must take to cheat death for an unknown amount of time, I stopped by my police department and located my Captain. I dropped the note on his desk and told him I needed to get myself pulled together and told him I'd be back in a few weeks and get back to work. I wasn't about to admit that retirement was eminent, not yet anyway. I didn't want to show my hand just yet.

On the long drive home I began to think of the last 36 years and how I had lived them in a police uniform or playing the role of a dirt bag as an undercover officer. The good times, sad times, violent times, and the people I had met — those I had done battle with, those I had saved and those whose lives I have changed. I had an unlimited list of stories, most involving Pig and I coming up with clever ways to fix, deter, arrest, and save people. Pig and I had more than once mentioned that we should keep track of these stories and put them into a book before age stole the memories, never to be shared with anyone. How many times after doing a job did we say "You just can't make this shit up" and "I can't believe they pay me to do this?" I didn't want to regret and say to myself someday "I wish" or "I could have, would have, should have done it," wrote that book.

Arriving home I sealed up the house like I had done hundreds of times before when working graveyards to trick my mind into believing it is night to help myself sleep. Only this time I did it not to sleep, but to remember. I opened a well-aged bottle of wine and simply sat in the dark pondering my next move.

The wine and dark was doing the trick and soon memories began flooding back to me of the last 36 years. I grabbed a legal pad and a pen and began writing down some of the stories of two "Small town cops".

I watched him dress in his work clothes, lace up his heavy work boots, throw a coat over his broad shoulders, and gather up the thermos of coffee and lunch my mother had hastily prepared. Prior to leaving he would always run his big hands over the top of my and my brother's shaved heads and say "take care of your mother," then kiss my mom and disappear out into the dark of night and the fury of that storm. He was going to gather with other men of like character to rebuild, relight, and help his community recover from what was about to hit.

Chapter 2

In The Beginning

I'm not sure why I wanted to become a cop. I've never understood where in my life I decided but when I came to the right age I knew it; I wanted to become a cop badly, very badly.

I remember at eight years old sitting in the front room of our home watching black and white television. The phone rang and I watched my father turn to my mom and say "bet that's a call out". As he stood up he sighed a bit and made his way to the kitchen to take the call. All in my family – my mother, my brother and I knew it was the power company my father worked for who was calling him to come into work. After all the weather outside was relentless and the lights had already flickered with every gust that swept by. All I heard my father say on the phone was that he was "on the way".

"I'm on the way." I had no idea how many times I would not only hear those words and absolutely no clue that in the not so distant future I would be the one speaking them into my phone.

My father was leaving the comfort of our home and the company of his family to head out into the storm and the dark of the night. We all did. It's what he did, but none of us knew that this time, it would be different; it would be days before he returned to us. The storm was a rare hurricane that had fallen upon the great Pacific Northwest and in the coming days that storm would earn a generation's nickname as the Columbus Day storm of 1962.

I watched him dress in his work clothes, lace up his heavy work boots, throw a coat over his broad shoulders, and gather up the thermos of coffee and lunch my mother had hastily prepared. Prior to leaving he would always run his big hands over the top of my and my brother's shaved heads and say "take care of your mother," then kiss my mom and disappear out into the dark of night and the fury of that storm. He was going to gather with other men of like character to rebuild, relight, and help his community recover from what was about to hit.

He was a hero, my hero, and maybe that is where the seed to become a cop was planted within me at an early age. The sight of him was etched in my mind – his fearless, confident swagger as he made his way to his old truck to face the oncoming rage of a storm and do everything he could to help people not known to him; to recover and rebuild.

Shortly after he left we lost our power – lights, telephone, and television – but we had been through this before and my mother was a pillar of strength and made sure we were cared for in my father's absence. The night quickly passed, then the day turned into days and still our father had not returned and the storm continued to rage. Our home shook at times and the hurricane winds pelted our windows with rain and storm debris. On the third day the winds subsided and the rains stopped, but still my father was gone. We had not heard from him, only constant reports over a 12 volt radio that the storm was wide spread leaving death and destruction throughout the area.

On the evening of the fourth day the headlights of my father's truck drove into our driveway. The man that climbed out of the truck was my father but he looked as though he had been in battle. Caked in layers of mud, cuts scattered about his face and dried blood on one of his hands. His eyes were hollowed and sunk deeply into his face and the gasp of my mother told me she too was shocked. My mother helped him to a chair and began helping remove his boots and wet clothing. He calmly asked if we were okay and then stated that he only had eight hours and needed to eat and sleep before returning to work as they were far from done. He spoke quietly to mother and she intensely listened to his description of the last four days and nights. He was careful to guard the information from us, however.

But here he was: bloody, battered, and dented, and taking a knee on the sidelines. Time to gather himself – eat, rest, and in a short eight hours would re-enter the arena and work to right a wrong.

It wasn't the first time I had witnessed this from the men in my life. I was but a small boy when my oldest brother guided a ski boat to a dock of frantic and crying kids that screamed their brother had slipped beneath the dark cold waters of Hood Canal in the great Puget Sound. I watched my brother dive beneath the waves and disappear into the darkness below and on the third time he reappeared pulling the body of a lifeless boy to the surface. I witnessed his frantic attempts with others to resuscitate the lad, only to find out hours later that the boy had died at the hospital.

As a boy, powerful heroic actions are deeply etched into the fiber of your life when you witness them first hand.

My father slowly stood and walked towards my brother and I. He stopped to place his large hands on our shoulders and asked us if we had been good and if we watched over our mother. After a quick exchange, exhausted, he made his way to the bathroom for a much wanted shower, be it a cold one.

My mother was busy putting together a meal that would please my father and make him feel better.

She was a handsome woman, five and half feet tall, her hair was impeccable and she would never be caught in public without it neatly curled and combed. She was a beautician and business owner in Sumner and many knew her.

I recall that she once drove to my grade school and told the bus driver he was to stop in front of our home and pick me up. She did not want any of her kids standing on the Orting Highway waiting for the bus after three girls had been hit and killed by a car close to our home. The girls had been walking along the shoulder of the Orting Highway. Our home was located on Meade Cumber, a half block off that highway.

I knew this had been a warring topic at home and she was not bending on the matter; the driver would stop or there would be hell to pay.

The weekend had passed and now it was Monday morning and I was ready for school. I walked with my mother to the edge of the road in front of our home. We crossed Meade Mc Cumber and she made me stand next to our mailbox. I waited for the bus as mom disappeared into the front door of the family home. I then could see her standing in the front window of our home, watching, waiting.

She had told me, with authority, not to move, even if the bus passed me by; my orders were to stay put. I was frozen as I saw the bus approach. I somehow knew from the look in my mother's eyes and her intensity that I was the bait in a battle plan.

As the bus inched closer all I thought about was the driver. I hoped that he realized the consequences of his actions if he failed to stop. I was seven years old, and I knew.

As he got closer it was apparent that he wasn't going to stop, and didn't, till he got to the Orting Highway. I watched the bus pass by and followed it with my eyes till the stop sign at the Orting Highway. After the bus stopped I noticed the front side boarding door open, but no one was there; he was waiting for me. I didn't move a muscle, except to look back at my home and the sight of my mother (already wearing her coat and scarf) emerge from the front door. Still, I didn't move.

She hurriedly made it to the middle of the road and signaled to me to join her, as she glared at the back of the bus stopped a half block away. I think that was when the driver realized he had maybe crossed the wrong woman. The door to the bus closed, and he was off.

I had orders to get into the car and did, but mom was already inside; car started and in reverse. As she backed out onto the road and the bus was several blocks ahead and turning left and would be at Maple Lawn Elementary in moments, so too would we.

When we arrived at the school I spotted the bus parked out front and kids still unloading; the driver was also unloading and making his way to safety of the front office.

"Go to class," she intently stated, and I looked at her face. Her eyes were forward and focused, the muscles of her jaw bulged beneath her near perfect skin and she walked with purpose. This, even at seven years old, I knew, was not going to end well.

I couldn't help myself, I tagged along acting as if not to care, but desperately wanting to watch through to the conclusion of what was about to unfold. I watched mom storm by the secretaries of the office and the Vice Principal. The door to the principal's office was closed; it didn't matter, and she knew the bus driver was hiding in there and his ass was hers', and she burst through the door like she owned the place.

I strained to hear the heated conversation but couldn't from the hallway. Soon another bus driver entered the office and was walking directly towards the principal's office. If he was their backup they would clearly need help, more help in fact since mom was a ferocious woman, and would not back down in matters of safety for her children.

The next morning I had to be ready and at the bus stop, the one in front of our house, now on the same side of the street as our house. Minutes after arriving at my stop, a big yellow school bus coming from the opposite direction appeared and the doors to the bus opened directly in front of me. I recognized the driver; he was the driver that had entered the office after my mother was in there. He had negotiated a peace plan.

I looked over my shoulder and saw my mother standing in the window of our home, sipping her coffee. She had won!

Thinking back to those days when growing up and noticing the actions of my parents and brothers, I now realize I had the willingness to be in the arena – the compassion to help those that so desperately needed it, and the ability to wage violence when I had to. The tools had been imprinted early and without knowing it then, I was given control of my own destiny; a policeman.

Chapter 3

The One That Got Away

The sun felt good as it warmed the October afternoon of 1982. Summer had crept away and fall chased in behind and was still holding winter at bay and I was in a ticket writing mood. Actually, my chief was on my ass for not writing enough tickets so I was out to make a wrong, a right, and get him off my ass.

Some days it was easy, in an hour's time one could write four or five tickets; other days, nothing. Lucky if you caught one. Today was somewhere in between and my luck varied. I was in one of my favorite "fishing holes", next to Sunset Chevrolet in about the 700 block of Traffic Avenue – north bound, south bound, and two lane road that was highly traveled.

It was a matter of who saw whom first. If they were coming from the north and speeding, they make the curve; and if I saw them first, I'd lock in the hand held radar and bingo, mine for the cleaning. If they came from the south and I saw them first, they'd crest the hill speeding and again, locked and again, mine for the cleaning.

I usually wrote a ticket on every other traffic stop and when I did, almost always dropped it down to "5 over" the speed limit. By doing so it would give the citizen a big break in cost, they probably would just pay the fine. Other than this, they wouldn't climb out of their car and try to kick my ass. This is the best part, actually.

Small town cops work alone, plan ahead, and this was a good plan and usually always worked. Now and then you'd get some guy that wasn't going to go with the program and by the time it came to write the ticket I would already know he was going to be a problem, so he'd get a full meal deal, no breaks, and if he didn't like it, tough. If he wanted to take the conflict to a whole new level, so be it.

I needed one more ticket and I had just let a guy go with a warning, next one to bat would get it and the chief would be off my ass for a couple of weeks and I could go back to my routine of sipping coffee and chatting with the locals, sneak off with a snitch somewhere out of sight, and get the latest scoop of the criminal element in town, or just drive around waving and smiling. "Small town cop stuff".

And whoosh, into my trap he drives and I'm on him. He was driving some overly clean mid-sized car ... 37 miles per hour in a "25 miles per hour" zone. This would be a slam dunk, write a quick ticket for five over and be on my way.

As I approached the car I noticed it was an older model, at least ten years old but the paint hadn't dulled yet, still glimmered and mirror-like from cleaning and waxing, cared greatly for by its owner. The windows had no smudge and were as clear as the day's air. The interior was sharp and clean.

"License and registration please," I asked.

He was young, 20 something, tall and skinny. He looked as though he had to fold himself up in order to fit himself into the car.

"Do you know why I stopped you?" I inquired.

"Speeding" was his one word response.

He wrestled a small money clip from his pants' front pocket that held his driver's license and carefully folded bills in place, and reached over to his glove box and unlatched it. Inside the compartment was like the rest of the car: neat, clean, and orderly. He then handed me the license and carefully unfolded registration. He had a goofy look about him, but not a hair out of place and neat as a pin.

When I get ready to screw some guy over, I usually find a way to toss in a little sweet talk foreplay and make the trip more comfortable.

"What brings you to our little town today?" I asked.

He responded by saying "I took the civil service test for police officer here and I wanted to get to know a little about the town before tomorrow's oral interview."

I knew there was an opening, as predicted Jensen had bailed when he couldn't handle working alone. I was unaware or uncaring of any testing going on but if this guy had been called in for an oral interview, he was then a contender for the job and a ticket would be a knockout to his chances. Suddenly, my need for one last ticket was countered with the thought of another man's future in the balance.

There was silence as we looked at each other, one having the fate of the other "in hand." Write the ticket, game over, let him go, and he had a fighting chance. I looked at his license.

Got to be kidding, "Pigman," I said quietly, "hell of a name for a cop" I blurted out not thinking.

I had left him an opening for complaint but he didn't take it and said "yeah, I'm going to catch hell on that for my entire career."

Clearly this was a man that was hell bent on being a cop, if not in this town then somewhere else; it was what he was going to do. I like that in a person – sight set, now go get it.

"Wait here, I'll be back in a few minutes" I said, and turned and walked to my patrol car.

I sat motionless in my cruiser looking at the man in front of me. He didn't move, he probably was glancing at his rear view mirror but I couldn't tell. I thought of what to do, after all in the rotation he was to get a ticket. Every other one was my rule and he was the other one and due, but something held me back.

He was smart enough to do well on a civil service exam, impressive enough to get city leaders to call him in for an oral interview, clever enough to check out the town before the interview; so he would have some knowledge prior to the interview. Clean, orderly, and well kept; comfortable with his career choice even though he would be hassled throughout his entire career with the oddest of last names for a cop and it didn't faze him. I liked that.

My mind was made up, he was going to get a warning and I got out and swaggered to his car door.

"Here you go," handing the license and registration back, "this one is on me."

His face showed relief, "thanks" was his response and as carefully as he had removed his license and registration, he returned them all neatly in their proper place. "Thanks," he said again, "could have been a deal breaker" he remarked.

"Good luck on the test" and with that we parted company: he looking for a career, and me, one more victim to please my chief.

Fast forward about 30 years, it was May 31st, 2012. I stepped out of the back of the Puyallup police department that I had worked for so many years. I was decked out from top to bottom, all my medals of victory and accomplishments were worn on my chest, my hat, and like Carl's I wore it low, shadowing my eyes; my Harley boots made me tall. Beside me was my nephew – smaller, younger, and few medals, and he was growing into his hat. And of course Pig was there with me. It was my last official patrol and it would be of course, on foot through downtown and end at city hall where I would be honored for my service of over 33 years at Puyallup and neighboring Sumner. It was time to retire.

As we walked, people noticed. It had been years since they had seen old school cops, standing tall, round top hats with black gleaming brims. They had grown accustomed to cops wearing jumpsuits and baseball hats. This was a blast from the past as we made our way along our small town main street heading for my end.

My health had caught up with me and my white flag had been raised and the torch passed to a younger version of me, Kevin. We had had our cry in the elevator moments earlier after I had left my office for the last time; we controlled the elevator till we had our emotions in check, making sure that not even at my sunset would weakness be displayed. Now, we were going to finish it.

We entered the fifth floor of city hall and many people were there to greet me: family, friends, and cops, some long retired and had come to see me off. As the proceedings moved on, several high ranking speakers spoke. The Police Chief I had help train as a kid cop was now praising me for my stellar career and accomplishments, and near the end my best friend stood to speak.

It was Pig and he told a story about how he was stopped 30 years earlier by a kid cop in Sumner, how he had talked his way out of a ticket and eluded what few are capable of doing, and claimed to be "the one that got away." He spoke of the traffic stop, both he and my eyes watered, but nothing more, kept our weakness in check. The crowd loved the story, and some had heard it before.

There were two endings, mine and of course his: mine, claiming mercy was justified; and his, claiming he had simply out maneuvered the crime fighter.

One thing we both knew, it was a beginning of a lifelong friendship, commitment, and the willingness to die for the other, if need be. Our friendship would be tested by others and we always overcame the odds. Hell, we even tested it, our in house "domestics" were legendary, cop on cop and yes, there were times we had to be separated as the conflict had gotten physical, but in the end, we would apologize, and move on. I've told him several times I wished I'd wrote him that damn ticket, it would be my prized possession and it would have been mounted to the wall in my office. Then, I could simply point at it when he started a fight.

Recently a young detective came into my office and asked about Pig and I – how we managed to put together amazing operations, all the while during the planning process as we fought, bickered, and argued. "I've never seen anything like it, grumpy old men" he remarked. "Then when the operation begins, the fighting, bickering, and arguments stop and everything goes smooth as hell" he continued. "It's a process we use to get the best out of each other; you'll find your way someday and if you do you will be seated here where I am now" I replied.

When we began working narcotics I was a shoe in to do undercover work; I was comfortable being un-comfortable. I looked like crap if the roll was needed or to appear business-like if that fit the lie, but Pig ran the circus every time. Not one thing he over looked, nothing left to chance.

He could watch me work a deal: buying stolen cars, buying or selling dope, whatever it was and see just by my body language if the deal was going good or not. I often wondered just how much of my thoughts he could read. I didn't care, he had my back and I was very pleased with myself that I had not written that ticket so many years ago.

My attention wandered back to Pig, finishing his version of the story. There was a loud, cheerful applause as he finished, and I stood to greet him as he walked towards me. As I reached for his hand to shake, he pulled me forward and embraced me with his big hand and armed across my back and said "I miss you already." I quickly responded, "I left a path for you everywhere I've gone, don't wait too long to follow this last one, ok?" With that, I turned and walked to the podium. I looked at the faces in front of me. Family, friends, and cops – all had somehow played a role in me being here; others, like my wife, had un-wavering support for me and would have always been here. The faces I missed were that of my parents, some old time cops that had helped raised me to this position, and of course, Carl.

I adjusted my hat, so that the brim shadowed my eyes, and reluctantly said my goodbyes.

No One Gets Away With It

Justice ... a word people fight for and long to see. Some continue to believe; some have given up hope. I myself have become frustrated many times because of the injustices I have seen, more so those that were beyond my control.

The next stories are stories of justice served, in one way or the other. And for those who thought they got away with it, let me tell them something. I believe that there is a greater justice than what we have here. Everybody will pay for what he has done. No one gets away with it.

Having gotten all I needed, I switched back to a primary channel and listened for updates. Seattle, I thought, which way would he go? Since this was a bold crime and most likely for revenge, the shooter would think his victim to be dead thus delaying any type of police response, therefore he would continue to perform boldly and take the simplest and easy way home, down highway 410 and directly through my town.

Chapter 4

Shooter

It was late September, 1981 when I rolled into the police department parking lot. There was Carl, hat tipped back, left foot hiked onto the back bumper of his Pontiac Lemans' patrol car, smoking a cigarette. He was getting off at 11 pm and was about to go home.

Carl was a tall, lanky, cowboy type; quiet and soft spoken. He was well over six feet tall, slender and always smoking a cigarette, with his rolled-up long sleeved uniform, and eight point police hat and badge. He would always pull his hat brim down just enough to shadow his eyes. Carl had been a Sumner cop for almost as long as I had been alive. I used to watch his every move, especially in bars or a fight. He was the closest thing to "Cool Hand Luke" I'd ever known and I wanted his knowledge, and paid attention to his every word.

"Hey, keep an eye on that new kid tonight, ok?" Carl stated.

He was speaking of a new guy we had hired and was a couple of months out of the academy.

"Will do Carl" I responded. "Get outta here, I got this covered" telling Carl, and with that I coded my way through the back door and disappeared into the police department.

Jensen was just getting dressed – short blond hair, rosy cheeks, and frisky as they come. We had found him in some King County town working as a Police Explorer. When he turned 21 he was recruited by several towns but he tested best here in Sumner, and thus he was ours for the time being.

There was not much to brief him on except the usual, do bar checks and back each other up. Good to go, I left and was back out working. I was working the much sought after 8 pm till 4 am shift. This shift was usually held by the Sergeant, Tuesday through Saturday night, giving two officers working together in this small town. The Sergeant was on vacation and I was the pick to fill in.

The night progressed smoothly and was much like the previous Saturday nights that I had worked in Sumner. I grinned when I thought about what Carl had said, "Keep an eye on the new kid tonight," like I was some sort of old time salt. Well, I had been a Military policeman for three years and now a cop in Sumner for less than three. Couple kids out here running around, but none the less we could and would handle what was coming our way.

At about 0145 hrs dispatch put out a distressing call that there had been a shooting in Bonney Lake, a small community just five miles from Sumner off highway 410 on the hill to our east. Pierce County Deputies were responding as were neighboring police departments, including mine. Jensen was rabid about going and wanted me to agree. I wasn't the supervisor but I knew if I went, he would follow, leaving no one in our town. Damn kid, "Go" I responded over the radio and in moment he was racing off with lights and siren, fearlessly charging into the night and the unknown.

I wanted to know more so I asked dispatch to move to a private channel. When the dispatcher got there I wanted to know the full story.

I listened intently as the dispatcher told me that a woman living alone had answered a knock at her door. When she opened the door, the shooter opened up and shot her in the face. Deputies and neighbors responded quickly and the victim had still enough breathe and fight in her to give up a name. Neighbors described the car, and the information was put out on various police channels. The shooter was a previous boyfriend from Seattle, apparently pissed off about being dumped and wanted revenge.

Having gotten all I needed, I switched back to a primary channel and listened for updates. Seattle, I thought, which way would he go? Since this was a bold crime and most likely for revenge, the shooter would think his victim to be dead thus delaying any type of police response, therefore he would continue to perform boldly and take the simplest and easy way home, down highway 410 and directly through my town.

I sped to an on ramp to 410 from the Orting Highway and sat up shop. I parked in the dark above the freeway on the on ramp, lights off and waited for a blue 4-door Dodge to come by. How many could there be? I didn't wait long, in fact I believe it was the first car I saw drive by, but I knew all hell was now at my door, and I was going to open it.

I quickly sped down the on ramp and merged onto the freeway. I could see the taillights in front of me, he was not in a hurry, good sign, I thought to myself. I moved into the passing lane, and slowly, ever so slowly caught up to the vehicle just enough to see his license plate. Bingo!

I contacted dispatch and informed them of my situation and asked for confirmation of the suspect's vehicle plate. They confirmed it instantly and the tone of their voice had suddenly sharpened up, knowing full well of what was about to occur. I asked for back up, most of them were on the hill, in Bonney Lake. I told dispatch we were exiting highway 410 and now entering northbound onto highway 167, towards Seattle.

Dispatch notified me that my call for help had been heard and everyone was on the way from Bonney Lake. "Thanks", I muttered, thinking about the fix I was in. Help was over five minutes away and in five minutes I'd be in King County with little or no radio reception.

It was a strange moment in time. This section of 167 is straight and flat 2 lane highway back then and you can see for miles in either direction, yet I saw no tail lights, no head lights. It was me and the shooter, 55 mph, one behind the other, both playing chess in a "life or death", "winner take all" moment.

He had boldly walked to the front door of his ex-girlfriend, calmly knocked on her door, cold bloodily shot her in the face, then turned and walked back to his car. Now he didn't hide anything he did, to the point of driving the most direct and open route back to Seattle. He probably grinned at the sight of speeding police cars passing him en-route to the shooting scene.

He was underestimating the police and me, or was it me under estimating him? Was I about to flip the switch to spring his trap? I reached down and activated my overhead lights. Checkmate, but for whom?

I had already called out by radio, "112 Sumner, traffic" I stated with confidence. I quickly gave my location and I think I heard a collective gasp as I hung up the microphone. I was on my own for the time being.

His right turn signal began blinking and he slowly drifted from the highway and came to a stop on the shoulder of the road. I watched the silhouetted figure in the front seat, he didn't move, not a twitch. I climbed out of my patrol car that I had parked at an angle to offer protection to an officer on a traffic stop. I watched the silhouette, no movement, but I knew he was intently watching me. I gave him what he needed, without being obvious; I showed him my hands, no gun in my hands.

Most assuredly a cop would not walk up onto a shooter without a gun in his hands; I hoped he thought I was ignorant of the shooting that had just occurred. By the time I had gotten to the back of his car, my headlights no longer revealed me, I stepped into his blind spot and directed my flashlight beam, held in my left hand, into his driver side door mirror. I caught him looking and in a moment of blindness I turned my gun hip away from his view and quickly un-holstered my stainless steel 357 Rugger and slipped it behind my right thigh, near my butt.

"Good morning, do you know why I stopped you?"

His left hand was on the steering wheel and his right hand on the thigh of his right leg. Unlike me, no gun was in his hands.

"No officer," he answered.

"I noticed, you have a tail light that's been flickering off and on, might cause a problem in heavy traffic," I lied.

"Thank you officer, I had not noticed that" he calmly replied.

"Is that a registration I see in your passenger visor?" Glancing up as I said it.

Then he looked to his passenger visor and started to speak. I glanced down to the floor of the car and spotted about 4 inches of gun barrel protruding from beneath the seat. No more fucking around!

His eyes turned back to mine at about the same time my 357 had cleared my back and was now brought to bear on his head.

"One wrong move and I will kill you, do you understand?" My voice had changed. That helpful officer smile had turned immediately intense, with the will to be violent, as needed.

"Yes sir," he responded.

"I know there is a gun under your front seat, even lean that direction I will kill you, understand?"

"Yes sir."

"Slowly put your right hand on the back of your head" I ordered.

Slowly, ever so slowly he did as he was told.

"Now, use your left hand, reach through the window and unlatch the door FROM THE OUTSIDE" I emphasized. "Slowly," I said.

He followed my demands and slowly reached through the driver's door window and twisted his hand to maneuver the latch, and the door popped open slightly.

I had quickly slipped the flashlight from my left hand to the sap pocket of my pants on my left leg. I grabbed the front door and swung it open, and then using my left hand, grabbed him by his left wrist. As I began to pull on him I quickly re-holstered my pistol, then my right hand grabbed his right hand, still on his head and along with a patch of hair. In one sudden move he was yanked from the driver's seat, landing face down on the shoulder of the highway. He offered no resistance and in seconds, he was handcuffed and searched.

I reached behind and slammed the car door shut, then stood him up. I looked at his face, some abrasions and one small rock imbedded into his cheek, considering what else could have happened, not bad.

It was the first time I really took notice considering it was his hands I was so interested in moments before. His eyes were lifeless, nothing home, and his skin was pale. His mouth lay open and he looked like death warmed over.

"You're under arrest for murder," understand?"

Nothing, no nod, nothing, he just stared straight ahead, straight through me.

I noticed a glint of light down the highway and looking closely it was apparent that the Calvary was in full charge mode, heading directly to us. In the excitement of the moment I had failed to notify my dispatch that I had one in custody and I was upright and breathing. They were clearly worried. I reached for my portable radio, but in the struggle of extraditing the murderer from his car, it had been knocked from its holder and was currently MIA, missing in action. There was no time to get back to my patrol car so we both watched and waited.

Out of nowhere, the suspect calmly asked me, "Think they'll be able to stop?"

"Hope so," I responded. "Come on, let's move way out front of your car," and away we went.

There we were, he had cuffs on, I had a grip on him and we stumbled through the dark trying to keep from being run over by those that came to save me.

Of course it was Jensen leading the charge. He had maneuvered his vehicle in behind mine and at some point realized he would not be able to stop in time. He veered further off the road and the vehicle spun out of control, sending rock and dust everywhere. His car came to rest next to us with headlights lighting up our position. A deputy's car came to a smoking squealing stop next to the suspect's car and the remainder of the troops filed in safely behind.

Jensen was pissed, not sure if it was over his loss of control of his car or the fact that he had missed out on some serious action, but he came out of his car bitching. I really didn't give a damn. Deputies seemed pleased and I never saw the murder suspect again.

In a moment I had gone from one of the most dangerous things I had done in my life, up until then, to dead quiet. I sat quietly in my patrol car and watched the activity outside. Deputies stopped by my car and shook my hand, telling me "great work".

Finally Jensen couldn't take it and stormed in my direction. I rolled down my window and waited to receive his complaint. I knew what he was mad about and part of me agreed, but his youth betrayed him, he had yet to learn the fact that he was a cop in a small town and sometimes, you can't wait for help, it won't be there in time.

"This is bullshit, it's not the way you are supposed to do things, you don't stop murder suspects in the middle of nowhere and alone" he harped. He continued his rant about the way cops did it where he had come from and finally it got to a point where I stopped him.

"You're right, don't change your mind and do what I did, and when you calm down I will explain to you why I did it, but you're right." I rolled up my window and turned around, and sped off, back to town.

Jensen had come from a place up north, where there was lots of money, lots of cops, and lots of training, he hadn't quite gripped the understanding that this was a one horse town and sometimes, every so often you simply had to cowboy up and get it done, alone.

Jensen would have to adapt or move on.

One year later he was gone, big city, big money and big problems, but we found a replacement and hired some goofy looking guy with a funny last name for a cop, Pig.

The clerks had made a photo copy of the Texas driver's license and the copy was given to detectives. They were certain the picture on the driver's license was that of Wilcox. We had found our man and confirmed he was here. The detectives quickly collected all cash in the office, any documents that Wilcox might have signed, and got access to any lobby video and parking lot video that the hotel could provide. As the detectives were leaving, one of the clerks mentioned that someone from room 128 had made a long distance phone call to Plano Texas a couple of hours earlier, before our arrival.

CHAPTER 5

Taxi!

I could hear running; heavy boots impacting the floor on the second level of the police department, unusual for the detective division, unless something serious is going on. The thuds hastened until they came to a stop at my door; it was my Captain.

"Sergeant, quick in my office; get Dan" and with that he hurried off.

Dan was the sergeant of general detectives, general investigations; I was sergeant of SIU, Special Investigation Unit. Dan's people wore suits, clean cut, and reeked of cop. My people, some looked like thugs, some skinheads in appearance, some had that "normal" look to them. At a moment's notice anyone of them could slide into an undercover role if needed.

Dan and I arrived at the Captain's office at about the same time.

"Come in, shut the door," he ordered.

Now seated, he explained that patrol had just received information that a serial bank robber was in a room 128 at Extended Stay Hotel in the industrial park, just north of downtown Puyallup. The information was thought to be credible. The FBI wanted us to confirm that the man, Mark Wilcox, out of El Paso Texas, was there. The Captain handed us a photo of Wilcox along with an FBI description of him and a special note that jumped out at the reader. It was in bold letters at the bottom of the flyer, "Caution, considered armed and extremely dangerous."

Captain continued, "Take your best guys and go to the hotel and see if you can confirm Wilcox is still there and if so, seal the place down and we can call SWAT to come get him out. There is a confirmed FBI warrant out for his arrest for bank robberies, many of them."

I began reading the synopsis of Mark Wilcox's activities on the second page. The first known bank robbery he committed began in El Paso Texas, 19 weeks earlier. Judging from the location of the banks and the dates, Wilcox had simply drove on highway 10, westbound through New Mexico, then Arizona, into Southern California and then North on I-5, landing now in Puyallup Washington. Along the route he had struck 17 times and his 18th attack was yesterday, in Vancouver Washington, Bank of America, approximately 100 miles to the South of Puyallup Washington. He was going to hit us next unless we got him first.

Wilcox – a bold, smaller man with a long dark coat, would walk briskly through the front doors of a bank, open his coat, and swing his double-barreled shotgun to bear on tellers and customers alike. Wilcox would throw a nylon bag onto the counter, yelling at the tellers to put cash into the bag and no dye packs, or he would return to kill people. He would be out of the same doors and vanish in under a minute with clean cash in hand. So far, he had a plan that had worked.

"Ok Captain, we'll get it done" and we left, our pace quickened.

There were seven of us, seven detectives and one marked unit parked near the only way in, only way out of the hotel parking lot. The marked unit was to post at the exit in case Wilcox got out and into a vehicle before we had a chance to grab him.

Two detectives went to the lobby and asked if a man looking like Wilcox had checked into the hotel recently. The picture of Wilcox was provided and the female clerks quickly stated that Wilcox had checked in extremely early this morning, perhaps after two. He had arrived by taxi, had one large bag and one small bag. He had given the clerks each an extra $20.00 for allowing him to stay because he had no credit cards, but did have a Texas driver's license with a different name. Wilcox got a key to room 128.

The clerks had made a photo copy of the Texas driver's license and the copy was given to detectives. They were certain the picture on the driver's license was that of Wilcox. We had found our man and confirmed he was here. The detectives quickly collected all cash in the office, any documents that Wilcox might have signed, and got access to any lobby video and parking lot video that the hotel could provide. As the detectives were leaving, one of the clerks mentioned that someone from room 128 had made a long distance phone call to Plano Texas a couple of hours earlier, before our arrival.

The phone call made from 128 was no doubt made by Wilcox and later I would learn that Wilcox has a brother living in Plano. The FBI had figured this out and had tapped the phone in the brother's home. Wilcox didn't know he had made a big mistake or didn't care.

A SWAT boss arrived and met with us. Dave was a young, sharp sergeant and well on his way to a cushy job in administration but had some career hoops to clear first, SWAT boss was one of them.

Dave was briefed with the information that detectives had already obtained to include floor plans of the hotel and a floor plan of room 128. Room 129, next door to Wilcox was vacant but the other rooms around and behind Wilcox had been rented out and now we needed to clear them. This was going to be a long day and had a possibility of ending in a shootout with police. Any occupants in those rooms would be forced to move, quickly and quietly, without alerting Wilcox of our presence.

A plan and steps to execute began to form. In fact, the execution had already begun when the patrol officer at the entrance to the hotel announced over the radio that a taxi had arrived and the officer had stopped it right there.

The officer stated that the taxi had been summoned to pick up a passenger in room 128 ... Wilcox! Dave reported back to the officer, "Turn him around, no fare to pick up here." By now I was damn near sprinting to Dave's location and I brought my radio up to my mouth and told the officer not to let the taxi leave.

"Get it back and get him to me."

There was silence on the radio. Then the officer responded, "will do."

I arrived at Dave's location and he, along with the others, had puzzled looks on their faces. SIU detectives already knew what was about to happen; it's what we do.

"What you got in mind?" Dave asked.

"Fucker wants a taxi, he will get one," I responded. "I'll drive the taxi to the front of the room, park front end in, outside the window with passenger side slightly angled towards his door, making it look inviting and customer-service like. I'll knock on the door and when he opens it he will either have his hands full or will have two bags nearby. I'll tell him I'm popping open the trunk for luggage, then turn and walk to the rear of the taxi and open the trunk. I'll look busy to him and I guarantee he will come out, probably with bags in tow. When he gets five feet out the door and we see no gun, we drop him there. Case closed! No one gets hurt."

"What happens if he doesn't have his bags and he just needs a ride?" Dave asked.

"When he gets to the passenger side, I'll act like I need to unlock it, by then I'll expect your ass and friends to be on him," I told Dave.

Quiet, nothing said. We all just looked at each other, thinking about it.

"What about cover?" Dave asked.

"Take two hard hitting detectives with you; the three of you sneak quietly into room 129. Listen and watch for the right time to take care of business, one of you have a rifle for cover. Then put another detective with a rifle on the top floor just to cover the passenger side of the car where we will ambush him. It's a perfect "L" shaped ambush," I answered.

Again, silence.

Dave then broke the quietness, "Good plan and I'm game."

"Great, get this thing set up, I'm going to go make this cabbie think he's the hero in this plan and get his cooperation," I said as I turned towards the taxi.

The driver was like most cabbies in this area: rough around the edges, un-shaven and un-kept, and protested me driving his cab. I promised him I'd write a letter outlining his cooperation and that he was the key to this operation. If he still wouldn't cooperate, I'd extract his ass and take the cab anyway.

He gave me the keys, and said the keys will open the trunk and assured me there were no weapons in the cab. I checked anyway.

I then grabbed a Mariner's baseball hat and thigh length black canvas jacket that was already dirty from my Escalade, a vehicle donated by a drug dealer. The cap would hold my long hair back and out of my way and the coat would conceal my weapons. I was ready.

I sat quietly thinking in the cab, awaiting Dave's green light to begin. This plan has one major flaw: Pig wasn't here to oversee it. I'm superstitious. Dave asked over the radio if everyone was in place and ready, and they responded that all were ready. My turn.

"On the way," was about all I needed to say. I slipped the radio between my legs and slipped the gear shift into drive. This will be fun, Pig or not.

I rounded the end of the building and was now on the back side of the hotel, exposed to room 128. I quickly glanced up to the second floor and could make out the detective that had made his way there. He looked like any other guest, having concealed his rifle somewhere under his clothing. As I nosed into an open parking space directly in front of room 128, I angled the car as planned, and glanced at the moving curtain in the window of room 129.

I put the taxi in park, turned off the engine, and grabbed the keys. No movement. The shades still drawn to room 128, as it had been earlier.

I opened the door, turned off my police radio, stepped out with my left leg, and slid the radio under the front seat, concealing it. Once out I shut the door and walked to the front of the car, past the window to his room, and knocked twice on the door bearing the numbers "128". I then stepped off to the side and a bit back.

The shade moved and Wilcox looked out the window, glanced at me, then the cab. The shade is closed, and the front door opened about 10 inches.

"You called a cab?" I asked.

"Yep, give me a sec." He responded, and closed the door.

With that I turned and walked along the passenger side of the car to the trunk. I dug out the keys and gave un-caring glances at the door to room 128. I took my time.

I slowly slid the key into the lock and slowly turned it. I wasn't about to walk up to that door again. But the door stayed closed. *What was he doing?* I thought to myself, *taking his damn time!*

I lifted the lid and bent over, moving and pretending to move crap around. Acting busy is easy for a government worker like me.

I quickly glanced up and to my right. The detective up there no longer looked cavalier, his face had become hard and he was watching and waiting. As I stood I noticed the door to room 129 was ajar, ever so slightly; I would not have noticed had I not known it would be ajar. The door to room 128 opened!

There was Wilcox, hip length dark coat, one small bag in his left hand and he was struggling with the big bag in his right. I pretended not to notice.

I glanced around the side of the trunk and noticed that Wilcox finally cleared the door to his room.

I asked, "Hey, you wanna put your bags in the trunk?" as he started to walk towards me, now free of the door jam.

He responded, "Probably the big one, but the small one is staying with me."

Gee, I wonder why, I thought to myself knowing exactly why; gun.

I noticed movement. It was door 129 swinging open and Dave, rifle coming up and stepping swiftly to his left to get me out of his field of fire, followed by two ex-football players turned cops that really missed the violence they had fallen in love with on the grid iron.

Wilcox was about two seconds behind everyone else, but his expression began to change when he looked at me. My normal cabbie "don't give a shit" look had changed, an evil smirk to it he now saw. Just as he began to turn his head to his left was about the same time the linebackers with badges laid waste to him. The small bag was fumbled completely out of his hand and the big one was released on impact. He was no match. He was nothing without his guns.

I hoped Wilcox felt the fear, be it for only seconds that he had imposed onto his victims of all 18 banks he had robbed!

The commotion in the parking lot brought curious onlookers that had but moments earlier, been cradled safely in their rooms, completely unaware of the activity that had been going on just outside their doors.

Shades opened, doors crack opened, and now we were on a stage with an audience. All they saw were two enormous men playing with a guy that was being twisted like that of a "Gumby" toy.

The FBI had arrived quietly in the middle of the operation and now paraded themselves center stage with their gold FBI badges displayed forward on the belts of their suits and dark wind breaker jackets with the letters boldly scribed to their backs "FBI".

They know how to steal a moment, and this time we didn't mind. They wanted it all – evidence, the bad guy, and they even brought a crime lab unit with them to process Wilcox's room. Hell, we had all the fun and we were more than happy to leave the work to them.

There was some unfinished business with the cabbie. He had checked his car and found a rather large dent in the passenger side rear door from the impact of two cops and Wilcox.

"Hey Sergeant, what you going to do about the dent in my cab?" he asked.

"I heard you talked your way into the surveillance van, you get a good view?" I asked.

"Very cool, he sure got his ass kicked" he responded with much excitement in his voice.

"Here's my card; tell your boss what happened here and if he wants to file a claim for damages, I'll help him figure it out, ok? And frankly, the dent matches the car's other dents," I said.

"I know it's a piece of shit, but it's his piece of shit" the cabbie said.

"I know, give him my card, thanks, gotta go." With that I turned and left the parking lot.

The owner of the taxi company never called.

I spotted one of the reserve teams moving slowly towards our position. Three men in the front carried large shields with police boldly stamped to the front. Two officers, one right handed, the other left handed, advanced with the shield with rifle barrels pointed towards the house. The left hander would be deployed to the left of the shields with weapon pointed towards the house, and the right hander on the right side of the shield wall. Behind the shields was an officer carrying a throw phone. The phone is contained in a steal box, about a square foot in size with a handle, opening instruction in various languages and a hand held phone inside, already turned on and ready to go. Another rifleman would cover over the top of the shields and be next to the thrower.

Chapter 6

Four, Three, Two, One, Execute!

I found a place to park just outside the police lines and the uniforms that turned away traffic. I could see Pig, already arrived and was moving quickly around his rig, retrieving carefully packed gears with a system he had practiced many times before. All around me, they were the best of the best, S.W.A.T. cops. All of them are going about the quiet business that they had practiced over and over again, preparing for a high risk activity that could very well lead to the death of a criminal or themselves.

This S.W.A.T. callout would call for the arrest of a savage that had only hours earlier called his estranged wife to meet him in the front yard of the home she had just rented near Olympia Washington, then shot her several times and stood over her body and glistened into her dying eyes as she slowly lost the grip to her life. He then left her body in front of the home where her children would find her. Fifty miles later he stopped in the driveway of his home in Bonney Lake Washington, entered his home, locked the doors behind him, climbed into his bed, snuggled with his gun and whiskey, and awaited the cops. We would not disappoint him.

I began to gather my stuff from the back of my soccer mom type van with blacked out windows to conceal the reality of what lay hidden behind them. We had referred to the van as a Trojan horse, like the one used to conquer Troy; and we used it to take down criminals.

I wasn't nearly as organized as my buddy Pig. His gear was not only carefully stowed away but was polished clean to perfection. He'd always make rude remarks about how I "comfortably" stored my gear and it was never to his standards. I simply referred to him as a "shiny bitch" and we seemed to work well within those parameters of insults as friends do. Many referred to us as the odd couple, Felix and Unger.

Those that had gathered began the routine. Heavy military style boots, camouflaged pants, and hard shelled knee pads – all held together by a reinforced heavy nylon belt that could be used in rappelling. Up top would be heavy body armor covering our vitals, and thick metal plates just big enough to cover our heart inserted into the armor, secured by pockets. All this would be hidden by camouflaged blouse that displayed our name, department patch, and rank, if any. Another heavier belt with padded suspenders complete with holsters and ammo pouches are strapped down to our thighs. Over that we wore a large load bearing vest that snapped together with large plastic snaps located in the front. More pockets for gear, food, ammo, first aid kit, and water. Radios with ear pieces and boomer mics atop our head and all covered in a Kevlar strap down helmet. Goggles and balaclava topped off the basics. On the left thigh were gasmasks and sorted flash bangs we called bangers, and more pouches. On the right thigh, most wore semi-automatic pistols and of course, more ammo. Gear, more gear, and then more gear. Cool stuff.

This was Pig's arena. I'd put him up against any animal that walks the face of the earth. Pig would not only have more gear, but the gear you really need. Case in point, one time we were on an operation and I detected the faint sound in my ear of a hearing aid, battery failure. Damn, I don't have any hearing aid batteries with me. We were lying in the bushes, waiting to ambush some well deserving crook when I looked at Pig, "Hey, you got any hearing aid batteries?" I said it almost half-heartedly and then watched in amazement as a small infrared light come on, and in a few short seconds Pig handed me a single tiny hearing aid battery. Are you shitting me? Got to love a guy like that!

Pig soon arrived at the slider door to my van where I stood working at getting ready for the upcoming task. He poked his head into my van and then pulled it out.

"Stinks in there, smells like shit, you been smoking cigars and farting again" he bitched.

"It's what I do," I responded, pulling a final thigh strap tight on my right leg.

"When are you going to clean up this piece of shit?" he continued.

"I thought you were going to do that for me?" I rallied in return.

"Yeah right, not happening; let's go, ready?" he said.

"Yep, let's get this son of bitch," I fired back and we were off, heading for a field briefing and the violence that patiently awaited our arrival.

I looked around at the gathering and took in the moment. About 35 uniformed SWAT cops stood ready, all looked alike except for height and it's hard to tell us apart; for an outsider, impossible. A command vehicle to our front, latest in all the tech equipment, and a parascoping camera system had the house covered. Captains, Commanders, and Sergeant were standing around in uniform and intently watching the proceedings. An assistant chief was in total command and would make any last minute high up decisions, if presented with one. As the SWAT boss began to speak I nudged Pig and said "we've come a long way since Sumner, Dorothy." He nodded in response.

The SWAT boss provided a run down as to the situation that had brought us to the location. All were provided the latest intel on the suspect barricaded within the home. Cops then broke down into their four and five man teams; and team leaders would brief his team on the team's goal. Our team and one other team had been tasked with entry, when and if it was needed.

There were a total of ten SWAT cops making entry to the home when the time came. Other teams would deploy for sniper coverage and 360 coverage of the home.

Everything, absolutely everything, would be coordinated through SWAT command at the motor home. Two teams would be held in reserve, ready to respond to a need at a moment's notice. SWAT events are well organized, choreographed operations and with military type structure and absolute precision. There is no room for mistakes or failures.

Sniper teams and their spotters were first to leave and replace patrol officers that had been watching the home. Once the sniper teams got set up in their assigned locations they would put "eyes" on the suspect's house and look for any sign of the suspect using high powered scopes and glassware. When the coast was clear the entry team would be moved into a location close to the home and the entry point, but in a position of cover and concealment. There they wait for the most dangerous mission, entry.

We had studied a floor plan of the home attained by intel folks. We had even used large chalk sticks and drew out a full scale floor plan in a closed off area of a neighboring street. We then practiced time and time again our movement through the home. We had developed a plan and had practiced it. I would be number three on the entry team; Pig would be number four of the 10-man team. The biggest strongest one on the team, Gabe, would be the ram man and would batter the door open for our entry. As Gabe would hit the door, bangers would be deployed through most all the windows as would gas canisters via 37 mm launching rifles. For now we just hunkered down and awaited orders.

The plan was to open up a line of communication with the killer. Negotiators would try to get him to talk and if they accomplished that they would then try to bring this entire matter to a peaceful end, and the suspect would simply give up and surrender. That's where a problem arose. The killer was not answering his phone! Apparently it was going directly to voice mail, so command was unsure if the phone had been turned off or not charged up.

One of the teams held in reserve was ordered to provide cover for a negotiator that would be moved closer to the home and attempt contact with the suspect by using a bull horn. I watched intently as the team arrived. They moved in a tight "V" formation using natural cover to a point that the bull horn would be effective; however, nothing came in return. Snipers and spotters saw no movement and there had been no noise from the home.

All power, water, and cable had been cut off to restrict the killer from getting anything. Television was always the first to go. Television news air crews always seemed to arrive during an operation and in an attempt to get the breaking news first would expose our positions from the air, and if the suspect was watching he would know our locations and could prepare for a strike.

The team with the negotiator withdrew back to command and it was decided that a throw phone would be deployed next.

By now the sun was high in the sky and we were on the wrong side of the bushes for shade. I felt over heated as if I was slowly baking and I knew that all of us were feeling the effects of the heat, but no one complained. We'd just take it and sip our lessoning supply of water. At times like these I hated balaclava head gear. Mine was soaked in sweat. It had been six hours since our arrival in the area and we had been under the sun now for the better part of five hours. In two hours the reserve teams would be activated and directed to go practice in the chalk house and then would be sent in to relieve us, that is if this operation was still not resolved.

I dug through a pocket on my load bearing vest and found a spare fully charged battery pack and quickly changed it out as my radio battery was showing signs of depletion. It's odd to lay around in the dirt with nine other men. We can't talk; only listen to our radio mics in our ears. We communicate by writing on tablets, hand gestures, and eyes. Surprising how much can be said using any means other than voice. I've learned you can tell a lot about a person by just looking into his eyes. Fear, confidence, questioning, and anger are easily spotted by the eye, of the eye.

I spotted one of the reserve teams moving slowly towards our position. Three men in the front carried large shields with police boldly stamped to the front. Two officers, one right handed, the other left handed, advanced with the shield with rifle barrels pointed towards the house. The left hander would be deployed to the left of the shields with weapon pointed towards the house, and the right hander on the right side of the shield wall. Behind the shields was an officer carrying a throw phone. The phone is contained in a steal box, about a square foot in size with a handle, opening instruction in various languages and a hand held phone inside, already turned on and ready to go. Another rifleman would cover over the top of the shields and be next to the thrower.

They would work their way to a window and the phone would be thrown through the window into the house. They would then retreat and a negotiator would ring up the throw phone hoping that someone would answer.

This time when the team got to the house, the rifleman covered the left shield flank, let his rifle hang, and quickly did a break and rake of a bedroom window with a hooligan bar. The thrower then threw the phone through the open window area and they retreated retracing their steps. Now we just waited.

Another half hour passed by and no communication from the home had been established. Command decided that pressure needed to be amped up.

There were a number of possibilities as to what was going on with the killer. First it was thought that he could have already killed himself and we were being held at bay by a dead guy. Two, he was incapacitated by drugs or alcohol or both. Three, he wasn't there but neighbors saw him arrive in his car and never saw him leave. And four, he had nerves of steel and was simply waiting for us to come get him and then all hell would break lose.

Command ordered that all 37 mm launching rifles be loaded with gas and prepare for deployment. Every one of us knew the next step, after the gas deployment we would be given entry orders.

A couple more minutes went by and command stated that gas would be deployed on count down beginning with "four, three, two, one, deploy gas" and with that the 37 mm launching rifles roared to life.

"Prepare for second volley" came the order. Moments later a second volley roared to life. And the entry orders came, "entry team, prepare for entry."

Balaclavas were removed and replaced with gas masks, and helmets got strapped down. Once the team leader got a "thumbs up" from each team member, he radioed command that the entry team was ready.

There are many glancing eyes behind the windows of our gas masks, made it more difficult to read those around you, but the atmosphere was definitely amped up. Minutes seemed like hours. Then command gave orders for entry team to move into position. We moved in a static line. Your every move is dictated by the man in front of you. If his rifle is pointing off to the right, yours then is to the left. We work together in our movements that we have practiced over and over again. As our line got to the front door we came to a stop. Gabe was moved to the front and waited for the count down. Team leader notified command that the entry team was in position and ready.

In the moments we waited for whatever was behind this door, I reached back to my training and prior experiences. I'm well trained, well equipped, experienced, and I can fight and never quit even if injured. Honestly, I never felt more alive than at these very moments.

I thought about how many times I had done this very thing. The first couple times you're frightened to death, but by the third time you become euphoric and your fear is no longer present, and your confidence has changed. It's difficult to describe these seconds before the entry; if it were a drug I'd be an addict!

There was nothing but quiet. The command is in full throttle, and snipers and spotters are focused looking for any movement, anything that might help us. Nothing! Suddenly, command gives the order, "entry on countdown, four, three, two, one, execute!"

There is a reason Gabe is a breacher; in one solid swing of the ram the front door explodes open! Gabe steps back and we begin our entry. There is no hesitation. As I clear the door jamb, the door itself swings back into me and catches the end of my gas mask and the seal is immediately broken and I can feel the sting of the tear gas. Since the mask has been compromised and is now more blinding to me, I simply grabbed the front of it and peeled it and my helmet off tossing all to the floor. I kept moving, holding my breath as long as I can, but staying on task.

The number one man and number two man entered the first bedroom door on the left, I continued past them till I reached the next door, on the right. As I turned into the room I immediately spotted the suspect, lying flat on his back. His pistol is lying on the bed next to him and a shot gun leaning against the wall next to the broken out window. I immediately recognized the window. It's the one broken out by the officer just before the throw phone came through it. I noticed a large amount of blood on the bed and face of the suspect and saw a nasty gash to his head.

I then figured out what had occurred! The killer got hit in the head with the throw phone box and he is out! Down for the count and I'm sure the half empty whiskey bottle helped keep him there.

He is quickly handcuffed and moved onto the floor. A stretcher is brought forward and the suspect is placed onto the stretcher and moved outside for medical treatment because of the gas.

We just stood there for a moment looking at the room, trying to figure out how this must have looked like when the phone came flying in. Clearly it caught the suspect by surprise and hit him perfectly.

The SWAT boss entered the room and gave me a look. He stepped up to me and asked about my helmet and mask.

"It tried to kill me coming through the front door so I dumped it".

"L&I would have a fit if they found out you're running around in here without a helmet" he stated.

"Don't tell them," I responded.

"Is the gas even fazing you?" he asked.

"Not really," I answered.

"Figures," he stated and wandered off. I didn't point out that he too had no mask on nor helmet and he did not look any worse for the wear. *Tough bastard,* I thought to myself.

Detectives from Thurston County had arrived at the scene and quickly asked us to move out as they wanted to begin their investigation and SWAT cops were in the way. Pig and I met up in the front yard. Pig made mention of the high tech equipment and training that we have and we use, and this asshole gets taken out by a throw phone. Funny actually, probably saved his life as it looked like he was preparing for a fight.

"Was the shotgun loaded?" Pig asked.

"I don't know, got kicked out before I could check, but the pistol had a mag in it so odds are it was," I responded.

"Let's get out of our gear before debrief, I want to get comfortable" Pig said, and with that we made our way back to our rigs.

The motions we went through hours earlier now were in reverse. I was done first because I "comfortably" put my stuff away and Pig of course, neatly. We arrived back at the command van and the bullshit flowed uninterrupted. Soon the SWAT Boss asked for officer Sandle to stand. Sandle was made the official phone thrower for the SWAT team "from here on in" claimed the SWAT boss. Sandle was the officer that launched the throw phone through the window that knocked out the suspect. It was a fun moment.

As Pig and I made our way back to our police vehicles, I mentioned that I was not going to be able to stay on SWAT much longer because of my age. Fifty was the cut off and I was almost 51 years old. I had only been allowed to stay past 50 because only one SWAT officer had beat me on the physical fitness test, the SWAT Boss, but clearly my time was coming.

Pig asked me, "what you going to miss the most?"

"The thirty seconds prior to and hearing four, three, two, one, execute." I answered.

"Really?" Pig asked.

"Really, that moment makes me feel so alive," I responded.

"I'm hungry and little thirsty, beer and pizza on me," Pig said.

"I see no reason to argue with that offer, I'll follow," I was quick to respond.

I retired from Metro SWAT seven months later, after 13 years of service. I still miss it, terribly.

He was a monster! Every bit of six foot six, 250 pounds I guessed. *Pig, don't fail me now*, but he too soon rounded the corner. There we stood, eye to eye. "Detective Sgt Gill, Puyallup PD, checkmate, you're under arrest!" I spoke with authority. Dave, we learned later of his name, simply stood there. He was clearly shocked! For me there was also a moment of hesitation; we stood face to face, hunter to hunter, stalker to prey. I felt revitalized and the frustrations of the hunt suddenly dissipated and were replaced with satisfaction and success.

Chapter 7

The Step Ladder!

I read the report in astonishment. How could this happen? How could a person sleeping quietly and contently, not have a clue that there is a man hovered above, within inches of him and his wife? How could they have not noticed it until it was too late? That intruder would go through the person's wallet that is placed on the nightstand, taking loose change, then move to the other side of the bed and stand over the man's near naked wife, sleeping peaceably next to him.

The cat burglar would then systematically search the second floor apartment, gathering anything of value and placing it into a bag. He would then leave exactly as he had come: out the sliding glass door onto the balcony, climb over the rail, step down onto a ladder, and slink off into the night.

First there was one report in May of 2010, then by June the reports would almost come every other day. The reports are all the same – all second floor apartments, all the sliding doors had been left unlocked, all victims had been asleep in their beds and un-witnessing of the event that was unfolding in their presence, yet unaware till they awoke in the morning to suddenly learn their secure world, was not!

I learned that similar burglaries had taken place not only in our little town of Puyallup, but it was pretty much county wide and nothing, not one slip up, not one witness, not one fingerprint. Damn spook!

I kept track, read, re-read reports, made notes, made Pig read the reports, looking for that one piece of info. And on July 1st we found a path that would lead Special Investigation Unit (SIU) Detectives to this creep's capture. The step ladder!

It wasn't that the ladder was so special. It was almost identical to the ladder that I, as a boy, had used 48 years earlier in Frenchman's Waste way at Potholes reservoir located in Eastern Washington's inland empire. It gave me height on the river as I waited patiently for a carp to swim by, allowing me a shot at it using a re-curve bow and specially constructed fishing arrows. I was using the ladder to give me an elevated position to ambush fish, much like the cat burglar was using it to get to his sleeping victims.

It was where the ladder had come from that was the key. They came from cable television and communication trucks and vans that were parked in the parking lot of the apartments.

Investigation found that employers would allow their workers to drive these trucks home at night and park them in the parking lots of apartment buildings, if that is where the employee lived. There were few restrictions. In fact the only restrictions were placed on my detectives. Telephone and cable companies would not cooperate with us, unless they were served with a search warrant or court order. I had directed the detectives to find out where cable/television employees lived, and only those that lived in apartment complexes, but the door had been slammed in our face.

To prepare a court order or search warrant would take time: Detectives would work feverishly on the warrant, then wait patiently for it to be reviewed by a prosecutor, adjustments made, reviewed again, and then the warrant would be produced to a judge for a signature. I was quite familiar with the routine and had used it many times in narcotics. Following all that the warrant would be presented to the companies, they would demand time for their attorneys to review the documents, and again, time would pass and more nights would come and go.

All I could think about was while we scrabbled over bureaucratic bullshit; more victims would awake to the horror that their secure life was very, very vulnerable.

I shivered at the thought that some night a lone female would be caught sleeping, dreaming of her life to be, only to be awakened by a creep in the night that had elected to up his game from cat burglar to rapist and possible murder to satisfy his lust for power and control over the helpless and unsuspecting.

Bullshit, I told Pig. I know another way. We had been "narc" cops way too long not to know tricks. And we had been cops for over thirty years and therefore knew secrets and people's weaknesses, which is usually money.

I directed Detectives to find a snitch in the cable companies, a flirty secretary that liked to talk. Take her to lunch, get the information we so desperately need and then slip her a couple of crisp $100.00 bills, and assure her that silence is golden.

We purchased two sources of information and had all we needed in a short afternoon's work. Back at the police department the information was dissected, and apartment complexes with work trucks and vans were identified. Apartment complexes that had already been hit by the burglar in one list, and those apartment complexes with work vehicles that had been untouched by the burglar on the other list.

Pig and I used satellite images to locate apartments that we knew to have second floor sliding glass door balconies that had a greenbelt behind the apartments, giving the suspect the feeling of cover as he climbed to the balcony. We found six suitable in our area and felt confident that he would strike and we, well, we would be waiting.

More politics and funding problems arose; not surprising. It was the fourth of July weekend, my detectives would be off and the department would not pay overtime to 12 detectives on what they felt was less than a 50/50 chance of success. Then I learn that a TV camera loving Captain had jeopardized the entire investigation by announcing on the news that Puyallup Police would be out in force over the holiday, complete with plain clothes detectives in apartment complexes hoping to catch the sneaky cat burglary. Of course it was all bullshit; the department had already told me no overtime for detectives, so my department was making up a lie to keep the burglar at bay, at least through the long weekend.

Not only had the Captain tipped off the suspect, he had alerted an already nervous public that plain clothes' men would be in the apartment complexes hunting another plain clothed man! Damn it, common sense out the door!

I needed 12 detectives; I needed 12 volunteers willing to put Fourth of July on hold and stand watch throughout the rainy night that was in the forecast.

I got them, almost immediately; they stepped up. Of course Pig practically broke my office door down to get on the list and the remainder followed suit, led by Rob.

Honestly, I knew that if I had told them I had an arrest warrant for the Devil and I was going to hell to serve it on Christmas morning they'd show up to help, rifle in one hand and a shot of tequila in the other, ready to get it on. The blood that pumped through their bodies was vivid blue.

Six "two man" teams were deployed in and around the complexes. All teams were made aware of the latest intel that had been developed and the best guesses at which apartments would be targeted in their assigned buildings. The hours slowly melted away and each hour got longer to pass than the prior; and when the sun began to rise we slipped back to the police department all unnoticed. The first night was disappointing, nothing. Nowhere in the county had there been a burglary on the nature of what we were looking for.

Then more politics and legal issues arose. I received a phone call from union bosses stating there might be a problem with detectives working overtime, not getting paid for it, and the "what ifs" started: What if they got hurt? What if they hurt someone? Is this even legal with OSHA? "And what if I don't give a shit?" was all I could muster. Then I said, "Give me an hour, I'll get back to you."

There is always a way around any problem, especially paper shufflers that had over inflated views of their importance, and how insignificant their job was to me. All I demanded was honesty of my Detectives, especially honesty with themselves.

"What you need?" my Captain said answering the phone.

"Compensation; instead of paying overtime, give my guys 15 hours vacation and comp time for every 10 hours they work the balcony burglary case, deal?" I asked.

There was a sigh and then he agreed. I didn't even bother calling the union boss back, keep him guessing and worrying about nothing was my plan.

As we had done the previous night, 12 detectives met, quietly assembling in the briefing room held in a secluded one way in, one way out room. After the briefing, detectives slipped away into the night, six "two man teams", looking for trouble. This night we would find it.

As predicted, the night was full of rain in the Pacific Northwest and there was a slight wind out of the southwest. It's where most weather-related problems attack.

Pig and I knew from studying the suspect's modus operandi that he would strike on the secluded side of an apartment complex. He would first remove a step ladder from the work vehicle found in the parking lot then figure out which apartment he would try to gain entry. If the slider was open he'd be in, if not, he would move to another apartment sliding door.

Of the six apartment complexes we had identified, we chose the best one that I personally felt would be hit. It was perfect in every way.

Arriving in the parking lot on foot and having left our vehicle several blocks from the area, we entered undetected by all. We found the work truck and noticed all the ladders were secure on top of the vehicle and unlocked. We walked the back side of the entire complex, remaining un-noticed and using hand signals for communication; this wasn't our first sneak and peek and it would not be our last. All our movements were calculated and tactical.

We settled in a spot concealed by brush and trees and watched using binoculars, trying to stay dry and monitored the other five teams by radio. Nothing! There was absolute silence, with the exception of traffic that buzzed around the area, and the occasional siren of police, fire, or medical services. Now and then a loud pop or thundering bang of fireworks would go off. Even though the 4th was only 1 hour and thirty minutes old, people could hardly wait to light off their fireworks.

Pig and I were taking turns returning to the work truck to make sure the ladders had not been disturbed, and so far the night was yielding nothing. One of my young detectives contacted me. He was growing impatient; weakness of youth. He had several fixes in mind and ran them by me for a response. I simply replied "Have patience my young Jedi." Pig grinned a little by my response.

"Remember when we were kid cops?" Pig asked.

"How could I forget? Three or four radio calls a night, sparkled with bunch of traffic stops; and no damn supervisors. Are you kidding?" I responded.

"Simple times" he quipped.

"Smokers," Pig said looking through his binoculars.

He was watching two women on a second floor balcony puffing away.

"I could never understand why people would smoke," he carried on.

"You married one, dumbass," I responded, even though they had long since divorced.

"Yeah, I was young and dumb but I won't even date a smoker, not even if she is the hottest thing on the planet," he boasted. "They even taste like smoke," continuing with his complaining.

"Is this your way of breaking up with me?" I asked, grinning.

"You and your damn cigars; just don't smoke them around me," he continued.

Then I glanced at the women on the balcony, then movement to the balcony to their right. This was a second floor balcony and next to where the women were smoking, but hidden from them due to a large wood barrier between the balconies. It was a man, large man, six and a half feet tall, large frame, wearing a light colored jacket and carrying a big white cloth bag that appeared to be full of something. He was sliding open the balcony door and stepping out onto the balcony.

As I watched, he moved to the rail and threw the bag over the rail but never let it go; just let it dangle outside the rail. Then he slowly and deliberately began climbing the rail. I glanced down and saw the step ladder beneath him.

Pig was still bitching about smokers and all their pitfalls but my slap to the back of his head got his attention.

"Look, balcony to the east" I spoke.

He quickly scoped in on my view and simply said, "I'll be damned!"

There would be no hesitation, and as we had done hundreds of times before we quickly broke into a low crouched run, covering ground fast. I continued to watch as the man stood with both feet on the top step of the ladder, one hand clutching the bag, the other the base of the balcony. Then I watched him let go of the balcony and with the slow precision of a tight rope walker he bent at the waste and slowly moved his hands to the top of the ladder and slowly began to step down the ladder.

By now Pig had been on the radio giving direction to responding units and information to dispatch. In the distance I could hear the roar of big V-8 engines kicking to life with the news that we had the balcony burglar in our sights. Those V-8s were, without a doubt, police cars rushing to help.

We moved quickly and silently along the back of the apartments. I stopped us at the apartment under the smoker's balcony. I glanced over my shoulder at Pig; he was close and still on the radio. As he got to me I mouthed the words "I'm going," he simply nodded.

I came around the corner in time to see the suspect step off the ladder. I was now behind him; he had no idea I was there. How befitting, a man that prided himself in his ability to move in stealth, into and out of un-suspecting innocent people's apartments was now himself the victim of two masters of stealth, and our collision would not be pleasant.

I moved quickly now, not caring if I was detected; it was too late for him. As he stepped around the corner and out of sight, I too ran around the corner. He had turned and we were face to face.

He was a monster! Every bit of six foot six, 250 pounds I guessed. *Pig, don't fail me now*, but he too soon rounded the corner. There we stood, eye to eye. "Detective Sgt Gill, Puyallup PD, checkmate, you're under arrest!" I spoke with authority. Dave, we learned later of his name, simply stood there. He was clearly shocked! For me there was also a moment of hesitation; we stood face to face, hunter to hunter, stalker to prey. I felt revitalized and the frustrations of the hunt suddenly dissipated and were replaced with satisfaction and success.

The white bag dropped onto the wet grass and with a sudden jolt he was running, running fast and I was hot on his tail with Pig in behind on the radio yelling "foot pursuit, eastbound behind the apartments!" This guy was huge and running like a gazelle. A 5-foot lead was soon 10 feet and with every stride his lead increased. Soon Dave found an opening between the apartment buildings and he rounded the corner heading to the parking lot trying to out distance us but all he found was a wall of blue, uniformed cops, the ones whose V-8s I had heard earlier had arrived and with Pig's direction had listened and moved into a capture position, and Dave simply ran to them.

As quickly as it had started it was over. Dave was at the bottom of a pig pile and soon there would be no struggle, just the sounds of happy cops high fiving each other and running around with the excitement of boys on a playfield.

Minutes later all SIU detectives had gathered in the parking lot and we retraced the foot pursuit path looking for anything else Dave may have discarded while he was being chased. We only found the big white bag.

The bag contained the spoils of Dave's adventure that early Fourth of July: game boys; DVDs; laptop computers; two of them; jewelry; and even an antique silver spoon.

I sent uniforms to knock on the front door and they got no response. Pig and I were outback and could hear the cops banging on the door and yelling police. Blue lights flashed in the parking lot and yes, even a loud speaker attempted to summon the occupants of the apartment; nothing. Everyone else in the complex was awake, but no, not these folks, happily sleeping away completely ignorant to the turmoil outside.

"Maybe no one is home" a detective said.

"No, the sergeant and I saw a skinny white guy playing video games around midnight in that apartment, he's there" Pig stated.

I nodded in agreement.

"Well shit, if Sasquatch Dave can climb up there and get in, so can I," I stated. "Anyone notice a cable truck around? I need a ladder." I smiled as I said it.

We walked to the rear of the apartment and the ladder had yet to be moved or photographed. We wanted to make sure as many people saw it as possible, kind of sink home the idea that they need to lock their doors and windows at night, even on the second and third floor.

Pig held the ladder and I climbed, followed the action in reverse that I had witnessed Dave make. Soon I was on the balcony, and a young uniformed man who had the same last name as I, joined me. Wearing gloves, I slid open the door and yelled "Police"!

No response. Damn it. My nephew and I both yelled Police at the same time and it did the trick. Soon we spotted the figure of a skinny white guy emerge from the hallway, shielding his eyes from our probing lights. He was followed by a scantily clad gal; they appeared to be mid-20s and clueless.

"What the fuck?" he mumbled.

"We are the police; look out your front door."

He slowly moved to the apartment main door and looked through the peephole and said "cops?"

"There has been an incident, may we come in?"

The young man's eyes quickly glanced about the apartment; he was trying to figure out if he had put away his pot from the evening of playing video games while riding smoke.

"Don't worry about it, you've been the victim of a crime and you don't know it."

"Yes, come in."

With that I held out my gold badge and stepped into the living room, relieved I would not have to climb down that damn ladder.

The lad opened the front door and in walked couple more uniforms and Pig, holding the bag of goodies that Dave had dropped. I asked the young man and his lady to look into the bag but not to touch anything. Pig held open the bag as they peered inside; soon the girl jumped and clasped her hand over her mouth and looked at us.

"That's my grandmother's spoon, how did you get it? It had been in my drawer in the kitchen."

Both of them now looked at us for answers, and they got them. Pig and I sat them down and told them of the last month and a half investigation and how our trail had led us to their balcony and how her grandmother's spoon got into the bag. We told them of Dave, what we had seen and what had happened. They looked at each other in utter shock and disbelief.

"Can I see your bedroom?" I asked.

They agreed, and soon I flipped on the lights and the bedroom was like most young people's room, cluttered and busy.

I looked closely at the floor on both sides of the bed then said "look, Dave has big feet with vibram soled boots with a trace of beauty bark; you can see his prints in the carpet."

Their shock was now absolute fear. The reality of the fact that a complete stranger had been in their bedroom standing next to them as they slept finally struck home. The girl shook at her vulnerability and the young man questioned his ability to protect her.

I took the moment and reassured them they had not been the only ones this had happened to, and now Dave was off the street and going to prison and they would be safe. Words I practically choked on, knowing full well it was all bullshit.

We stayed awhile longer, talking about safety and reassured them that the bad guy was gone and not to worry; Dave would never be back.

Pictures of the scene were taken, evidence gathered, stolen property photographed, fingerprinted, and returned to the owners. Dave was driven to jail and booked, and later held in the county jail for one count of burglary. A Captain got on the morning news letting the public know we had our man.

Dave gleefully pleads guilty to one count of burglary.

Dave was sentenced to one year in prison, given credit for time served, and was out in 10 months; yeah, 10 months!

Something to Touch your Hearts

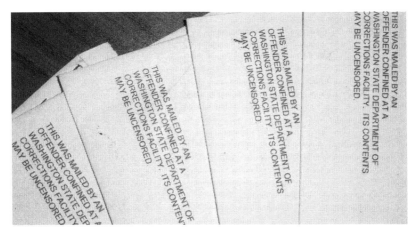

There are memories that will forever be etched not only in our minds but in our hearts. These are the memories that will forever linger because they have touched us deeply. In my years of service, there were a few stories that surely left an indelible print in my heart; some were heavy, some were light. Some still bring me to tears; some put a smile on my face. May these stories touch your hearts deeply, lightly, or in whatever way they will.

The question sent mixed signals. Here is a pathetic person whose life is shattered, his body completely damaged from the use of meth and the stress brought about by the relentless pursuit of using any method known to mankind to acquire it. Why would he give a damn about me? He was about to jump, an activity that would most assuredly snap his neck thus ending his tortured life, but he wanted to make sure he didn't hurt me in doing so?

Chapter 8

Sunrise Suicide

I awoke to the buzzing sound of my cell phone parked next to me on a night stand. A quick glance at the clock revealed it was 0330 in the morning. "I bet I know what this is about," I muttered to myself. True enough, it was Pig. I answered in a gruff voice, "Yeah, what you want?"

Pig replied, "Hey, I just got to the PD and need to write a search warrant. The road guys flushed some guy out last night up to no good and chased him to an address off 4th. They stumbled into a meth lab. I need your help, ok?"

"Yeah, on the way," I responded.

Climbing out of bed barely awake, my long hair wadded up and hanging down on my left shoulder, I saw myself in the mirror and surely looked like crap. I brushed my teeth, threw on some roughed up looking clothes, and headed out for my Lincoln Navigator donated by some asshole drug dealer, then off to begin the 45 minute drive to town.

Pig lived close to the department and always got there before me, which was good. He is methodical, organized, and neat. He loves structure, for as long as it's his structure and works well in that atmosphere. I, on the other hand, don't give a damn. I just want to get things done. Together we were a great team who had learned to work together years earlier. We can have a conversation with each other without saying a word. He knows me so well – if I am stressed, struggling, comfortable, or over my head – and he always has a plan in place to fix the problem. Many times before he had watched me intently as I worked an undercover deal, and he knew exactly what was going on.

As I got near the town, Pig radioed me the address on 4th and that he needed a complete description of the property, buildings, and vehicles so he could write the information on the search warrant. I knew the drill and his need for perfection.

As I arrived at the place I was greeted by a couple of uniformed men parked out front and standing guard waiting for the search warrant and lab teams that had yet been alerted.

"Where's the lab?" I asked. The officers directed me to the field behind the house. "I'll take it from here" I said, and they returned to their patrol cars.

I looked around the area noticing it was bordered on the back by railroad tracks, and the house to the front. The area was out of view of wandering eyes from the road and in a thicket of brush and blackberry bushes. In the middle of the thicket stood some old shacks, crudely made, and of course the tell-tale signs of a meth problem – the ever present blue tarps that made up the walls. Also in the middle was a rather large maple tree that looked unhealthy, probably suffering from the exposure to the toxic wastes of a meth lab being dumped on its root system. I moved a little closer and began searching my clothing for a pen and small notepad that I usually kept with me.

The sky was clear and the stars had faded as this day in January 2004 was about to be born. I could see that looming giant Mount Rainier from a distance, silhouetted by the rising sun. It was a stunning view that I never grew tired of and had stared at many times since I was a young boy growing up in the Puyallup Valley.

I turned my gaze back to the task at hand and got the detailed description that Pig would demand for his search warrant. I continued to let my eyes wander and noticed the obvious signs of a meth lab – scattered cans of "Heet" and different kinds of solvents, coffee filters, and quart-sized glass jars, some with bi-layer liquids in them. But it is what I saw next that made the hair on the back of my neck stand on end!

A single falling maple seed that, as it fell from the tree, spun like the rotating blades of a helicopter. I watched it intently, falling straight and true in the absolute calm of the morning. I knew I was not the only beast in the woods and whatever was here was directly above me in the tree. I reached up to my hip and felt my handgun concealed beneath my black leather vest and found my phone. I switched the ringer to off, deciding this was no time to be bothered by Pig. I still didn't look up. I didn't want to have a conversation about a search warrant right now and I was already wondering why Pig hadn't called me looking for answers. I did not want to let, whatever was above me, know that I was a cop. I looked like crap and was happy, very happy with that cloak. Whatever was there had allowed me to move about freely and I wasn't about to call it out. I decided however that it was time to at least get into a tactically better position without drawing attention that I was aware of his or its presence. I took several steps in reverse, cautious and calculating as I moved but trying not to look like it.

I pondered my position and situation I had wandered into. Whatever was above me had eluded the police and a tracking dog. Maybe it was nothing, or maybe it was a cat. Nah, I knew better. Someone was there, above me and watching. My sixth sense was on full power and it had never betrayed me before.

"Damn it, how did the uniforms miss this?" I thought to myself. I considered simply turning and walking out to a position where I could turn and look back, but would "it" allow me to? That became a clear concern. I'd rather see something coming than feel the hit from behind, not seeing whatever it was. Fuck it, I looked up!

I saw a slightly built man, with filthy clothing and long, greasy, tangled hair. He peered back at me and I saw in his eyes that same lifeless zombie look and immediately I knew he was a meth addict who was at the end of his rope ... literally. He had tied a fire hose around his neck and knotted it. The other end of the hose was secured to the large branch he was standing on. The bottoms of his bare feet were filthy and bloody. He was about 25 feet in the air above me and if he jumped, it appeared he would come up about five feet short of rope, thus easily snapping his neck and landing on me if the knot didn't hold.

"What you doing?" I easily spoke in a wondering tone, not wanting to sound too authoritative.

"I'm watching my last sunrise then I'm jumping," he replied.

The next question was obvious. "Why?" I asked.

"I'm not going back to prison, my life is ruined and I'm just done." Then he simply asked, "Would you please move? I don't want to hit you."

The question sent mixed signals. Here is a pathetic person whose life is shattered, his body completely damaged from the use of meth and the stress brought about by the relentless pursuit of using any method known to mankind to acquire it. Why would he give a damn about me? He was about to jump, an activity that would most assuredly snap his neck thus ending his tortured life, but he wanted to make sure he didn't hurt me in doing so?

I replied in a soft caring tone, "Sorry, I can't do that."

I recalled him looking at me with an intense stare, cropped by the greasy tangled hair that hung to the sides of his sunken cheeks. He held his glare then finally spoke, "You're a cop, aren't you?"

With a deep sigh, I replied, "Yeah."

He glanced again at the rising sun just beginning to peek over the mountains to the east. Not taking his eyes from the view he simply asked me "Why do you give a shit about me?"

I waited to make a response, pondering my answer. Do I use the authoritative side of me and give a policeman type response that has been grilled into us since the academy, or should I apply human nature and continue down the "I care" route? I decided a little of both was appropriate.

"Look, I have issues with this. We are both here because of other people: you on that tree and me under you. How we arrived at this point is no longer an issue. We are here right now. You want to kill yourself, and I, well I can't allow that as I have sworn an oath to protect and help people, even you. Besides I'm in a place known to most as a place between a rock and a hard spot. You've got your "out" figure out, but for me there is only my way."

He slowly took his eyes from the rising sun and looked at me and stated "I won't sue you for letting me jump, I'll be dead and it's only you and me, no one will know, so move."

"It's not that," I responded. "If I let you jump I got to live with that choice, I've got to carry the memory of watching you jump, watching you fall, and hearing the snap of your neck! I have no more room in my memories for any more of those thoughts, I'm filled with those types of horrifying sights and I'm not moving!"

He looked away, watching the slowly rising sun. *I've got my demons too asshole*, thinking to myself. I asked him "what's your name?"

I could see his sigh, then a little grin, and he said "Nick." "Yours?" he asked back.

"Gill," I replied.

As Nick stared at the rising sun I caught some movement to my right side near the rear of the house and could see a uniform appear from the front of the house walking my way. Crap, I muttered. Not wanting Nick to see this, I discreetly waved at the officer to stop; he did, and then I pointed up. He immediately glanced up and immediately had a look of disbelief as he wondered some of the same thoughts I had just minutes earlier. I motioned him away and he quietly and without Nick knowing, slipped out of sight. The Calvary would soon be on its way.

"I had it all – wife, kid, job, shit I even attended church, and now look at me!!! What a piece of shit I've become, because I was too weak to say no," Nick spoke with a crackling voice and I could see the tears beginning to fill his eyes. "This isn't supposed to happen to me," he said with a heavy sad voice.

I was quick to respond, wanting to seize this moment. "Look, you're not the only one; many people have succumbed to this terrible drug, and to be completely honest with you, many recover when their life reached the depth that yours is right now. There is hope."

"Prison," Nick muttered.

Then with a deep sigh I responded, "Yes, there will be a price to pay, but if you are sincere about cleaning up your life, then that would help you rebuild, find your foundation for the remainder of your life, and hit the ground running when you get out." "You mentioned a family," I asked cautiously.

Nick responded, "I don't even know where they are at, what my son looks like, nothing."

It was the moment I had been waiting for, the chance for getting Nick out of that damn tree and freeing my mind of the possibility of watching yet another person "needlessly" die because of meth. Pick your words wisely, I muttered to myself. I also now knew Nick wanted to be saved.

"I'll make you a deal!" I responded.

Nick turned his gaze at me, and intently asked "What?"

"Deal," I repeated.

"Go on" Nick stated.

Without hesitation I responded, "come out of that damn tree safely, I'll walk you to my car, personally drive you to the jail, no cuffs, and walk you through booking; no one will disrespect you as I will not tolerate it and then I will personally track your family down. I will tell them of this morning and that I sincerely believed you when you told me you wanted to straighten your life out and spend the remainder of it making it up to them for your mistakes."

Nothing, no response, he just looked at me. Then Nick raised his head and began looking at the rising sun. Nick began, "Why should I believe you, your hair is long, you do undercover work, thus you make your living as a liar."

Damn, I thought, he still has a thought process and is somewhat intelligent. I had but one answer. "You're right," I responded. "I am an undercover cop; yep I am a liar when I must be, but I'm a husband, father and grandpa. Forget the cop part; I'm a dad reaching out to another dad right now, I just need you to reach back."

By now Nick was again looking at me ... looking for trust, looking for help and I knew he wanted to reach back.

"Ball's in your court Nick," I said. We held our stare for a few moments then I turned away and nodded at the sunrise. "I've lived here all my life and never got tired of watching that sunrise," I mentioned, trying to relax the moment but not stray far from the task at hand.

He was thinking, staring at the sunrise. Not a word was spoken for a couple minutes, seemed like hours. This was a tight spot, for both of us.

Then I said, "About the cop part of me, I'm like no cop you've ever met; I give a damn and once I've given my word to you, it's a done deal. I will find your family, swear it."

More minutes passed then Nick spoke. "There's a reason I'm on this tree this morning and there is a reason you are the one that found me, did I mention I used to go to church?"

"Yes," I responded.

"I think someone is reaching out to me through you," Nick said. "What do you think, Detective?"

"Honestly speaking Nick, I'm not a religious man but do strongly believe that some things happen for a reason; and yes this is definitely one of those times," I responded.

More time passed as Nick stared at the half-risen sun with a pinkish red glow. I too watched the sunrise as I kept a fleeting eye on my counterpart above, not yet sure how this was going to play out.

Movement soon caught my eye as Nick raised his left hand and began tugging on the fire hose that was knotted around his neck. He was trying to untie it while watching the sunrise and making sure that he does not lose his balance. He was struggling when he let go of the tree and was using both hands now, desperately, hurriedly pulling the knot free. He was suddenly anxious to untie himself, but in his haste he began to lose his balance and I feared that he would fall. How ironic that would have been to climb the tree to kill one's self then die accidentally after deciding not to take one's life. Would I be able to catch him?

Nick caught himself and the knot was gone; he had released himself. Slowly without a word spoken between us, Nick began climbing down. I had wondered how he had gotten up the tree in the first place as there were no branches or ladder; but nonetheless he had gotten himself up there and was slowly getting himself down.

Once on the ground Nick turned to me and reintroduced himself as Nick Ponders. I followed suit, "Detective Gill".

Nick was a whiff of a man. He stood five and a half feet tall, his body eaten away by his drug use. He looked pitiful and filthy, covered in scratches and bleeding; no doubt this was from running from the police earlier. He had open sores to his face, hands and arms, obviously from the meth that poisoned his body.

I was going to run him through my regular routine and ask him if he had any guns, knives or grenades on him, but clearly, he had nothing.

As Nick and I started to walk to my car, cops began appearing from all areas, some rushing towards me, some just watching. Pig was there also.

"What's up?" Pig asked.

"I've made a deal, I'm escorting Nick to jail; and I'll handle the booking. You got this, right?" I asked of Pig.

"Sergeant is not going to like how you do things," Pig responded.

"I don't give a shit what he thinks; I made a deal" I said.

Pig already knew what my answer would be to that and we walked together escorting Nick to my dirty green Lincoln. Once I pulled away from the curb I noticed I was being escorted by two marked patrol cars. Pig wouldn't have it any other way.

As I drove to the jail, I advised Nick of his constitutional rights from memory. I then asked him if he understood his rights and he quietly said "yes". I then said, "I'll find your wife Nick." He simply responded, "I know."

It was now mid-March. Over two months had passed since that morning in the thicket with Nick perched in a tree and in seemingly hopeless position watching and waiting on his sunrise suicide, and me struggling to find a way to talk him down. I had found Nick's wife and told her everything that happened that morning, and the promise I made to Nick about her. I have no idea what, if anything, she did with the information I gave her, but my promise had been paid in full.

Then I got a phone message from some attorney-at-law saying: "Detective Gill, this is Dan Slavens, Nick Ponders' attorney. I have a very unusual request, please call me."

This was unusual. There is a process and clearly Mr. Slavens was not following it. I checked into Slavens' background and learned that he was an experienced savvy defense attorney. Good attorneys come with inflated fees; Nick had someone with money helping him.

I contacted the prosecutor assigned to the Nick Ponders case and learned that the case was all but adjudicated and that Nick Ponders was rolling on it, pleading out for a lesser sentence. So what did Mr. Slavens want with me? The prosecutor told me to not respond and he would contact Mr. Slavens and find out what he wanted.

Several days passed and the prosecutor called me at work.

"Detective, go to the meeting with Mr. Slavens, Nick Ponders will be there also, so it will be at the jail."

"What's this in regards to?" I quizzed.

"Just go, I think you'll like it," was his response. With that, the conversation ended.

A week later I arrived at the county jail. After checking in I was escorted down long halls and up an elevator to a series of rooms with heavily hinged steel doors that bore large door locks. The guard stopped and opened one of these doors for my entry. Inside I recognized Nick, seated with his attorney, Slavens, no doubt, and a lady. After brief introductions I learned that the lady was Nick's wife. Until now I had only spoken to her by phone.

"What's this all about?" I asked.

Nick stood then spoke. "I asked to meet you Detective. I wanted to thank you for saving my life."

His wife quickly stated, "me too."

I was at a loss for words. In all my years I had never been summoned to a jailhouse meeting with a suspect and his attorney for a thank you. It was a very pleasant surprise. Emotions ran high with Nick and his wife and this was clearly their moment. After an exchange of a few pleasantries, I bid them farewell and wished them good luck in their future.

Six years later I was seated at my desk when my phone rang. It was the receptionist in the front lobby of the police department. She said there was a man in the lobby that asked to speak with me. She went on further stating the man did not want to give his name, just wanted to speak with me. I told her I'd be there shortly.

A lot of things had changed since that cold January day in 2004. I had been promoted to sergeant and supervised a Special Investigation Unit. We specialized in auto theft, store front operations, narcotics, and anything else they could fit onto my desk. Of course, Pig and Rob were the tip of my spear.

He was a short stocky man who wore construction clothing and a hard hat, with a grin from ear to ear. The grip of his hand shake was one of strength, and as he shook my hand he patted me on the shoulder and stated he had waited years for this very moment. He had me on my heels; I had not yet realized who this man was and he knew it, and delighted at my questioning look.

"You have no idea who I am, do you?" he finally said in a victorious manner.

"Sorry, look familiar but no, no idea" I responded.

"I'm Nick, Nick Ponders, former tree hugger" Nick said smiling on the verge of a giggle.

That's when it hit me, the guy from the tree at the meth lab. The pathetic, dilapidated man with the open sores and zombie look was standing before me. I was shocked! I had seen recovery before but not to this extent. Nick couldn't talk fast enough. He went on about his wife, his son, and new baby on the way. He was employed doing construction and was building a facility just down the street and decided it was time to stop by and simply say hi.

We spent his lunch hour walking the area and talking. Not much was said of the incident in the thicket in January 2004 but more on the struggles of his recovery from addiction and the fight to regain his family's trust and confidence. Nick was aglow with life and had that energy about him. As we walked, it was hard to believe, even now thinking about it, that this was the same man from the tree that night. The man that I had met was filled with drugs, hopelessness, and despair. This man I am with is a man filled with love, life, and dreams of tomorrow. "How could it be?" I thought.

Prior to Nick's leaving he mentioned that he does remember me saying that I had taken an oath to protect people, even people like him. He casually stated that he too had sworn an oath to himself: that he would never turn away from helping anyone, ever.

As quickly as Nick had arrived and spoke, he was gone promising to stay in touch. It was the last time I have seen Nick Ponders, although he calls at least once a year to check and see if I need anything, and to say thanks.

"You're welcome, Mr. Ponders."

Chapter 9

Footprints in the Snow

Spring had sprung and summer had invaded my small town. I was working graveyards alone doing yet another bar check of one of the eight bars we had in our little town. I had just entered the Club Tavern in downtown Sumner and made my way slowly thru the crowd, working them as I usually had done, taught to me by Carl. The bar had an "L" shape and at the end of the "L" was the entrance to the back of the bar and where the tender would be located. I usually met him there and we would small talk for a few moments, then I would continue to move thru the bar, "checking". Tonight would be no different.

There was a new face seated near where I was slowly moving. He wasn't new to me but to the bar. His name was Luke and never had a problem with him. I knew him and had made small talk with him along Main Street when I would walk the downtown area. It was a small town and I knew most, especially those that lived close to the downtown area. Luke was older than I and was a heavy equipment operator. In the last six months Luke had visited the bar nearly every night, sitting alone at the end of the bar drinking beer till he could barely walk, then he would close the bar by leaving out the back door and stagger home. As I entered the bar Luke would look at me and when I return the look he would look down, a sign of submission. I would catch him looking at me again, and again he would always look down. I never asked him why he was drinking so heavily but I would listen if he ever wanted to talk.

I continued slowly moving, acting as though I owned the place and slowly walked behind Luke, past him to the end of the bar where I would engage the bartender in small talk. Tonight was no different. As my short un-meaningful conversation ended with the bartender I once again moved slowly behind Luke; and as I just got past him he whirled in his bar stool, grabbed my left arm, and pulled me a bit towards him. This was odd behavior, very odd; people don't grab cops like that.

"It was me," Luke spoke with emotion. "It was me that left the footprints in snow that night," he spoke like a man confessing something, but what?

"I don't understand what you're telling me," I responded.

"The car; the one upside down along the freeway near the Orting highway overpass, the one with the girl inside," he pleaded to me. "The snowy night, the car was in the low spot between the on-ramp and the freeway edge, the one flipped over" he continued, "those were my foot prints you found in the snow that night, remember?"

Then it hit me. I stepped up to the bar, grabbed a stool and sat next to Luke, pulling the event out from behind the walls where I had hidden it in my mind. I began reliving that night.

Dispatched had called me and asked that I check for a possible accident on highway 410, near the Orting highway over pass. I recall hearing the time, 0232 hrs. The January night was bitterly cold and rain had turned to snow and the wind blew. The roads were slick and the ditches full of near frozen runoff. A male citizen had called and said there was a car flipped over on its roof and spun into the ditch, and police needed to check on it. The caller hung up without giving his name. As I arrived I found what had been reported: a single car, flipped upside down in the wide ditch full of freezing water. Not only had it flipped, it had spun and was now facing oncoming traffic. I notified dispatch that I had arrived and to contact state patrol, this would be their report for the taking.

As I approached, I used my large well-used flashlight of those days and noticed, as I advanced, footprints in the snow leading away from the car. The prints were larger, a man I figured. I waded into the water and to the passenger side of the car where the edge of the ditch was yet to fill with water and more snow, more footprints. My first thoughts were that the driver had gotten out of the wreck, inspected his predicament, and left the wreck walking. I knelt in the snow and peered into the car with my flashlight. At first I saw nothing, but slowly I made out clothing. Laundry was my first thought, then a saw glint of a human arm, a small human arm afloat in the water that filled the car.

I grabbed my radio and loudly stated "I have one person in the car, appears to be pinned upside down, head in the water; send me a tow and fire department immediately."

I figured a tow truck to lift the car if I couldn't free the person. With that I made a little toss of my radio to the bottom of the car that was facing skyward into the falling snow. I grabbed the door latch but it would not open. I swung wildly at the window shattering it with my flashlight. With a quick raking motion I cleared the remainder of the glass from the window opening, diving head first into the cab of the car, and the girl inside. She was seat belted into the car, most of her lower body was above the water but the most important thing was her head and upper shoulders dangled in the water. I forced myself under her head and shoulders and pushed her head up towards the floor of the car, frantically trying to get her head out of the water. It worked but I was using a huge amount of force. I reached down fumbling for my ever present boot knife, bringing my right boot ever so closely to my reaching left hand. With a quick flip of the snap the double edge razor sharp knife cleared my boot. With a frantic swipe of the knife I cut the seatbelt holding the girl upside down and she dropped full weight onto me. Now her head and shoulders cleared the water. I now found a flaw in my plan; I was now pinned under her, under the water holding my breath. I had experience this before as a lifeguard at the high school so I was able to keep my wits about me. Her weight was dead weight. She was small but her weight seemed as though she were large.

I reached my right hand wildly up looking for the steering wheel column and found it. I grasp the steering column and in a huge effort pulled my head from the water and with my left hand I pushed the girl off me towards the passenger door and the open window. We both had our heads above water now but only I was breathing. I worked my way till I was on top of the girl all the while keeping her head above water. I took a moment and to breath three breaths into her mouth. I began wiggling in reverse and pausing only moments to blast more breaths into her mouth. Then I heard words behind me, outside the car, voice of a man that I had known as a small boy. It was Les, a tow truck driver/owner who had arrived ahead of fire department aid and state patrol. Not surprising if you knew Les.

"I'm going to pull you out by your boots; do you have a hold of her?" Les asked.

"Yes!" I screamed "pull me out!"

And with that Les grabbed my boots and frantically dragged me and the girl out of the car onto the snow. Les and I worked frantically on her. He was compressing her chest and I desperately tried to breathe life into her as snow fell on us and wind whirled about our pile of humanity. Minutes passed by and the fire department arrived followed by an ambulance. Our duty was finished and the girl was now in their capable hands.

The cold and wet hit me and I began shivering uncontrollably. Les was suffering also. We just looked at each other: an old tow truck driver and a kid cop.

"Yes, I remember that night Luke, terrible night," I said.

"I didn't see her in the car when I checked, didn't see anything," he continued. "I walked all around that car and believed no one was in it." Then Luke said something that answered an earlier question I had of him, why he was drinking himself into alcoholism for the last six months. "I let her drown in that car that night," Luke spoke quietly. "I walked away and let her drown."

I wasn't about to let that traffic fatality claim yet another life; no way was I going to let that happen. I might not have been able to save that girl that night but damn it, Luke wasn't going to drink himself to death over it either.

"Luke, look at me," I spoke. "She didn't drown, she died of a broken neck, and she was gone when you walked around that wreck that night."

"Are you sure?" he asked. "The paper said she drowned."

"They had it wrong; I even thought she had drowned. I wrote in my police report that I believed she had drowned, but an autopsy later found she had died from a broken neck due to the whiplash of the crash."

Luke's eyes filled with water. "Are you sure officer?" he asked.

"Yes, the local newspaper read my report and reported it that way," I told him.

Silence; Luke searched me, wanting to believe me.

"There was nothing you or I could have done; her fate was out of our hands," I said.

Luke pushed his beer from in front of him, pulled out a twenty dollar bill, and placed it under the half drank glass of beer. I stood as he did and we shook hands. Luke walked out of the back of the bar that night. I never found him in a bar again, drinking. I had been lying, not willing to lose yet another life to that traffic accident that night.

Six years later Luke lost his life in a work related accident. This story of a small town cop would have never have been told if Luke was still alive. He died without having the guilt of that night.

"Don't Make Me Tell the Truth"

Please don't make me tell the truth.
It happened so fast, it is but a blur.
"So help me God," to the court I will always say,
but this time please Lord, let me stray.

Please God, don't make me tell the truth this time.
Release this child's life back to me.
I worked so hard to not let her drown.
Please lord, don't let me down.
Don't make me tell her parents of their loss.
Please Lord, give this girl back to us.

It's only a car upside down in a water filled ditch.
So please Lord, let me change my next pitch,
to a line that I can say to her mom and dad
that she will be fine.
I beg of you oh Lord,
Don't make me tell the truth.

Sometimes I see things and I just turn my back,
But other times it is much worse,
something happens; I must attack.

Checking the rise and fall of covers,
When a child dies there is so much grief
And their parents I must brief,
And help them through the sorrow and pain.
This news would kill me if I were not the police.

Walt had heard that I was a truck driver that had been stealing pseudoephedrine from my truck loads and was selling it for $2500.00 a case. Pseudoephedrine was a "gotta have" to make methamphetamine. Walt had gotten in touch with me through a police informant and a meeting was set up. Walt had brought a meth maggot with him and used the meth head to walk to my car. The meth head introduced himself and said Walt didn't want to meet me the first time but said cops can't use dope so if I wasn't a cop I'd surely use some dope for proof that I wasn't a cop.

Chapter 10

Letters from Prison

I arrived at work as usual, and the first thing I did was check my mailbox for any department information. It was a letter this time, a letter from Jose Herrera. Name looked familiar but till I opened it; no idea who Jose Herrera might be. The return address was from Monroe, a Washington state prison. 'Hate' mail? Mail bomb? I stepped back outside in the parking lot and slowly, carefully opened the envelope. Inside was a carefully folded letter, hand written with broken English and miss-spelled words. It read:

Hello Detective,

My name is Jose Herrera and about a year ago you arrested me for unlawful possession and distribution of narcotics. You owe me nothing but I would really appreciate it if you could send me the pictures that were in my property. They were of my parents, brothers and sisters. There was some mail with addresses with the stuff and I would like to be able to find them and let them know I'm okay.

I know you're busy but if you would just take a moment it would mean much to me and my family, I know they are worried and have no idea what happened to me. I'm glad you stopped me. I came to America to make a better life for them and all I've done is screwed up. Please, take a moment and send those items to me.

Thank You.

Jose Herrera

I returned inside the police department and made my way to the second floor and my office. I ran "Jose Herrera" into the data base and his case popped up. I learned he had been arrested 17 months ago and I was the lead detective. I searched the property sheet and found "box of papers". If there had been pictures and letters, they were probably there.

I then called the property room and asked about the property in Jose Herrera's case. After waiting about five minutes the clerk got back on the phone.

"Since that case has been adjudicated, all the property has been disposed of," she said.

"Define disposed?" I asked.

She was in no mood to educate me but answered "dope would be destroyed, firearms destroyed; and any money, valuables and stuff would be stored, letters sent to last known addresses and if we get no response, that stuff taken to auction."

"So it's gone?" I asked.

"Yes," she responded and our conversation ended.

I slid his letter and envelope into the round file trash and began to work on my latest case.

Several years past by and I found yet another letter in my mailbox, not from Jose Herrera but from a guy named Walter Henderson, also from a Washington state prison. It read:

Dear Sir,

I'm Walter Henderson you arrested me for dealing in dope and now I'm in prison. I have been here for almost a year and wanted to send you a note to thank you for stopping me. I was on a dark spiraling path that led to nowhere. My life was out of control and I needed help stopping. Again thank you for that. When I get out in a couple of years I will be transported back to Minnesota for a crime I'm wanted for there. If and when I get out I want to stop by and thank you in person. Anyway, thanks, I hope to see you soon.
Respectfully,
Walter Henderson

It had always bothered me that I had not written Jose Herrera and at least tell him I tried to find his stuff but elected instead to simply, coldly throw his letter away with absolutely no regard for he or his family. I had promised myself no matter what the letter contained, from then on I would respond.

I looked up Walter and found it was a reverse hot pop that had occurred two years prior at the local Fred Meyer Store in Puyallup. Walt had been lured to that area by detectives and a trap had been set up.

Walt had heard that I was a truck driver that had been stealing pseudoephedrine from my truck loads and was selling it for $2500.00 a case. Pseudoephedrine was a "gotta have" to make methamphetamine. Walt had gotten in touch with me through a police informant and a meeting was set up. Walt had brought a meth maggot with him and used the meth head to walk to my car. The meth head introduced himself and said Walt didn't want to meet me the first time but said cops can't use dope so if I wasn't a cop I'd surely use some dope for proof that I wasn't a cop.

"What you have in mind?" I asked. I watched intently as he took a small plastic baggie containing a white crystal substance, meth, and carefully lined in up on a foil gum wrapper using a razor blade. My mind was whirling, *how was I going to get this done? No way no how was I using this crap but if I could make him believe I did we would be good to go.*

"This is not a good place to be doing dope; cops everywhere and on bikes too," I warned.

"I'll be look-out" he responded still fanatically trying to make a perfect snorting line, and then carefully handed it to me.

"Go ahead," he ordered.

"Ok, you watch out the rear windows towards the road," directing him to look away.

I immediately dumped the dope to the left of my pant leg and snorted away, at nothing. I jerked my head back and faked a good hit as I had seen other meth heads do.

"Fuckin A, that's some good shit, your man makes this stuff?" I asked.

"Yeah he's a great cook," he answered.

"Hold it," I said. "This is a good hit," and does he have any he would like to trade?"

"Yeah, he's always holding," the kid bolstered.

"Tell him I got three cases, he can have all three $6500.00 and an ounce of this shit, see what he says, ok?" I told him.

With that he got out of the car and walked through the lot, almost skipping. He stopped and got into what looked like an old Camaro. After a couple of minutes the vehicle backed out of its parking space and made its way to me. The vehicle stopped directly behind me lining up the trunks; I figured this is a good deal. The meth head jumped out of the Camaro and opened the passenger door to my car. He threw an ounce baggie of crystal methamphetamine onto the seat and a wad of cash, all hundreds. A quick count found $6500. I hit the button letting the trunk to my car open and in seconds the three cases of pseudoephedrine were placed into the rear trunk of Walt's car. The next thing I did was a signal all had been waiting for; I reached and turned around my NY Yankees baseball hat. It was the signal the deal was done and Walter was ripe for the cleaning. Of course all hell broke loose.

Immediately cops appeared out of nowhere, Walter slammed his car into gear and with spinning squealing tires and rich blue smoke was screaming through the lot looking for a way out.

"What the fuck is going on?" I asked the bewildered kid watching the scene unfold before him and I acting as stupid as possible. He began to get twitchy, "keep cool kid, keep cool," I urged him. "Cop's aren't after us."

Moments later two bike cops appeared from out of the wood line next to us and just as the meth head made a break for it he was gang tackled by what would appear to be Seahawk line backers. You know what the best part was? The dumbass was yelling at me to run, "it's the cops, run Don," he shouted all the while getting a parking lot ass kicking.

Soon he was subdued. As he lay face down on the pavement bleeding, I walked over, knelt down, and dropped open my badge wallet: "that's Detective Don," meth head. He turned away realizing finally what had happened.

After a short pursuit and a few gun shots Walter surrendered after his car spun wildly out of control. No one got hurt but for a few cuts and scrapes. My three cases of pseudoephedrine were retrieved from Walt's trunk and could be used again in another reverse drug case.

Reports were written, evidence submitted and Walter was helpless. Cops had a solid case so he just rolled on the plea and was placed in prison.

My return letter read:

Hello Walt,

I'm glad you came to your senses and I hope you mean it. It won't be easy when you get out and temptation will be at every turn. Consider getting out a chance at a new start, just don't screw it up. If I'm still working and haven't retired, you're welcome to stop by and say hi. Look forward to it.

Good Luck Walt!
Detective Gill

It was the last time I heard from Walt but more letters came, from different people; different cases and most of them thanked me, even though they hated prison they understood why they were there. Then I got a letter from a guy named Rudy. The letter read:

Detective, I use the word lightly with because you lied to me. Cops are not supposed to lie, yet you did and did it so well that I fully believed you, never even thought you were a cop. You looked like me, how is it you cops say, dirt bag. You're worse, a lying dirt bag. I hope you're happy, my life is ruined and I'm going to rot for years in this hell hole you put me in. When I get out I hope I RUN into you.

Rudy didn't sign the letter but clearly he was upset and somewhat threatening. I looked up his name and found the case. It had occurred almost two years earlier and I was the undercover detective that did him. He was now doing a seven year stint in prison for car theft; apparently we had done a good job on him. I read on.

I had heard of Rudy through a police informant, snitch. The snitch told me that Rudy was stealing cars, mostly Hondas and Toyotas and was selling parts from the cars then dumping the car someplace. Rudy had bragged to the snitch that he loved the rush he got when stealing cars and that one time he stole eleven in one night for transportation from Bremerton to Puyallup.

An investigation into Rudy's activities began and detectives learned that Rudy had already done couple years in prison for auto theft and burglary. Further, we learned that lately in the last six months seven stolen Hondas had been recovered in the vicinity of Rudy's residence. All the cars recovered were Hondas and all were missing parts. I called the snitch to set up a meeting that eventually led me to being introduced to Rudy in person. The moment I shook hands when I met Rudy, I was lying and manipulative. I convinced him I was buying stolen cars, shipping them to California where they would be given a whole new look and identity. I told him that if he wanted to work with me he had to deliver the cars in tack, stereos in the dash, nothing stolen out of them, and no broken windows as it would cost me money as the cars' value would be reduced. I told Rudy that I had a small warehouse where I collected the cars for shipping and I had two other guys working for me.

Rudy bragged to me now. He claimed to be the best car thief in the area and he could outperform my other two guys put together. Rudy even bragged about being in prison and how he had learned a lot and could not be caught.

Rudy then asked me a question, "when can I start?"

I wrote down my phone number and handed it to him, "call me when you have one."

"Sure thing," Rudy spoke back and we parted company.

Detectives withdrew from the meeting and reports were written. Operation planning had already been planned out and we already had found a small currently unused warehouse that had an automatic metal roll up door with a drive up ramp. This wasn't our first car operation and would not be the last. About three hours after I had met with Rudy we got a call from him; he had us a stolen car and wanted to meet for delivery and payment. An hour later I pushed the button to raise the door to the small warehouse and Rudy proudly drove in his prize. After a quick inspection Rudy was paid and sent out the door. Over the next week and half Rudy delivered six stolen Hondas, all caught on film as he drove them into the warehouse and reached out to accept the money I offered to pay him for his services. Each time Rudy would leave through the side door on foot being followed, except after he delivered the sixth and his final car. After accepting the money I handed him, he turned to leave and was greeted by five big men and a lady that had until that moment been hidden. Rudy tried resisting for a moment but he got his ass kicked and his time in prison was just a few court room stops away.

I wrote a letter to Rudy and it read:

Greetings Rudy,

By now I'm sure your attorney and a few of your cell mates have told you cops can lie during undercover operations such as I did in your case. You were a car thief, had already done prison time for being a car thief and had learned nothing from the previous experience. So when you got out of prison you simply started stealing cars all over again. The only thing you learned this time is this: I'm better at doing my job than you are at stealing cars and there are many more cops just like me out here waiting for you to do what you do.

I'm going to give you some advice, I hope you take it. Look in the mirror and then be totally honest with yourself and say, "I'm in prison because I stole cars." That will be your first and probably hardest thing you must do. Then figure out what you want to do, legally then pursue it. You clearly have mechanical skill and a like for cars that should give you a clue as to what you might want to look into.

Stay in touch Rudy, if you need help with anything let me know. I truly hope the best for you on your release.
Detective Gill

I didn't hear from Rudy for well over six months then another letter from prison; it was Rudy.

Detective,

I have given it a lot of thought and you're right. I'm here because I stole cars and you did a great job catching me. I read everything I can get my hands on that has to do with auto mechanics. If you need a good mechanic in the future just look me up in the phone book, under auto mechanics.

Thanks.

Rudy

A couple more years passed by and I received a letter from someone I knew on the outside of prison: a person I had worked with, met some of his family, and had spent a great deal of time talking to. This letter from prison truly shocked me. It was Dale.

I had met Dale years ago when he was a self-employed pressure washer contractor that made a living cleaning just about anything with a pressure washer. At the time he had just gone through a divorce but he was granted weekends with his daughter that he clearly adored. I didn't know his ex-wife but I had heard she was a psycho and Dale had more than once sported a black eye to prove it, but he never called the cops.

When Dale was going through the divorce, money dried up so he had walked into our office and offered his services as an informant. He knew people in the marijuana business, having been a frequent user but nothing in the dealing area. Dale knew of locations of grows and soon he made money from information that had led detectives to many grows, and the money helped fill in for the divorce costs. Then as the divorce ended, so did his business. Dale stopped at a local big box-type hardware store and while shopping inside thieves had taken his truck; the truck held his entire business and any means of making a legitimate business now faded. Dale stepped up his police informant business to make ends meet.

Things got interesting one day when he found a man that made money at stealing cars and trucks. Dale had a revenge interest and became entwined with the fellow and fed us the information. Finally one day Dale introduced an undercover police detective to the car thief and in the middle of the meeting he fell apart. Dave hit the "duh" wall and the detective was sharp enough to fill in the blanks and we were in. Later that night we were in business and had purchased our first stolen car. Dale got paid and was officially out of the deal but brokered a deal that gave him $100.00 for every car we recovered. Eighteen cars later and four men arrested from a car theft ring, Dale practically knocked me to the ground with the hug he gave me when he got paid.

Dale used the money and some he had been saving to restart his business, and soon he was back on his intended path. He had met a girl and told me one day he was once again in love. I ran into Dale at the park one day; he was there with his daughter enjoying the afternoon having taken it off from working. Dale was happy; no longer worked for the police unless he came across something that bothered him. He once learned of a guy selling marijuana to junior high kids and Dale made quick work of him using us.

When Dale came to us to first ask to be a police informant we did a complete background on him and found nothing. He'd gotten the usual traffic tickets but he was unlike the others in this business: no arrests, no signs of violence, nothing

This is why the letter I got from Dale was so shocking. It was a letter from prison, Dale's prison. What could this quiet, shy, non-violent man have done that landed him in prison?

It had been a domestic violence situation that appeared to have gotten well out of control and the new lady of his dreams had paid a dear price for it. She had been severely beaten by Dale. I knew Dale was not the sharpest pencil in the box but this; this was completely out of the norm.

I wrote Dale back asking him what he had done. His response was he had been set up by yet another psycho woman and now he was in prison, separated from his daughter with nothing. I pressed about what had actually occurred and Dale stated that he could not speak with me about it via a letter or internet as all the lines would be read by guards and he had become very distrusting of the system which began with his court appointed attorney.

Court appointed attorneys are for the most part questionable. They really don't give a rat's ass about these people, only the check from the tax payers. Win, lose, or draw, they still get paid, thus they really don't care. I'm sure there are excellent defense attorneys out there working hard for the less privileged on the tax payer dime, and to those of you out there doing that, I do apologize. But think about it; if you earn a law degree, why will you end up working for government wages in a meat grinder facility for a fraction of what you could earn in a private practice? The question is "why". Is it laziness, incompetence, lack of drive or confidence, or a mixture of excuses? Nonetheless, we pay them and so do the accused with time off their lives. I have heard of street lawyers, lawyers that represent the homeless people and the ones that have no means of support, let alone hire an attorney; to those attorneys I have nothing but praise. Unfortunately, I have not met them. **In all fairness to attorneys I know of cops that are exactly the same way, useless and lazy.**

In the back and forth letters Dale shared with me, he clearly was upset with his court appointed attorney. Dale told me he did things on Dale's behalf that were never made clear to him; things just happened and soon the snowball effect was in full force.

In one of his more recent letters, Dale wrote that it had been his 2000th day anniversary of being in prison. Sometimes his letters are upbeat; sometimes I could see he was weakening with the 23 hours he spent in a room with nothing but his thoughts. Some of his letters tell me of his latest appeal and he can't understand why the court system is so slow; not even sure his appeal has been filed and not sure about when or if he ever gets out.

Dale speaks constantly of his daughter – how he misses her and his ailing mother. He also worries about when he does get out, finding employment, or trying to get his new business started; and the little things like a driver's license, a car, and a place to stay.

"You know they just dump us back onto the street," he wrote. "No wonder most of these guys in here are repeat offenders," he wrote on.

In Dale's earliest letters he was upbeat, having full faith in the system and that he would win on appeal as the real truth had not yet been revealed due to limitation put on his defense. His attorney was optimistic and continued fighting, according to Dale. But over time I slowly read about his eroding optimism, slowly whittling at his spirit to fight on. After the 2000th day comment in that letter, Dale's next few letters led me to believe he was giving up – that there is really no more tomorrow, only the current. Dale had always boasted that he stayed to himself; the less contact with these people, the better off he would be when he gets out.

I had always been supportive and encouraged him to read and educate himself with all the time he had on his hands; but his time out of cell was limited.

Dale and I have exchanged many letters over the last five years. I have decided Dale will be a project, one who I will help and show that someone gives a damn. Dale will not be "dumped" back onto the streets; I'll be there to pick him up and help him rebuild. I don't know exactly what happened that night he got into so much trouble; but before he gets out I will review the case and see if he lied to me, or if in fact there are holes in the case and that a lazy ass attorney let the cops slide and Dale paid a terrible price.

Until then I will continue to receive and answer his' and others like him, their letters from prison.

Chapter 11

Play Ball

I slipped my truck into park and turned off the ignition. As I opened the door I could feel the fresh salt lined air around my ears, something I miss when I have long hair. There is simply a feeling of freedom with a new haircut and shave after spending the last eight months looking fury. Then I felt something that never changes, no matter the length of my hair: the phone impatiently buzzing in my pocket, demanding attention.

Opening it I see it's the patrol sergeant's desk number and I'm tempted to ignore it but I can't.

"Gill", what you need?" It was sergeant Steadman.

"You get a haircut yet?" he asked.

This is where I could lie and say no, but I owned up and said, "Just got back from one, I'm a shiny bitch right now."

"Good, we need a day shift sergeant for tomorrow's shift, 12 hours overtime, you game?" Steadman asked.

My first impression was to hang up. I hadn't worked patrol for several years, didn't even have a car, meaning I'd have to get a loaner from the fleet at the city shops; but the thought of a 12 hour shift in a uniform and a car felt like I was getting back to my roots so to speak.

"Yeah, I'll do it," I responded.

"Thanks, we need the help," and with that he hung up.

Then I came to the realization that I didn't have a uniform prepared or a gun belt that was up to my standards, thus requiring me to rush around for the next couple of hours putting theses' items together and seeing if I could come out of it looking decent.

I gave up on the jumpsuit; it was nowhere to be found. I suspected it was somewhere in my locker at work, but I did have a long-sleeved dress shirt still in the plastic wrapping from the cleaners. Trousers were next on the list, almost as easy to locate as were the shirt. The gun belt was of heavy leather, as was the handcuff case and spare bullet speed loader case. Hell, if I'm only doing one shift I'm going to wear what I used to wear in Sumner 20 years earlier. The only modification I had made since then was I had added heavy suspenders to take the tension off my lower back.

Award pins, name tag, and badge were quickly located; and 45 minutes after the phone call I was ready for work the next day. I kind of got a tickle thinking of it, back to my roots

The next morning I left home extra early and at the motor pool found an acceptable car, one I could smoke a cigar in without pissing off the entire department. I parked in the spot marked for the patrol sergeant and out of the car and thru the backdoor of the police department. It was 0530 hrs on a quiet Sunday morning in June. I shouldn't be this excited, but I was.

I had gotten to work a half hour early, wanting to prepare for the briefing of the squad of officers I would be working with and to re-acquaint myself with patrol duties as their sergeant. I greeted the night shift sergeant and learned they had been busy, slammed, as he put it till about 0330 hrs and then it dropped off to nothing.

"You should have a quiet day," he said as he practically skipped out of the office.

Absolutely nothing felt right; the chairs, desk and surroundings made me uncomfortable so I elected to run this show out of my office, just a locked door and long hallway away. As I found my comfy familiar chair, desk, and key board, I quickly opened the computer and read about the past 24 hours of Puyallup Police Department activities; huh, the usual.

I returned to the sergeant's office and was greeted by the officers that had already arrived. They were talking about their last four days off the just plain bs-ing until they saw me. Then their conversation of humor turned to pointing out my short grey hair and that "freshly" look. Some thought I looked younger, some older, but they made it clear I was an old fart. I was older than dust with this bunch of grinning over-educated kids

I spoke of the last 24 hours and of any updates the department put out; then I said, "be careful out there," and left. There was a police series that had played out on television and at the end of the briefing the character playing sergeant would always end it with that line, "be careful out there." I liked it and had always used it when working patrol as a sergeant.

I found a quiet coffee shop, grabbed a cup of coffee, and ordered up some breakfast. I sat quietly in the corner of the restaurant, back to the wall with a complete view of anything or anyone in my area. This routine of survival occupation in a restaurant was used in any restaurant I ate at, on duty or off. It just made sense to me and most cops. The radio was quiet, a traffic stop now and then, and a call for theft report came over the air several times.

The day had progressed well; easy money. Then at about 1300 hrs I heard a radio call: "Go to one of my officers." Apparently, an elderly lady was upset; she had returned home and as she walked to her front door a baseball struck her windshield, destroying it. It appeared that there was a baseball game going in the field next to where she lives and an errant baseball had landed in the middle of her windshield and she wanted an officer to make a report. She sounded like she was very upset. It was just down the road from where I was at, so I answered back to dispatch.

"Sam 5 Puyallup, I'm close I'll take that."

"Received Sam 5" was their response.

As I arrived I located the lady in the parking lot of the senior home. She was in her seventies, walked with a cane; but what struck me the most was her fingernails that were painted bright red, as well as her silver grey hair that was neat as a pin, in tight with well-made curls. She reminded me of my mother. She had tears in her eyes as she showed me the damage and how she had little to no money to fix the car.

"Heaven's sake, I need my car" she said.

"Heaven's sake," I don't how many times my mother had used that term. I fell instantly in love with her. She pointed to the ball game going on next door and while doing so I could see people in the stands watching us and her pointing their way.

I was glad I took this call. If one of those over-educated kids had taken it they would tell her it was a civil matter; and there was nothing they could do for her and leave. That would leave this little old lady to anguish and bitch about lazy cops and that damn ball field located next to her old folk's home.

"Let me see what I can do," and with that I turned and began walking towards the baseball field and more eyes now came upon me.

I removed my wallet, found a five dollar bill and folded it then put it into my right front trouser pocket.

This is not my first time dealing with this kind of situation. In fact, this would be my third baseball game interrupted when a car window had been shattered and the previous two worked out fine. I suspected this one would have the same results. As I neared the field, the pitcher hurled yet another high speed fast ball towards home plate. He found his mark as the ump yelled sstttrriike! These weren't kids but a young men's team, made up mostly of 20 something year olds. Wives, girlfriends and buddies were in the stands. This must have been a highly contested game as the place was packed, several hundred people at least. *The more the better* I thought to myself.

The only thing that can trump an ump on a ball field during a game was a cop – tall, slender, uniform that showed years of service, cowboy boots, and an old school hat with black shiny brim pulled down enough to shadow his eyes.

The moment my right foot stepped onto the field the referee jumped out from behind the catcher and yelled "time out" with great theatrics. The ump looked like an umpire –short, barrel-chested, and a no bullshit man. I walked directly to the pitcher's mound and reached out, "give me the ball and stand down," I said with a wink. He backed down off the mound, tossing me the ball. I pointed to both coaches and the ump and summoned them to the mound. They all knew too well the topic of conversation would be the windshield.

The ump was the first to speak, "takes a lot of nerve to walk into the middle of my game officer."

"It's Sergeant, and I'm here to make a wrong, right," I returned. "The little old lady with the car over there, the one with the broken windshield is very upset, I want to fix this."

"What you got in mind?" one of coaches asked.

I removed my hat and held it upside down in my left hand. I reached into my right pocket and pulled out the five dollar bill, making sure everyone saw me in the ball park; unfolded it, and placed it in my hat. I handed my hat to the coach to my left and told him "go to your people and pass the hat and when you're done give it to the other coach so he may do the same."

Both coaches walk together for a bit, talking, and then parted ways. I looked around and noticed an outfielder already had his wallet in hand and was rummaging through for some bills; some folks in the stands were doing the same. Some just stared at me. Then I saw what I had hoped I'd see, a couple young cops standing behind me, just off the field, grinning and learning, I hoped.

The ump said "not the first time you've done this sergeant."

"Third time and it always works," I responded.

"Well it's a first for me," the ump noted, "and I like it". He pulled a fresh dollar bill from his wallet.

Soon the other coach walked out to me and handed me the hat. Full of bills and I even noticed a twenty dollar bill in the mix.

I asked the coach "you have a wife or gal I can borrow for 5 minutes?"

The coach turned and yelled "Cindy" and flagged her out to the mound. She gleefully ran to the mound dying to know what was going on and why she was needed. I suspected she was an ex-cheer leader in a previous life.

"Cindy, take my hat and count the money, ok?"

"Ok," she responded. "Three hundred and fifty three dollars," she said.

"These are some generous and nice folks," I remarked. I took my hat and replaced it on my head, pulled low to conceal my eyes from all but those near me. "Now Cindy, will you walk with me to that little old lady over there with the broken windshield? And when we get there I want you to give her this money and tell her everyone passed a hat to help pay for her windshield."

"Sure," she excitedly said.

I still had the ball under my right arm bicep, and I relaxed it enough to drop the ball to my waiting left hand. I looked at the pitcher, still standing near the mound, with a little toss the ball landed in his mitt. I looked at the ump "thank you gentlemen, now play ball." I turned and surrendered the mound and heard a few claps from the stands. Cindy bounced along next to me.

When I got to my car I stopped. "Cindy, you know what to do and you're going to feel great doing it and make sure you give the credit to all those folks in the ball park, ok?"

"Ok," she excitedly said.

I opened my car door, took off my hat and tossed it onto the passenger seat. As I started the car I could see Cindy and the little ole lady hugging. Then Cindy turned and began bouncing towards the ball field, blowing me a kiss as she did.

Take a Break and Laugh

A cop's job can be very exhausting, not to mention challenging; so moments that made me laugh or 'shake my head' are very precious to me. It surely gave the job some balance; some reminder of what humanity is really all about. It reminded me to take a break and smell the roses. I want you to do the same now. After reading all the previous heart-wrenching, emotion-stirring chapters; it's time to loosen a bit now, relax, and have a good laugh. Call it funny, gross, or stupid; it will still make you laugh.

I swung the door open and motioned for one of the firemen to grab it, the door was now well above my head. As the door opened, it sucked a huge cloud of smoke from the interior of the car revealing the damn driver. There he sat! Hands holding the steering wheel at ten and two, eyes staring intently out the front window, left foot planted firmly on the floorboards, right foot planted firmly on the gas pedal!

Chapter 12

Burning Rubber

It was a Saturday night, about 0200 and I was working alone. Sumner was a small quiet town, and on most occasions it only took one officer to keep the peace and quiet.

I had noticed from an earlier bar check that Marge was working alone at the Waterhole Pub located East of downtown Sumner. Marge was in appearance a sweet little old lady with the usual odd quirks. But make a mistake and she would snap a knot in your ass. Still, she was an older lady so I felt a certain sense of responsibility to look in on her, all the while knowing full well I'd be on thin ice. Still, it was odd she was alone but if you knew Marge, she would be ok. I elected to check on her however, even though I knew she wouldn't need me checking.

As I walked in, there were a few patrons getting ready to leave and Marge glanced up and peered at me over her grandma-style glasses perched low on her nose. No hi, how you doing, no greetings at all. She simply said "we're closing, and if we were open I wouldn't serve ya, you look too young to drink." I could hear patrons snicker from a distance. God, I loved her smartass attack style personality.

"Heck Marge, I was just checking on ya" I returned.

"I got nothing worth checking" she responded.

"Considering your sweet personality I bet you don't even have tip money" I mentioned. I detected a little upturn in the corner of her lips, she liked the banter.

I wandered to the back of the bar and checked the bathrooms and storage areas making sure no one was hiding, waiting for Marge to lock the front doors. Satisfied, I returned to the bar area and was about to make a smartass remark before leaving when I received a radio dispatch.

"Sumner 112," dispatch enquired.

"12 Sumner," I responded.

"Traffic accident reported in the 900 block of Traffic Avenue. Car vs. tree and reports are that the car is smoking heavily, possible fire. Fire Department has been dispatched".

"12 received," I answered.

Marge was quick to respond to the news. "Good, now get your ticket writing ass outta here and I can drive like a woman-possessed home!"

"Knock it off Marge, no time for sweet talk, gotta go," and with that I left.

As I did, I heard a quiet "be careful" come from her direction, but she would have never admitted to it.

I quickly jumped into my Pontiac Lemans, Carl's favorite car. As I sped from the parking lot I found the three dangling toggle switches that hung under the dash and managed to locate the correct one to activate the overhead blue lights.

I liked to drive fast, blue lights flashing, get kind of pumped up while en-route. This kind of excitement I displayed would annoy Carl, after all he has been around awhile and it all was in a day's work ... nothing more, nothing less.

I arrived just ahead of the fire department. It was a Chevy, full size car that impacted a city tree planted well off Traffic Avenue in a well groomed green belt area that bordered between the road and two sets of North South running railroad tracks. The area was covered in smoke. As I walked to the car I could smell the burning rubber, and now hear the racing engine that sounded as though it were at full throttle. Odd situation, I thought to myself when I saw that the tree was about a foot across at the base.

The car had hit the tree dead center, but instead of breaking off, the tree had angled over somewhat enough to allow the car to basically climb it. I stepped back a minute and could see that most of the weight of the car was now settling in on the rear bumper and the spinning rear tires were buried into the dirt completely engulfed in smoke. I only needed now to figure out where the driver was. Something told me "alcohol was involved."

A couple of young fireman ran to my location and they were about as surprised as I had been. I shouted to one of them that the smoke was coming from the tires, probably no fire.

"Where's the driver?" asked one of the fireman, looking at me.

I didn't respond. I was staring intently at the center of the driver's door window which was at my eye level. Smoke absolutely choked the interior of the car and I couldn't see anything inside. I reach for the driver door handle, the firemen stepped back. The door was unlocked.

I swung the door open and motioned for one of the firemen to grab it, the door was now well above my head. As the door opened, it sucked a huge cloud of smoke from the interior of the car revealing the damn driver. There he sat! Hands holding the steering wheel at ten and two, eyes staring intently out the front window, left foot planted firmly on the floorboards, right foot planted firmly on the gas pedal!

Drunken fool thought he was still driving! Slowly he began turning his head to look at me as I guess he had not noticed my presence after I opened the door. He had a very surprised look about his face, never moved his hands from the steering wheel and never let off the gas. I don't even think he knew he had hit a tree.

I had seen enough, it was time to do something about it. My lungs were filled with rubber burnt smoke, and my eyes burned from the smoke as my ears ached from that screaming damn engine. I grabbed the driver by the front of the shirt and back of his collar and with one forceful yank, ejected him from the driver's seat. As we both sailed backwards, him now airborne, he slammed into the fireman that was caught gawking at the scene from behind me. The fireman tumbled to his butt, and the driver landed facedown with me on top of him. The car idled peaceably and rear tires slowed.

Apparently the violence of my action must have made the driver suddenly aware that he was no longer driving, but face down in the grass wearing a cop. He began struggling to free himself but I was having none of it. I had already secured his right hand behind his back but he was flailing about with his legs and left arm.

Carl had taught me a way to inflict terrible pain on a fighting suspect that would usually force the suspect to submit. The driver was lying face down and he was facing the car he had been driving, exposing his right ear to me. I simply placed my right thumb to the base of his skull, in line with his right ear lobe and applied direct pressure. The driver exploded in screams and flailing but even his drunken ass had had enough. He quickly threw his left arm to the small of his back and the struggle was over. Cuffs were applied and I told him to stay there and not move.

I quickly inspected the interior of the car and found no one else. I turned off the car and removed the keys. A tow truck would soon arrive and the wreck would be removed. The firemen wandered off, dragging the equipment with them. I smiled when I noticed grass stains to the bunker pants of the one that had gotten knocked on his butt.

My belligerent drunk driver was beginning to perk up, having forgotten the pain I had just inflicted on him. I stood him up and we began walking to my car. He started in on me, about how much of an asshole I was and how he could easily kick my ass, etc. etc. etc, I had heard it all before. After searching him he was politely stuffed into the rear seat of my car and the door shut.

I hesitated a bit, then looked up and saw the face of a sweet little old lady seated behind the wheel of her Buick, with the driver's window rolled down. I noted that her granny glasses were slid far down her nose and she lowered her head a bit and peered at me over the top of them. It was Marge! I gave her a smile and then she said "I was just checking on you," then she floored it and was quickly breaking the speed limit as she disappeared into the dark.

Damn, I love this little town.

It was mid 1980s and smoking in bars was perfectly acceptable but damn, if this place had a smoke detector it had given up before noon, and the bar was packed for a Saturday night. We moved slowly through the crowd, watching, making eye contact but not holding it, just long enough to let them know, "yes, I see you" then move to the next. I usually stop and give the bartender some time; people in the bar would see us talking and in appearance to them, as though we were working together, so to speak.

Chapter 13

The Comancheros

I could hear the distant sound of a motorcycle, sounds like a Honda 350 and it was heading downtown. I had been out wandering around on foot and had just arrived back at my car and the motorcycle was coming my way. It was noisy! Just prior to it passing me, it slowed quickly as the driver must have figured out that I was a cop standing next to my well-marked patrol car. As he passed by I could see that not only was it a Honda 350, as I had figured, but it had two big men on board.

Seeing two people on a motorcycle was common sight, man and woman, but two fat guys was just a weird view. They looked familiar and I was pretty sure who they were. They both had helmets on, much too small of helmets for the size of their heads; kind of gave them that "baked bread" look. Their faces budged from out of the helmets and part of their ears was showing. Their hair was braided long down their back and they both wore sleeveless jean jackets with some sort of motorcycle gang patch displayed on their backs.

The motorcycle turned right off the road onto an alley that led to the rear entrances of downtown watering holes. I slid into my car and made a few notes and was looking over a police report I had finished earlier, checking for errors.

That motorcycle again, getting louder, and soon I watched in my driver's side door mirror the motorcycle coming out of the alley and turning back towards me. As it slowly passed me I noticed that only the driver was aboard and between his legs was a helmet, empty of course and he was still wearing his'. My headlights were on and this time I could make out the name of the motorcycle gang identified on the back of the motorcycle's driver, "Comancheros".

I had a suspicion as to what was going on. I elected to stay put and I turned off my headlights and my patrol car with the driver's window down. I peered into the night, looking and listening down the dark street lined with single family homes; then I heard the approach of the Honda 350 coming back at me. I got out of the car, wanting a good look at what I was sure was coming. It was the same motorcycle, same driver, but a different passenger who had the same helmet on as the first passenger. He, like the first, is a fat guy with long hair but not braided. He also had the same patch, as the others, on a jean jacket.

I had this figured out but needed to confirm it. I climbed back into my cage and took my time driving to the rear entrance of the Club Tavern in downtown Sumner. The motorcycle was just leaving, only the driver aboard and his passenger were walking through the back door of the tavern.

Precious! But working alone; I had no one to share this with and it would be another half hour before Pig arrived for his graveyard shift. I could wait, after all it was only 2230 hrs and the Comancheros would be around till at least 0200 hrs.

Pig arrived at work and I was waiting in the Police parking lot for him.

"Time you got here, get dressed, I got something cool for you to see," I said.

"What is it?" He pried.

"I can't make this shit up or explain it, you need to see this for yourself," I returned.

"Ok, give me a minute," he said, and with that he trotted off for the locker room.

Minute my ass I thought, Pig was worse than a woman when it comes to getting ready; hair and uniform will be perfect. Hell, he is even going to vacuum out his car.

About 20 minutes later I heard him check in via the radio and then he asked for me. I answered up and soon we were parked out front the Club Tavern. I had already got to the sidewalk out front and was waiting for Pig. As he walked to my location I couldn't help but notice that he glistened and sparkled in his uniform, shoes and leather gear all gleaming with the care of an obsessive man. We matched up well, mutt and Pig.

"Let's test your power of observations tonight," I said.

"Ok, what do you have in mind?" he responded.

"Let's bar check the Club; I post, you rove," I said.

"What's going on? That's pretty standard stuff," he returned.

"As you move, count all the bikers with Comanchero colors on, ok? Then go out back and match your count with the amount of motorcycles there; do the math and give me your answer, ok?"

"Got it" he said with a fiendish grin, and I swung open the big heavy front door.

It was mid 1980s and smoking in bars was perfectly acceptable but damn, if this place had a smoke detector it had given up before noon, and the bar was packed for a Saturday night. We moved slowly through the crowd, watching, making eye contact but not holding it, just long enough to let them know, "yes, I see you" then move to the next. I usually stop and give the bartender some time; people in the bar would see us talking and in appearance to them, as though we were working together, so to speak. When I was doing these alone, I would move through a bar slowly and deliberately, as though I owned the place, something I had learned from Carl. Pig was learning this and he walked as if he owned the joint. I watched him closely; he moved well but I could tell he was counting "outlaw" bikers. After about 5 minutes he wandered out the back door. He hadn't been long when he returned. As he entered the main bar area he made eye contact with me, and a bit of a grin. Pig worked his way to me and said "one bike, 8 bikers." I winked and told him to post.

I worked my way to the back of the bar near the pool tables and spotted one of the Comancheros at a back pool table. I recognized him as a kid named Gaylord. Gaylord was big, six foot three and outweighed me by about 75 pounds, but I had never had a problem with him. What the hell, I figured and wandered his way. I reached out to him and he shook my hand.

"I didn't know you had a gang," I said.

"Oh yeah, first time we have worn our colors out and about," he responded.

"Are these all your members?" I asked.

"We got a couple more guys but they couldn't get out tonight," he responded.

"Well, stay outta trouble," and with that I moved on.

I must admit, they looked the part, big and nasty, but damn, one bike, and it's a 350 Honda. The "real" bikers I had met in my few short years would intimidate other patrons in a bar, basically taking it over then they could do as they please, or at least till the bar keep called the police. And there was protocol for contacting them. The young bikers were like new cops, wanting to prove themselves; and I would ignore them and look for the leader of the group. Since I was usually alone I would negotiate a settlement that didn't involve me getting my ass kicked or them getting arrested. I had learned to look directly at them when I spoke and would not be intimidated, professionally fatal if a cop let that happen. Over the years I had gotten very good at speaking to bikers and listening to them. I knew most of them by name and I kept book on them. I knew what all the patches on their jackets meant; it was a rank and honor system that told others, who, what, and basically how much of a bad ass they were, and they rode Harley Davidson's, and rode them as good as anyone could. No, the Comancheros were not a bad ass biker gang; they were men pretending. It was a damn good thing a real biker had not entered the bar. Upon seeing the Comancheros all hell would have erupted. It would have ended with the Comancheros' patches on the back of their jackets being cut off after a complete ass kicking. You do not pretend to be a biker, nor a cop, and flaunt it in public. The price on both counts would be high.

As I neared Pig I glanced at him and motioned to the door and we worked our way through the mass to the front door and exited.

Once outside he said "ok, what's the catch?"

"One guy drove the bike and gave rides to the remainder of the gang," I said.

He looked at me and grinned, asking for clarity. "One guy drove and gave the other seven rides to the bar on one motorcycle?"

"Yep," I responded.

We agreed to be in the area when the bar closed. Pig wanted to see the gang in "action".

We had found a spot near the road close to where I had first saw them riding tandem towards the bar and waited. By 0215 hrs nothing, not even the sound of a motorcycle; then we noticed movement where the alley and the street intersected. We counted eight people walking and as they got closer, we counted eight "bad ass bikers". One of them was pushing the one and only motorcycle. As they got to our location I spotted Gaylord and I just couldn't help myself.

"Gaylord, what's going on?" I asked.

"Our motorcycle is outta gas," he answered.

"Motorcycle? Assuredly you have more than one motorcycle don't you?" I pressed on.

"No, just the one for now," he responded.

"I'd lend you gas if I had any," I told Gaylord.

"Thanks officer," he responded and they continued their quiet journey home, on foot, pushing their motorcycle.

Pig was fighting back laughter, as was I, at the sight of the eight men walking and pushing their motorcycle. They were a fearsome looking bunch, but had not a pot to pee in nor a window to throw it out of, so this was their way of spending their wild Saturday night, pretending.

"Like I said, you can't make this shit up, nor adequately explain it," I mention again to Pig.

He responded, "I hope they never have kids."

Note to reader: There is a group of motorcycle enthusiasts that have named them-selves "The Comancheros". The author means no disrespect, or similarities to my little group of Comancheros described herein.

Chapter 14

Oops

Certain things happen as you travel life's path. Sometimes something is said that is not planned, and sometimes you are involved in it. There is only one word to describe something like this – whenever it happens, and whatever it may be. That word is ... "oops".

Here are the top five "oops" that don't include someone getting hurt or killed.

Number five

It was O dark thirty and the dispatcher, a female, asked both of us to respond to the police department. She had a problem. Pig and I arrived and entered the department through the front doors and met the dispatcher's problem. He was a drunken fool that had wandered by and noticed the front doors unlocked and a lone dispatcher seated inside. This has always been a concern of officers working for Sumner Police Department, the vulnerable front office as it was never locked; so checking on the dispatcher was paramount.

The dispatcher stated that he had twice tried to come around the counter and had made lewd statements and gestures towards her. She wanted him out and now. Of course he didn't want to leave but he did, understanding how close he was to being arrested. So he gave a bit and stepped outside and then began the usual bitching, cussing and all, that was just a super pain in the ass. He then put down a gift box that he had been carrying and on top of it he placed a bag where he kept his personal items in: wallet, glasses, keys, cigarettes, etc. The guy continued on walking the grey line between arrest and walk away. He was not local but had ended up in our town through the means of hitch hiking and now we were stuck with him. His original destination, Seattle, was altered when a driver that had picked him up earlier became upset with him and kicked him out of the car at the edge of our little town, and now here he was irritating the hell out of Pig and I.

As I tried to reason with this idiot and get him to move along, I noticed Pig was sizing up the bag that was on the ground. As I watched I noticed that he began moving off to the side and stepping back about six feet. Suddenly I realized that he was taking up the stance of a field goal kicker – head down, arms swinging free at his sides and his left foot stepped out in front of him. In a sudden move, Pig looked like that of a field goal kicker moving to the ball, in this case a bag. Pig's right big boot caught the bag and with a great follow through lofted the bag high into the air. The bag arced perfectly and landed in the northbound lanes of Alder Avenue in front of the Police Department. The three of us just stood there. Then, as if it was perfectly planned, a semi-truck rolled by, in northbound lane of Alder Avenue. The passenger side front tire ran directly over the bag, the duly wheels of the tractor next ran over the same bag and then followed by the duly rear tires of the trailer towed behind the tractor. All three of us were silent. I do believe I uttered the word "oops".

The guy finally wandered out to retrieve his bag.

I mentioned to Pig, "If we have to do paper on this I'll let you do it, there is no way of explaining this."

"He's done. Reality just hit home; he's worried about his own safety, he wants out of this town," Pig said.

As he finished talking the guy walked back to him and said, "I can't believe you did that."

"The next thing I'm kicking is your ass so I recommend you leave town," Pig responded.

"I didn't do anything wrong, but you kicked my bag into the path of a moving truck," the man claimed.

"You made lewd remarks and gestures towards our dispatcher and by the time I'm done arresting you, you'll need medical attention," Pig responded with coolness of a cop that really thought he had an air tight case.

Finally the fool shut up and assessed his position. "Which way is the freeway and which way to Seattle?" he asked.

"Grab your crap, I'll give you a ride," I answered.

No way was I going to let this idiot wander around our little town after what we had just done to him. After checking him for weapons he climbed into the back of the car. I left for the freeway.

"Your buddy is a fucking asshole," he told me.

"I know, that's why I like him," I responded.

I pulled off the edge of the highway in the middle of nowhere.

"Why we stopping?" he asked me.

"Edge of town, as far as I'm going," I responded.

"I thought you were taking me to Seattle" he mentioned.

"It says police on the side of my car, not taxi" I responded. He protests as he climbs out of my car.

"Do you see that glow of lights?" I asked, as I pointed North. "That's Seattle," I said. "Don't come back to our town, ever, we won't be as nice next time," I continued, as I climbed back into my cruiser.

I turned the car around heading back to Sumner; I glanced in my rear view mirror; the idiot was walking carrying his box and his bag of crunched up stuff over his shoulder.

Number four

Spokane's narcotic task force had put out a notice that they had seized a large quantity of marijuana smuggled across the border in a semi-trailer from British Columbia, making it some of the best pot that could be purchased; BC Bud as it's known. The case that Spokane had seized the pot under was adjudicated and now they needed to get rid of the dope. They offered it to police departments, task forces, and DEA to be used in reversals conducted by police. A reversal works this way: if a buyer is located, the police act as marijuana sellers and when the suspect shows up with the money for the pot we basically rip him and he goes to jail and the city seizes the guy's money. In this area where the pot is produced, it sold at that time for around $2,400.00 per pound. Do the math and you will see why city coffers like it when police do reversals. When an offer for fresh BC bud comes across the wire departments, it usually freshens up their inventory.

Rob, Pig, and I loaded up in an SUV that had been donated to us from a drug dealer and off we went. I'm not sure what we were thinking at that time, actually we were not thinking. We had been tasked to grab 250 pounds of fresh, uncompressed BC bud and bring it back so it could be distributed to narcotic departments in the Pierce county area when and if needed. A pound of uncompressed BC bud is about the size of a couch pillow. Multiply that by 250, and put it into an SUV containing three large furry cops, gear, and windows that are not tinted. That's the part that we clearly had not thought about until we arrived in Vantage Washington, the halfway point between Spokane and Puyallup.

Spokane had arrived driving a large pick-up truck with canopy and cardboard boxes filled with pot in the back of the truck. Clearly, this is not their first time.

We began unloading them and we stayed quiet about the growing problem till one of the Spokane guys said "we are not taking any of this crap back with us."

"We'll get it in there, no problem," Rob defended us.

Spokane is unloaded and in a hurry, not wanting to stay and watch how we are going to manage to pack the dope into the SUV. Pig and I remained busy, finding little spots where we could stuff yet another pound into the SUV. Rob's job was simply to guard us. We were behind a gas station but still, that was a lot of pot and we were "a lot paranoid". Rob was a spot on weapons handler and came from a hunting background, so clearly this was his duty.

Pig and I stuffed pot under seats, around seats, into pockets of seats and in between seats. Soon the back of the SUV was absolutely jammed to the ceiling on top of our gear. The rear passenger seat behind me quickly filled to the ceiling. We still had more pot.

We had been sipping on Howling Monkeys, a "Red Bull" type energy drink that we had gotten from a distributor after we let him watch a hot pop in Puyallup. He thought it was so cool that we let him watch so he kept bringing us Howling Monkeys and we were now addicted to the stuff. It is a big mistake drinking those things, makes you want to pee and thus our "oops" moment would happen somewhere down the road.

Finally having no more room it was apparent that Rob would need to take his spot in the rear passenger spot behind Pig. Rob climbed in, bitching all the way. He and I stuffed more dope on and around him to near the bottom of the window to the floor around his legs. Next Pig got into the front passenger seat and the last of the "pillows" were stuffed around him. As I jumped into the driver's seat I couldn't help but notice that Rob reminded me of that "ET" character in the 1982 movie except for one thing, Rob was not happy and his glare proved it.

"Rob, you look like ET from that movie," I said with an antagonistic tone.

"Fuck you," was his response.

As I slip the SUV into gear Pig mentions "probably not one of the smartest things we've done."

"Duh," I responded.

We pulled out on the access road and soon we are west bound on Interstate 90. About half hour into the drive and no one speaking, Rob pops out "going to have to pee soon, find a place to stop."

The Howling Monkey factor was coming into play.

"Me too," Pig follows up.

I had to go also but I wasn't about to admit it. "I'm not going to drive any faster; all I need is for a young state trooper to pull us over, then orgasm as he gets to the clear windows of the SUV. No way would that end well," I commented to the others.

We get over the Snoqualmie pass and it's a short run to a 'stop and rob' gas station at the east end of North Bend near a trucker stop. Taking the exit and a few short turns later I pull to the side of the gas station to park and hopefully out of view from nearby customers, then the "ah shit" occurs. Rob, not holding back and absolutely not waiting for us to unload "him" simply bails out of the back seat scattering no less than thirty pillows onto the pavement. He was a man possessed as he broke into a run. His right boot caught a pillow and sent it two parking spaces over just as a car containing two college kids pull into the spot stopping just prior to running over the pillow. Pig was still carefully putting pillows into my seat so he could get out without creating the scene Rob had left behind. The two college kids in the car had eyes the size of silver dollars and mouths that gaped open looking at the pile to the side of them. It was a definite "oops" moment as I walked over in front of the kids' car and casually picked up the clear pillow containing a pound of marijuana. By now the kid's driver's window was down as he watched me walk by. "Oops, dropped my baggy" I recall saying to him as I tossed the pillow into the now vacant seat belonging to Rob. My badge wasn't visible but the barrel of my gun was visible from under my leather vest. The kids slowly backed out and slowly drove off watching our every move.

"I think we are bad for business," Pig mentions as he starts picking up pillows.

"Think they might call police," I mention.

"Yep, we'll probably be prone on the pavement any minute now," Pig offers.

Rob returns and retakes his spot in the back seat and soon we have him packed into place. Pig gets his turn in the restroom then it's my turn. No time to wash hands, anything extra; down load and go was our mission!

I slipped the SUV into drive and soon we make our escape and back to Puyallup. If we ever make that run again we will take a box van with no rear windows. Bunch of dumbasses.

Number three

It was a packed night at the Puyallup fair and I was part of a group of detectives working dope inside the fair grounds. Dealers were opportunists and selling dope in the arcade and carnival areas was too appealing for them and they would show up pedaling their trade and one could purchase whatever dope of choice he might want. We would move about the areas looking, watching, and when we found a dealer we would work it with an informant or a clever undercover cop. We usually get three or four arrests every night we run these operations. Following the arrest and the level of resistance the dealer offered we would move him outside to a booking van. Following his booking, a lead detective would place any and all evidence into a mobile police department, usually a motor home all dressed up in police garb. After all that we would take a break and usually stand some distance from the police vehicles in a shadowy spot.

We had just made an arrest and several of us stood in the shadows just out of sight from the peering lights of the red gate. I noticed a guy in his mid-twenties walking on the sidewalk next to the chain link fence lining the fair. We were across the street from him. As we watched him walking, basically because we had nothing else better to do at the moment, he slowed in the darkened area next to the fence by the art barn. The man then reached deep under the fence with the plastic bag he had been carrying, dropped the bag and then got up and trotted off for the red gate.

"You guys see that?" I asked.

They all replied they had, "you guys run him down, and I'm going for the bag" I said and began running towards the bag.

We have found dealers that had shoved a bag into the fairgrounds containing their dope so that it wouldn't be detected by fair cops or a drunk would slip a bottle of booze into the fair through the fence. We also knew too well that the terrorist level was always in play and when a crowd was present those warnings always played in the minds of watchful police.

As I got to the fence it was clear that I was not going to be able to reach it with my arm, but next to where the bag was located was an opening from a previous gate that I could possibly get through with my right foot. I slid my right leg through the opening and used the heel of my Harley boot to come down on the bag. I tried to drag the bag to a spot where I could reach it with my hand but it didn't move. I again impacted the bag, and again no movement. I repeated the action several more times trying to get the bag closer to the fence when the guy that had put the bag under the fence rounded the corner of the art barn.

"What you doing?" he yelled at me. "Don't touch the bag."

I returned showing him my badge. About that time the cops I had been standing with caught up to him and the bag he had now picked up. I pulled my leg from the fence and jogged to the red gate and finally made my way to the spot inside the fair next to the fence.

When I got there my cop buddies were laughing their collective asses off. Pig, barely able to speak, says: "the guy told us it was his lunch and when he came around the corner all he saw was some "old bum stomping on his lunch bag" busting out into another laugh as he finished.

The guy with the bag was still standing there.

"Let me see in the bag," and he opened it and displayed the crushed contents of his lunch to me.

"Oops" was my only thought.

I felt bad for the guy, working the fair to make ends meet and fair food was expensive. I took the moment to tell the guy about what we have seen smuggled into the fair and we take these matters seriously. He was understanding but hungry. My cop buddies were still giggling about the moment and continually repeated "some old bum stomping on my lunch bag". Considering the amount of money we get paid for working dope overtime, I did not hesitate to take out my wallet and pull out a twenty dollar bill.

"Here, lunch is on me."

Number two

It was late August and the city was getting ready for the fair to begin. Part of that preparation was getting the Puyallup Police Explorers up to speed on their bicycle handling skills, and this day I would be their one and only instructor as I was still a certified IPMBA instructor.

International **P**olice on **M**ountain **B**ikes **A**ssociation was the central hub of bicycle cops for training and equipment updates. If you were a bike cop you were a member of IPMBA. The Explorer group I led was made up of about ten youngsters that ranged in age from 15 to 18 years old. I usually like them – young, bright, and useful when you found a place to put them. We used one in SIU that was brilliant with computer skills and was smart with a great mix of common sense. When he turned twenty one he was snapped up by a neighboring jurisdiction; our loss, their gain.

This group had already been through bicycle training and simply needed a refresher course to get them ready for the fair. We rode out of the back parking lot of the police department. I had most of my long hair jammed up under a dew rag concealing my real use to the department, narcotics. I had my sunglasses, helmet, and an IPMBA Instructor shirt on with a sewn on bag to my left chest, a handgun, and a clip badge to my belt topped off with hand cuffs and case. We followed Meeker east bound to south Meridian where we turned right and moved to the east lane of the two lanes that were one way only southbound road. We pedaled easily along with traffic en-route to the Gold parking lot of the fairgrounds where we would do some training. We passed by Pioneer Park and it was spotted with families and kids. We continued in single file till we approached the Safeway grocery store complex that housed a hardware, cleaners, rental shop, and of course a teriyaki restaurant. I scanned the parking lot and noticed a guy in his forties intently watching a woman getting out of a car that was parked next to him. She gave him no attention as she walked by and disappeared into the store. We now were directly out front the Safeway store and I watched the guy walk over to the lady's car and in a quick karate style kicked spun and planted his right foot to the front quarter panel of the rather nice car the lady had been driving. The impact was violent and my immediate reaction was required. I entered the Safeway parking lot at the south end of the lot next to the Pink Elephant car wash and rode directly towards the man with all the Explorers in tow, probably wondering why there was a sudden course change. As I rode quickly through the lot I was now lined up with the suspect and he now had figured out I was the police and was probably coming for him. He didn't move, just stood there next to his car. I on the other hand had already partially dismounted and was riding with both legs on the same side of the bike. My left foot was still in the cage that we used on the pedals and when I would come to a stop I would simply put down my right foot to the ground, free my left foot from the cage, place it on the ground, and use the bicycle as a barrier between the suspect and I. This was pretty much standard police work and I had done it thousands of times prior, but this time would be an "oops" moment.

My left foot clearly had different plans than those instructions sent from deep in my brain. Actually the toe clip had wedged up my left boot toe and refused to let it go. There is no recovery from this except one thing, get up off the pavement after you fall. I hit the asphalt, then the side of the suspect's car with plenty of force, but I jumped to my feet making a quick recovery and acted as if nothing had occurred. It was a "do it all the time" routine but it had the attention of just about everyone in the zip code; the area was packed with people. As I confronted the suspect I couldn't help but notice those around me staring, wide eyed and mouths open. I had just presented an "oops" moment and acted as though it was nothing.

"Why did you kick that car?" I questioned pointing to the damage.

"Huh, I didn't kick it," was his stupid answer.

I grabbed him by the arm and said "step over my bike, get over here with me."

I wanted the bicycle lying on the ground behind him in case he bolted.

"Put your hands on the hood," I ordered and he complied.

As I patted him down I located a loaded semi-automatic Colt 380 pistol in his right front jacket pocket.

"Your day just keeps getting better by the second," I mentioned to him.

I placed the pistol in my right rear pants pocket and my hand returned to him holding handcuffs. The suspect was secured in handcuffs and I glanced at one of the older Explorers having a police radio. I pointed to my badge and mouthed the words "get back-up". Within minutes I had several marked police cars. Of course the Explorers couldn't wait to share the story of my rather unorthodox entrance with my cop buddies and soon they were all laughing and grinning at me. After the suspect was secured in the back of the police car I went inside Safeway and found the lady that had gotten out of the now damaged car that I had seen only minutes earlier. I explained what had happened and she briskly walked out of the store, looked at her car and the damage, then at the suspect.

"Do you know him?" I asked of her.

"No, not a clue," she responded.

She was clearly upset and really I can't and don't blame her. I opened the back door of the car and again asked the suspect why he had kicked the car.

"I don't even know," was his only answer.

"Did he say why he did it?" she asked me again.

"He doesn't know why he did it," I responded.

"What an asshole," she mentioned.

"That's a fair assessment," I responded.

I gathered all the information needed for the report. The suspect was taken to jail and I spent the remainder of the month defending myself from all the smartasses, and there are many of them in the police department.

Number one

I arrived at work at 2000 hrs and found a note left for me from the chief. The chief was basically saying they had hired a new guy and he had started tonight on swing shift. I was to get the new guy when I was ready to start my patrol. The chief explained to me that the new guy was an older man, 50ish, and has no police work in his background.

"Use patience, see what's there, and if there is anything we can use," the chief said.

He was warning me, telling me to be prepared then use patience. Considering the last few dumbasses he hired, we must be scraping the bottom of the pool.

One new recruit had recently followed me into a bar check. I had told him to stay quiet and just watch. As I moved to the back of the tavern there was a poker game going on. The recruit began circling the table then stopped behind one of the seated men. I about died when he spoke "great hand you have there." I quickly glanced at him and then the other men seated at the table. The man that had the "great hand" began to rise. We were within seconds of a free for all and considering what my idiot recruit had said would not end well. These were rough men that settled quarrels with fists. I moved quickly and positioned myself between the recruit and the pissed off poker player.

"He's new, stupid new, I sincerely apologize for what he just did, the next round of drinks is on him," I said loudly enough for all to hear.

"Good thing Gill is with you rookie; I'd beat the shit out of you, now get me and my friends fresh beer, and you serve it," the man said with a firm voice.

I glanced at the recruit and said, "Move it."

As the recruit walked to the bar tender I again apologized to the bunch.

"Why apologize, officer? Saved me some money," the player stated and the other three that would have lost laughed.

Holder of the "full house hand" was still not happy. I watched as the rookie cop turned bar maid served up the five men beer, getting an evil glare from the full house player. We moved outside.

"Next time I tell you to be quiet, be fucking quiet," I said spitting mad.

He didn't last much longer and a line was cast into the pool for another dumbass. Now it's this guy. He walks in the front doors of the police department after being dropped off by the swing shift officer and introduces himself to me. Honestly, I can't and will never remember his name but I do know who he reminded me of, Mister Rogers. He had to be his twin brother; they looked exactly alike. Mr. Rogers was an award winning host for a children's television show. The Mr. Roger I knew was a marvelous man and could entertain children for hours. The guy standing in front didn't even know that he already had a major hurtle to overcome.

Over the coming months Mr. Rogers had become a department project trying to get him up and running, but he just couldn't help himself. Not only did he look like the television host, he acted like him also. We deal with adults 99 percent of the time and one does not talk to adults like you are talking to a child. One time I watched him move through a bar acting like he was "bar checking" then I noticed he had a handful of scrap paper and would stop with a bar patron and hand a slip of paper to the customer. Mr. Rogers would utter something to the customer then move to another person in the bar and repeat it all over again. Every person Mr. Rogers gave a piece of paper to, would read whatever was on the paper and then toss it on the floor and glare at Mr. Rogers. I couldn't stand it any longer and motioned him over to me.

"What you handing out?" I asked of him.

Mr. Rogers handed me a cut piece of paper that had been surgically removed from the want ads of a local newspaper for a job opening.

"Outside," I said to him. "What the hell are you doing?" I asked.

"Well, I'm helping these guys find jobs," he replied.

"What makes you think they don't have a job or need or want one?" I replied.

"Just trying to show I care," he replied.

"Don't do it again, understand?" I said with great irritation.

On another occasion Mr. Roger is driving the patrol car. It is O dark thirty and we come to a "T" in the road with a decision to make, turn left or turn right after we stop at the stop sign. In front of us is a large warehouse and flower beds. Perched on top of the flower beds is a car, on its passenger side, with the rear wheel still spinning. Mr. Rogers does not see anything. Mr. Rogers turns on his left blinker, looks left, looks right and turns left and begins to accelerate.

"STOP" I yell. "Back up" I order him. He does. "Now stop" I say. He does. I jump out of the patrol car and make my way around to the driver's door and front windshield. There are two drunken guys inside the car, uninjured. About this time Mr. Rogers shows up and has that "deer in the headlights" look to his face.

"I didn't see the car," he tells me.

"Yep, understandable; I barely made it out myself" in about as smartass tone as one can get.

I couldn't take it anymore and Mr. Rogers was passed around the department like a whiskey bottle at a bon fire. Soon "the Pig" got him.

As Pig tells the story, he had Mr. Rogers in the front passenger seat riding shotgun. Pig was using a great deal of patience as he drove Mr. Rogers around, explaining observation techniques and how an officer has to always be aware of his surrounding, being ever so vigilant. Pig turned onto the West side access road that leads behind the Sumner Junior High school and makes the sweeping turn now eastbound on the single lane access road. Pig said he wasn't doing more than 10 or 15 miles per hour as he was explaining observation techniques to Mr. Rogers and about that very moment Pig learned that a cable had been put up blocking the access road. The first thing that hit the cable was the push bars on the front of the police car. Next the cable broke out both head lights and bounced up onto the hood of the patrol car. By this time Pig had "observed" the problem and was desperately trying to get the car stopped but it was too late. The cable impacted the windshield and smashed it in on the two officers as the patrol car came to a stop. Mr. Rogers then delivered one of the finest lines ever, "so now I get it". Oops!

Ten months after Mr. Rogers was hired, he resigned finally figuring it out that police work was no place for him. Best decision he ever made.

Chapter 15

Night Moves

It was one of those quiet nights in Sumner, not a lot going on and not a lot of folks out and about. I had completed all the required bar checks, noting the usual bar flies seated in their usual spots, drinking their favorite beverage. It was very "Cheers" like in the eight bars in town that were open that night. I elected to park my patrol car at the police department and do a little foot patrol. I moved quietly along, staying mostly in the shadows not wanting to be seen. I checked doors and windows of the downtown businesses walking the alley edges. I recall an occasional dog barking and the cats that fought on a regular basis. I noticed a few bar patrons leaving their pub family and making their way to their one and two room apartments that were scattered around the downtown area. Very few vehicles were moving. It was just another quiet night in small town America as the last of my citizens found refuge in their beds to sleep until a new day appeared, or so I thought!

As I found myself walking back to the police department and my car, I decided to stop for a quick visit with Caroline. She was a quick witted smart ass that let nothing slide. She lived in Sumner and like me knew most of the people in the area. She took a great deal of pleasure in tormenting me for how young I looked and her perception that I was naïve; therefore targeted me for any reason, be it one I provided or she would come up with a fictional weakness. Nonetheless, I enjoy the verbal sparring and tonight would be no different.

"What you been up to young man?" she greeted my entrance.

"Making my bar checks," I responded.

"Did they check your ID? You don't look old enough to be in those kinds of establishments," she said, launching the first attack.

I grinned at her and was struggling with a comeback when I heard the front door to the police lobby opened up. We had a visitor at 0230 hrs.

Our visitor was Mable. She was in her early sixties – slender, grey haired, and with manicured fingernails. At times, like now, Mable looks like she "painted" make-up on her face; but there had been times when she actually might have been sober when she applied the make-up almost normally. Mable always wore a knee length dress or skirt with nylons and dark pumped shoes, and of course a small clutch hand bag. She was one of the bar flies I have written about earlier. Mable lived off her social security income and her business, yes; I'll describe it as simply a business. She was in the business of providing "services" to the little old single men that also found family in the bars of my little town. Every once in a while, for a small fee of five to ten bucks, Mable would take care of "business". On this particular evening now morning, Mable had struck up a business deal with a younger man, say thirties or so. He was a young man that was seated at the Club Tavern with Mable chatting. I had noticed them earlier in the evening while doing a bar check.

The first words out of Mable's mouth were "I've been raped." She did not mention any of what I just described to you about the young man, just the words "I've been raped." I quickly moved towards Mable then I suddenly retreated nearly gagging as I did. Apparently Mable had suffered a bowel movement somewhere between here and wherever she came from, and now the movement was squished solidly inside her panties and panty hose. I asked Mable where the rape had occurred and she told me in the stairwell leading from the street to her second floor apartment above the tavern. Mable described to me that the man was younger and went by the name of Chuck. She further stated he was wearing a red bandana and a leather jacket.

"Was he armed?" I asked Mable.

"No" was her reply.

I knew who "Chuck" was and probably where he was walking to; home. He was the same guy I had spotted with Mable earlier in the bar.

"Mable, sit here. Don't move and I'll find Chuck and get to the bottom of this, okay?" I said.

"Thank you," she said then settled in, inside the lobby of the police department occupied only by the sharp witted smartass Caroline.

As I turned to leave via the backdoor of the police department, I glanced at Caroline with an evil smirk to my face; I winked. Caroline simply glared at me for leaving the smelly little lady behind to be babysat by dispatch.

This was not the first time I had met Mable at the front lobby counter of the police department. About once every two months or so Mable would bring in a bounced check, one written to her by one of her customers, a John that didn't have the funds to clear the check with the bank. Mable would bring it to us wanting us to collect the money from the "John". We had a limit to how much the check had to be for, and they never came to that amount. If she had brought in a check for 100.00 it would have been an interesting conversation on how she earned the money but that never happened.

I quickly drove to the location of the "rape" and did not see Chuck. I looped around into the alley behind the tavern and caught movement in the parking lot. It was a man walking away from the area; not in a hurry, just walking. He wore a leather jacket and a red bandana. I drove to Chuck and stopped him. He was soaked from the waist down.

"Why you so wet?" I asked Chuck.

"I was dirty so I simply hosed off before I left to go home," Chuck responded.

"I saw you earlier in the tavern and you weren't a mess then, what happened?" I asked Chuck. He was squirming by now, looking for a way to explain his predicament.

"Look" he said with a sigh, "she shit on me," he then blurted out.

"Shit on you?" I asked with a great questioning expression.

"You know, Mable," Chuck said. "She said she was going to report that I raped her," Chuck said.

"I need your side of the story Chuck, just tell me, only you, I, and Mable need to know," I said with a tone of a marriage type counselor.

"Well we got to talking in the bar, little bit of dirty talk, you know; then she offered to take care of my problem for ten bucks and I, you know, well, done her before so what the heck, do it again," Chuck stuttered out.

"And then?" I asked of Chuck.

"We left and well walked to the stairs and I didn't want to go to her room, smells like cat shit, and so, well, huh, well we got to doing it on the stairs and well, she huh, well she let go man, all over me," Chuck said struggling.

"She let go?" I asked, as in crapped on you?"

Chuck by now had his head down and was looking at the ground, "yes," Chuck said. "It pissed me off," he added.

"She got mad when I refused to pay her, even though I told her I couldn't continue with the act," Chuck said.

"Well you have a bigger problem right now," I told Chuck. With that I went on to tell him that she had played the rape card, and since she was sixty something and he was thirty something and she would claim he followed her to the stairwell and attacked her there, he would take a beating in the court systems. Chuck was starting to see his position was a bad one.

"Now what?" Chuck asked of me.

"Mable just wants to be paid," I told Chuck.

Chuck looked at me then reached for his wallet. He quickly opened it, one of those wallets that is secured with a bright silver chain to the owner's pants, and found a damp ten dollar bill. Chuck handed me the ten dollar bill and asked that I give it to Mable.

"Will do," I responded as I pinched the corner of the bill with my thumb and fore finger nails.

"Whatever you did with that hose over there didn't work, you smell like an outhouse," I mentioned to Chuck.

"I know, almost puked when it happened," he responded.

"Officer, you know I did not, would not rape her or anyone," Chuck said to me.

"I know Chuck, I know none of you would," I responded.

With that I left and drove back to the police department. I entered via the back door and "oh my god" the smell was horrific. I walked into the lobby and there sat Caroline with a Vick's laden hanky over her face and Mable, seated in a chair in the lobby with her feet crossed neatly under the chair.

"Here you go Mable. Chuck says he's sorry. Are we square?" I tell and ask Mable.

"Yes, thank you officer," Mable said and she quickly grabbed the ten dollar bill and left the lobby leaving her horrible odor behind. I watched her walk away from the building and disappear into the night. As I turned to gloat to

Caroline over my cleverness by leaving the well-dressed poop master with her, I also saw and felt the impact of the local telephone book to the side of my head. Caroline had found absolutely no humor in my actions. "You son of a bitch," was all I heard as I quickly ran from the police department; so much for the gun, bullet proof vest, and all the battle accoutrements that I wore on my belt. I just got my ass kicked by a pudgy phone book wielding pissed off dispatcher.

I quickly climbed into the protection of the interior of my battle wagon and as I left I noticed the front doors to the police department were propped open for airing out. I disappeared into the dark looking for more movement in the night.

My editor asked me a good question, "this is prostitution, correct?" I agreed but explained this was a family of people that spent time together rather than sit alone in their single room living quarters. Their gene of relation was that of alcohol. Thanksgiving and Christmas now meant more to them being able to share it and of course Mable would take care of business when one of the men had a "hankering". Mable would never been seen flaunting herself on a corner or sidewalk; she only took care of family.

Hold Your Breath!

Some stories are just more suspenseful than others. They are the near death experiences, the "you don't know what to expect" types of situations. Seeing them before your eyes is like watching a movie where you don't know if you will end up as the hero or the victim. These are stories that made me wonder if I could have done anything to stop it from happening; stories that made me feel so sorry for the families affected; and stories that made me believe that there is a higher being protecting me.

He too wasn't breathing but he didn't look nearly as bad as his younger friend. I began CPR about the time I spotted the first ambulance slowing to a stop. Behind that ambulance was another. In moments I had been relieved by professional life savers. The second arriving two medics asked me how many victims, besides this one.

Chapter 16

Who Lives, Who Dies

She spoke softly, quietly and with caution, all the while her eyes darted to the view out the front door of her first floor apartment.

"I heard someone just outside my window, I heard their clothing brush against the rhododendron bush that is growing there," she explained. "I saw the door knob to my front door turn slowly back and forth but I had locked it earlier," she continued to describe in detail what had occurred.

"Do you know who it might have been?" I asked.

She hesitated, and then looked down and to the right and quietly stated "no".

Why was she lying? I thought to myself. It was someone she knew, or at least figured it was a person she knew. She was using me, not to find the guy but to show him she was willing to call the police. It was her way of saying "told you" I'd call the police to whoever it was, and I figured he was watching us at this very moment.

"Ok, I'll stay in the area and keep an eye out, call if you hear anything else," I stated and we bid farewell as my radio burst with a sharp call for my response.

"112 Sumner, I'm clear, whatcha got?" I responded to the radio.

Dispatch stated that Washington State Patrol had called asking us to check for a possible accident on highway 167, they had only a report of an accident, but nothing further. WSP did not have a trooper working in the area and didn't want to pull a trooper from Interstate five corridors to check on a possible accident. I responded "en-route".

I hated these calls. Most of the time I would find nothing, sometimes there would be a traffic accident, and sometimes, like this one, could never be erased from a cop's memory.

I sped off and could move quickly as there was no traffic to speak of at 0315 hours in the morning. As I raced to the area I arrived to the on-ramp to highway 410, and then quickly exited to the on ramp of highway 167. In the early eighties 167 was a two way highway: one lane north, one lane south. As I rounded the high speed sweeping curve I came across what the State Patrol had been asking for, confirmation that this was in fact a traffic accident, and a terrible one.

I called dispatch, "112 Sumner, arriving, two car, two bodies lying on the highway, need aid" and with that I was out of my patrol car to check on the victims.

You never get used to finding people like this, sometimes breathing, sometimes not, sometimes only pieces here, pieces there and then there are the times like this. Three people, all struggling to stay alive, all desperately need some sort of help. Two men laying on the road and both were close to needing CPR. A 50 something year old lady was still pinned in her car had a leg bone poking through her skin just above her knee and apparently it had ruptured an artery as blood pumped freely.

Like most cops you get into the business to help people and this was a time when you were desperately needed by three; but that meant two would be released to their fate. Who lives, who dies?

I quickly un-snapped my gun belt straps, holding the belt to my trouser pants belt, then undid the buckle of the gun belt; and the entire weapon's belt fell onto the highway pavement. I next unbuckled my trouser belt and pulled it free from my pants and began wrapping the belt around her leg just above wound. If I could just slow the bleeding down, just enough till help arrived. She was still conscious and I showed her how to hold the belt in place, keeping the pressure on.

"Look at me. Don't look down; just keep looking at me, ok?"

She nodded her head at me letting me know she understood.

"I'm going to check on those two men over there, I'll be right back."

She blinks at me and with that I was off running to the others. I glanced back at her and she was still alert and watching. I told her to watch me and if I happened to see her head down I will know she is probably passing out and I'd have to return to her.

The first man I came to turned out to be a teenager. He was flat on his back, his head rolled over to the right side of his face, then when he would gasp in a breath his head would roll up facing to the night sky. When his breath left, his head would roll back to the right side of his face. It was rhythmic, and the rhythm was slowing. I noticed his right eye had dislodged from his skull and the top of his skull appeared flattened, but strangely no blood except from small cuts and scrapes.

I checked the third man and he too was lying on his back, struggling to breathe and was conscious. I looked at the woman and she was watching me but her head was low, she was struggling.

I looked at the man in front of me and I said, "hang in there, don't let go, hang in there, I'll be back."

I ran to my patrol car and pulled from my briefcase a kotex pad that I had always kept with me in case I had gotten shot and couldn't wait for an ambulance; I'd use it to control bleeding and drive myself to the hospital. Now seemed like an appropriate time to use it.

By the time I got to her, her eyes were but slits, but she was watching me. I slid the kotex over the wound and retightened the belt. This time I synch it down properly and it would not require her help, she would be unable.

"I can hear sirens, angels are close, fight, stay with me, ok?" I said.

She blinked acknowledgment and I ran back to the young man.

His head was just falling to the right, then nothing. I check his neck artery and nothing. As I did I looked to the other man, I saw no motion from him either. "Sorry" was all I said and I ran to the older man.

He too wasn't breathing but he didn't look nearly as bad as his younger friend. I began CPR about the time I spotted the first ambulance slowing to a stop. Behind that ambulance was another. In moments I had been relieved by professional life savers. The second arriving two medics asked me how many victims, besides this one.

"A woman in the car over there is bleeding out and that young man is gone," I responded. "The lady has a fighting chance if you get to her."

With that they gave a quick glance at the young man and turned and ran to the lady.

I took a moment and realized the truck had been occupied by the two men and had crossed the centerline and hit the lady head on. The two vehicles were probably doing a combined speed of 120 mph at the time of impact. "Amazing anyone is alive" I thought to myself.

Minutes later Washington State Patrol began arriving. Shortly this area would be shut down and a lengthy fatality investigation would begin. After I spoke briefly with the first Trooper arriving, I gathered up my gun belt and retreated to the police department to wash the blood from myself and equipment.

Shane didn't say much when I came into the police department. He was a young dispatcher working his way through college. The graveyard shift allowed him to study, enough time in the morning to grab a nap and he would then attend late morning and early afternoon classes.

"Pretty bad, huh? Shane asked.

"Yes, bad, very bad, don't want to talk about it," I responded.

"It doesn't get any better," Shane said.

"What, now what?" I asked.

"The lady with the prowler has been calling, she is pissed off. Says she hasn't seen you and she is still hearing noises outside, going to complain to the Chief tomorrow."

"She lives nearby; I'll wander over and check on her, how long ago did she make her last call?" I asked.

"Been about 15 minutes," Shane responded.

As I walked down the street towards her house I thought about what had occurred and what I could have done different. Really nothing, it is what it is and you can only do what you can do to get the best results possible.

As I got close to the house I could hear voices, talking coming from the far side of her apartment. I approached un-noticed and got close enough to hear the conversation. I learned that they were in a relationship and he stayed at the house off and on and they had a disagreement tonight and when he arrived at the house she had locked him out.

124 | Donald Gill

I stepped out of the shadows and asked her, "Why did you lie to me about not knowing him?"

They were caught off guard by my sudden appearance. "I wasn't sure" she stated. "Why didn't you check on me after you told me you would?" she asked.

"I was busy, you look fine, you don't need me, correct"?

"Not now," she responded in a snotty voice.

I walked back to the Police Department and came inside. Shane poked his head around the corner and said "they transported two from the accident scene to the hospital". I gave him a "thumbs up" and disappeared into the locker room.

It was time I left for home. My relief had shown up and was ready to go for dayshift. I left the Chief a note as to the night's activities and gave him a warning that there was a woman that was coming into the police department to file a complaint on me. With that I made my out of the back door and home was my destination.

My batteries were fully charged when I showed up for work and I found a note from the Chief.

"First of all, hell of job last night, the older guy is still alive but he is fighting and the woman is going to be fine. State Patrol said you performed well. Make sure you're in the office at 2300 hrs, the woman that made the complaint is coming down to the Police Department, and she wants to apologize to you in person." Chief.

Chapter 17

Shit Happens

I could see Pig parked just up the street. The sun was about to rise and morning was coming to this neighborhood. It is a typical little housing development with like houses built at about the same time, then filled with young families that would raise their children and turn their dreams of the perfect life into reality. That was the plan, at least until something or someone screwed it up and that's why we were there.

A young father had unexplainably fallen to the dark side and experimented with meth. His wife had hung on, hoping, praying, blinded by love and or ignorance, stayed with him and went through the motions of attaining the dream, all the while frightened out of her mind at what was really going on. The babies, toddlers, children just saw dad. They too knew something was wrong, but they had little lives to build on and dad and mom were their pillars and would not recognize dad's fall to weakness.

The radio crackled; it was Detective Browner announcing the warrant had been signed and he was on the way. Activity started to pick up, plans being made, and assignments being handed out. This was the routine of serving another search warrant for meth and the arrest of another meth dealer, dad.

Five hours earlier we had met dad in a remote parking lot on South Hill Puyallup and made our third controlled buy of meth from him. On each of the three buys we had made arrangements to meet for the purpose of buying meth, then detectives, that already knew were dad lived; followed him from this house to the parking lot. Dad would meet the undercover detective and an exchange would be watched, recorded, and photographed by other detectives. Dad would then be followed home, his family's house of dreams was about to be turned into a nightmare.

Evidence would be provided to a judge and a search warrant would be secured and we would do our jobs. This was familiar routine and we had done way too many times in our meth infected county.

Pig and I had been given the assignment to keep the home under surveillance and when the entry team approached we would move to the South side of the home and scale the six-foot wood fence. There, we would secure the back of the house and keep anyone from leaving or entering. Since Pig and I were watching the house, we had not attended the briefing; so, rules say, if you don't attend briefing you don't make entry to the house; but you can secure the perimeter. It makes sense. Then there is your ahhh shits!

A threat matrix found dad below the required points needed to use S.W.A.T. so we were going to take care of business ourselves. Most of us had been or were currently with S.W.A.T so this would not be a problem. The informant in this case had mentioned that dad had purchased a stolen rifle and the truck out front of his home was stolen but there wasn't much else according to Detective Browner. The Sergeant then called Pig and I on the radio, "we're moving, get ready." I climbed out of SUV and began moving slowly towards the front yard. I adjusted my body armor and thru the sling to my MP5 automatic rifle over my shoulder. As I moved I met up with Pig on the south side of the home.

The sky had color to it but there was enough light to see and soon we could make out the lineup of entry cops moving tactically towards the front door. Within seconds they were in place. Pig and I made our way to the fence, repositioned our MP5s to our backs and cleared the fence landing in the back yard.

As I cleared the fence, I heard the thunderous crack of a battering ram impact the front door to the home and the shouts of the word "police" told me they had gained entry and reality was in dad's house.

I also detected a problem, dogs. And, of course, not your common garden variety wiener dogs, but two pissed off Rottweiler's; Pig and I aren't that lucky. They had exploded into a run straight at us, snarling and growling. Their intentions were very clear. The last time I had witnessed this scene was in the 1970s, a movie called "The Omen".

There would be no time to re-climb the fence; they'd shred our family jewels and that wasn't an option. We simply turned and ran like hell towards the garage and a walk thru door that I was hoping to be unlocked.

I liked this plan; I was faster than Pig meaning he'd be "first steak". I had to get to that door and I did. It was unlocked and as I opened it I apparently wasn't moving as fast as Pig preferred. He slammed into my back side sending me sprawling onto the garage floor and he landing on me. I also noticed that a beast had attached himself to the toe area of my left boot and I was kicking like a madman trying to detach his massive shaking head as Pig tried to close the door.

It was no longer a scene from "The Omen" but one likened to that of "Jaws" where the captain of the shark hunting vessel is spoon fed off the back of his boat into the jaws of the massive shark. I know the dog is nothing like the shark, but at the moment the difference really didn't seem to matter. A well landed blow to the animal's snout by my right boot heel did the job and the door was shut; however the latch was busted from our violent entry and we had to hold the door shut.

Another problem presented itself, not like the one we had just evaded but a deadlier one, one that kills over time. We both immediately noticed it. Although it was dark in the garage, our eyes watered, throats burned, and every breath made our lungs scream. I swept the garage with my weapon mounted light and revealed our refuge was a cooking boiling red phosphorous methamphetamine lab.

We began holding our breath and suddenly the unthinkable option of killing the dogs was a clear consideration. We spotted another door on the opposite wall of the garage. As Pig held the door shut I managed to get to the escape door, unlocked it, and it opened. I stepped out in a space about four feet wide, bordered by another six-foot wood fence between dad's property and his neighbor to the North; but I could see the driveway and our escape. I motioned to Pig to get over to where I was and I held the door as I also knew the Rottweilers would be once again on his ass when they pushed the door open. It was about as fast as I had ever seen him move. I yanked the door shut as the dogs got there. We were able to breathe again. We kind of rested there for a moment, taking in what had just occurred.

"Do you recall anyone mentioning anything about damn big Rottweilers and a meth lab being at this place?" I asked.

"No," Pig responded.

"Let's find everybody," I said and with that I began stepping down the path towards the driveway.

About two steps into it I felt a stabbing pain in the ball of my left foot.

"Damn it, now what?" I said.

Leaning against the garage I picked up my left boot and looked. There was a small piece of plywood firmly attached to my boot by a rather large rusty nail that was now sticking into my left foot. There was also dog shit sandwiched between the board and boot. My left foot is taking a beating this morning.

"Oh it just keeps getting better," I mumbled and Pig pulled the board and nail out.

Checking the path, it was lined with many of the similar boards; booby traps no doubt. I wondered if Dad had let the kids know about it. We doubted he did. Dad was an asshole.

We made our way to the house. I recalled the carpet was white, rather clean till Pig and I arrived. We were coated with dog shit from the knees down and I could feel the bleeding to my left foot. We relayed to the Sergeant what we had encountered. His eye brows raised a bit when we mentioned there was fully operational red P lab in the garage and we had crashed into it. He turned to find Detective Browner.

"Browner, you me outside, we need to talk," ordered the Sergeant.

Clearly he was pissed off at the intel Browner had not gathered and it was safe to assume an ass chewing was forth coming.

"Now what?" Pig said looking at me.

I was about eight feet from him and glanced his way. What a sight. His hair looked like that of a cat ready to fight. It was sticking straight up in the air. His head was wet from sweat and he had sweat beads running down the side of his head near his temples. There was a large brown streak that ran from his right ear, down his neck. I figured it was dog shit. His clothing and body armor was a mess, bearing everything that we had encountered in the previous several minutes, and his boots were of particular interest. The vibram soles were what appeared to be nearly two inches above the floor, as if he were suspended. Dog shit curled out from under his boots looking like waffles being cooked in a waffle maker. The entirety of the sight and all of it standing on a white rug was quite the view. I smiled and snickered to myself.

"What you looking at asshole?" Pig said.

I glanced at his face and he was pissed off. Not a happy cop. Pig was one that was usually clean, gleaming, and polished, and absolutely nothing outta place; he was in no mood to be messed with.

I remember watching him use a leaf garden rake to rake out his footprints in his apartment carpet as we exited the front door. I remember that I used to flip the tassels out of the near perfect presentation of a throw carpet in his kitchen, being careful not to get caught. I'd grin as I watch him re-straighten those tassels back to perfection when he found them. Pig was fun to mess with, but I was pushing the limits here and now.

"You're worse off than me," Pig said.

"How ya figure?" was my response.

"You're bleeding from a rusty, shit laced nail out of a meth lab."

"Good point," I responded. "Probably should take care of that before it gets serious," I shot back.

The sergeant had re-entered the house and as he approached said "you two assholes look like shit and you're 'smelling' up my crime scene. Get out, and get that hole in your foot treated. Last time I checked they won't let me have a peg leg detective."

Without saying a word Pig and I turned and walked out the front door, leaving well marked shit footprints on the white carpet as we left. Once outside, we found a hose and helped each other wash dog shit off our boots. Pig was thoroughly discussed with the process as some of the water would spray onto him and was convinced of two things: it had shit in the spray; and I was doing it on purpose. He was correct on both counts. We always carried extra clothing in our vehicles, so changing clothes was the next option. During the process I cleaned up my hole in the foot and bandaged it, but clearly I would need to swing by the hospital for a professional re-due and tetanus shot. I was finished well ahead of Pig and found him still in his underwear wiping himself down; it was the closest thing to a shower he could find and he was taking his time getting it done correctly. When I pointed out that he still had a streak of dog shit on his neck, the one I had noticed earlier, I thought he was going to throw up. Life must be extremely difficult if you're a neat freak; but fun for their friends.

Pig finally found a somewhat acceptable level of discomfort with his current state of cleanliness, but I knew he wanted nothing more than to throw away all clothing he wore earlier and a shower. We walked back to the house of dreams turned nightmare to help with the task at hand.

Pig entered first, with me close behind. I immediately saw the family seated on the couch. Dad had already been removed in handcuffs and was in the back seat of a patrol car. Mom sat, not moving, staring into space. I could only imagine what was going on behind her blue eyes. There were bills to pay and mouths to feed. And what could she say to family and friends that had up until today no clue what Dad had been up to? Now that Dad was in jail, she would be tasked with breaking that news to family and friends and living through their reaction.

The toddlers clung to mom seated on both sides of her lap. The young boy standing next to the three also entwined with them. The children however were not staring off into space; they looked directly at me, tears in their eyes, frightened to death of me and the gang that I had been with. To them, we were intruders that took away dad. We were the enemy!

It reminded of a picture of a family in a third world country I once saw: a family clinging together because that was all they had left, each other, and had no clue what was going to happen next. My emotions inside were tearing at me. Should I feel ashamed? Should I apologize? Should I just simply not give a shit and leave and go help out; or should I do something a little different, check and see if I still have the reason I signed up to be a cop in me? For if it's gone, maybe I need to step back and re-think what the hell I'm doing.

I walked over and introduced myself. As I did, I knelt to one knee so not to tower above them and we could easily look into each other's eyes. I spoke softly and honestly.

"I'm extremely saddened by what has happened here today. I apologize for frightening you and your children. Sometimes we must serve search warrants and families are in the home."

Her first look of anger in her eyes began to disappear and the tears began to form.

"Can I answer any questions you may have?"

She was finding the strength to speak and finally asked "what's going to happen to my husband and why did he get arrested?"

I glanced over to the boy, he was about four.

"Would you rather do this in private?" I asked.

"No, there will be no more secrets in this family."

"He will be taken to Pierce County jail and booked for trafficking in methamphetamine, production of methamphetamine, and possession of a stolen truck," I responded.

"So that is what he has been doing," she stated. "He's been acting weird lately, I asked him if he was having an affair but he just stated he was busy at work and under a lot of pressure" she stated, and then asked "he has a meth lab?"

"Yes, in the garage," I responded.

She gasps and puts a hand over her mouth. "He wouldn't tell me what he was doing out there with his friends and kept it locked and even covered the windows," she claimed, but I believed her. "He just bought the truck last week," she told me.

"Maybe so, but it's stolen out of Olympia," I told her.

I could see her mind going a thousand miles an hour.

"Did you not notice a change in him; did you not know he was using meth?" I asked.

"I noticed he didn't sleep nearly as much as he used to and was losing weight. But his new friends were creepy, would look at me, stare at me, frighten me. And he would get a call, leave and be back in 15 minutes; those happened all the time," she spoke. "I don't know what I'm going to do now," she said.

"I'm going to put you in touch with some private and government programs for assistance and you're going to definitely need your family here to help you. You have family close?" I asked.

"Yes, they're all close and I will need to tell them about what happened," she responded.

I stood and pulled out a business card and wrote my cell phone number down on it. "Look, you run into any problems you can call me and I'll get the answers for you, ok?" I said.

She nodded and looked a little more relieved.

"I'll clean up the mess my partner and I made of the rug over there, don't worry about it," I said.

"Well, that's least of my worries right now" she said, "but much appreciated". She took my card and said thank you.

As I left the room she was dialing on her phone. I heard the first words, "Hi mom, I got some bad news….."

I found Pig helping with the search.

"What the fuck you been up to, playing social worker?" he asked.

"I was checking to see if I still had my humanity," was my response.

"And?" Pig asked.

"It's still there, needs a little work and I need some help," I responded.

"Ok, what you need, a fucking hug?" Pig offered.

"Let's clean the dog shit off her carpet," I said.

Pig hesitated, and then said, "My humanity can use a little work too."

We located rags, paper towels, and some cleaning solution and set in cleaning up a mess. All the while we could hear mom telling family members of what dad had been up to and what had occurred. She was pissed; not at us, but at her husband, the dad of her kids.

The floor was clean and looked as good as new. My foot had begun to throb, "time I go get this looked at," I told Pig.

"Been a long night," Pig said.

By this time the lab team had arrived and began setting up for the long process of taking down the lab. This lab would be difficult and the day would be a hot one. Detective Browner had his hands full and we didn't much give a damn. Normally I'd offer to stay and help but considering the shit storm Pig and I had gotten into with his sloppy work, we decided enough is enough and left.

I had one more stop to make, Good Samaritan Hospital in Puyallup to get my foot attended to. Usually they are pretty good about getting cops in to see a doctor over an injury, even a minor one, and this time would be no different.

"How'd this happen?" the doctor asked. I gave a brief run down and he kind of laughed at the dog chase part. *Real funny asshole* I thought to myself.

"Nail went deep," he said.

"Yeah, partner had to pull it off and there was a pile of dog shit between the board and my boot," I told him.

"Well we'll get you fixed up here, shot of tetanus and something for the infection that is about to happen, and you should be good to go."

"Thanks doc."

My phone began ringing. "It's my wife, gotta answer," I told the doc.

"Hi"

"Where you at?"

"Hospital."

"What the hell happened this time? You hurt or someone else?"

"Me, and it's minor."

"We served a search warrant and well, shit happens, tell you about it when I get home."

"Love you, bye."

"Love you too, bye."

The sudden move spun the man a bit and he slammed him into the door jam. He fought back pushing from the wall and door jam and now it was me getting slammed into the outer wall inside the foyer. All I could think about was *'hang on, don't let go, don't let go!'* I felt the hammer slam against the skin of my little finger and my adrenaline quickly filled my entire body. I pushed him back and slammed into the opposite wall all the while forcing the weapon up past my head and his'. I was a bit taller and it was the first time I really saw his face.

Chapter 22

C.Q.B.
(Close Quarters Battle)

I had this story pretty well hidden in my mind but it popped up during some thought process of another story. When I remembered it, the first thing I thought of was a line from the movie Gladiator made by Russell Crowe: "Death smiles down on all of us, all we can do is smile back." I do believe that night, when all was said and done, how close death had come for me. I did look up and say "thanks".

Usually when I came home off shift I'd tell my wife a funny joke I had heard at work or in a bar somewhere and she'd say "not funny" which puzzled me. She tells me "your jokes suck but your stories are hilarious, tell me a story," she would say. I never told her this story. The first time she knew of it was when she read it in the manuscript of this book. She had tears in her eyes when she finished reading it, "why didn't you tell me about this?" she asked. I answered her back and said, "It wasn't funny, it would have only frightened you for the next 30 years each time I left for work knowing that death looks down on all of us. One of these days we won't have time or ability to look back."

It was a warm summer night in the 1980s. I was working graveyard shift alone, had done my first round of bar checks, and had detected zero problems. Everything seemed to be going well inside and outside the bars. It was just another quiet night in a small American town.

Most graveyards are just as the word says it is, "graveyard" – quiet, calm, and serene. All that warm and fuzzy feeling went running off when I was dispatched to a disturbance at a lounge in the east end of Sumner. All dispatch could say is that there was a lot of yelling in the background as the caller asked for the cops to hurry. A fight was brewing in the lounge and police were needed. I hustled my cruiser to the parking lot, got out, and entered the lounge. The entrance had a foyer with a single glass door. Once inside the foyer there were two glass doors leading into the restaurant and bar area. As I stepped in, a man came running out the main double doors and ran by me – a good indication that he wanted out of the area and did not want to discuss the occurrence inside the lounge. I didn't stop him, although I was curious to see what vehicle he climbed into. He quickly entered a truck and with no hesitation backed out, revealing his license plate to me. I made a mental note to myself and turned back to the front double doors, and as I reached to push open the doors the door swung out wildly. What I saw next was not the man coming through the door but what he had in his right hand – a dark steel of the barrel of a four inch revolver, the hammer pulled back and his right index finger wrapped around the trigger of the weapon. A slight squeeze of the trigger and the weapon would explode sending a piece of hot lead out of the barrel.

There was no time to react to getting to my revolver, I had but one play. I reached out with both my hands and grabbed the weapon. My right hand grabbed the body of the revolver, my left the barrel. Sometimes you get lucky, and luck was on my side this night. My right little finger slipped between the hammer and the firing pin momentarily disabling the weapon but I could never let go. I hung on for my dear life.

The sudden move spun the man a bit and he slammed him into the door jam. He fought back pushing from the wall and door jam and now it was me getting slammed into the outer wall inside the foyer. All I could think about was *'hang on, don't let go, don't let go!'* I felt the hammer slam against the skin of my little finger and my adrenaline quickly filled my entire body. I pushed him back and slammed into the opposite wall all the while forcing the weapon up past my head and his'. I was a bit taller and it was the first time I really saw his face. Noodles! Noodles covered his face and hair! Weird seeing the noodles but I was fighting for my life at the moment and cared of nothing else. The only thing I cared about is to get the weapon no farther above us. I used every ounce of strength, fueled by fear and adrenaline, yanked the weapon straight down near the floor, and pulled the weapon immediately away from him. Now the weapon was free of his hands and completely in my hands.

The man continued to the floor into a fetal position, screaming and clutching his right hand. I kneeled down and with my left knee pinned the man to the floor on the foyer and looked at the weapon that is now firmly gripped by my right little finger. People now began to enter the foyer from the bar, crowding the place and standing above and all around me. I yelled at them to back away from me but there was little room to move, most wanted out of the bar and out of the foyer. I wanted the damn gun off my hand. I reached around the weapon and using my left index finger pulled the hammer back into the firing position locking it back. It released my finger and I simply then de-cocked the revolver. I opened the cylinder of the firearm and dropped six 357 hollow points into my waiting left hand. I stood and slipped the six rounds into my trouser pocket, checked the weapon to make sure it was clear, closed the cylinder, and tucked the pistol into the front of my gun belt securing it. The man was in agony and still fetal on the floor. My first thought was simply beat the living shit out of him; he tried to kill me and I was furious! I grabbed him and spun him so that he was now face to face with the floor and jerked his right arm behind his back. Then I noticed the reason for his pain and agony. His right trigger finger had completely dislodged from its socket. Ouch! Nonetheless he was cuffed and searched and all I found was a holster to his right hip. I stood and looked at the audience, those that had not left.

There was fire in my eyes when I asked, "What the fuck is this all about?"

Remembering the fact that I was alone, I called dispatch. "Get me backup, just get another cop here," was all I said.

"Already done, they're on the way," she replied.

"I need medical here also," I followed up with.

"They are being dispatched," she said.

The adrenaline that had filled my body has a side effect: shakes. I had ways of hiding the shakes of my hands as it would appear to be fear so I kept my hands busy so as not to be noticed by those around me. The man on the floor was still screaming and all I wanted to say is *"shut the fuck up, lucky I just don't simply kill you"* but those words would not be spoken.

"Okay, what happened?" I asked the group still gathered.

They all started speaking at once making matters even more confusing, coupled with the screaming of the man on the floor. Blue lights arrived in the parking lot as officers began to enter the building, checking on me.

"I'm fine but he's a bit banged up," I said as I pointed to the screaming man on the floor wearing hand cuffs.

An older deputy from the sheriff's department motioned at me to step outside with him. I didn't hesitate. Other officers separated the remaining group for questioning.

"What happened?" he asked me.

"Got a call of a disturbance and when I arrived this asshole nearly floored me with the door and he has a gun pointed low, under my armor, hammer back and trigger finger wrapped the trigger. I grabbed the gun and we battled back and forth till I got the gun from him" I said finishing. Then I simply said "damn, I just got lucky."

The deputy agreed and asked if I'm okay.

"Got the adrenaline shakes but fine," I responded.

"Do you want us to call your chief?" he asked me.

"No, let's find out what happened; something serious happened in the bar that set this guy off," I said.

"The deputy told me that they got the call over county radio that you were in a physical altercation with a man that had a gun, we were frantic about getting here," he added.

"Thanks," I responded.

With that we stepped back into the foyer as the fire department arrived.

"The guy screaming on the floor has a right index that let's say is fucked up," I told the first medic that arrived.

"You okay?" he asked.

"I'm fine," I responded.

Deputies and officers had formed a consensus as to what had occurred. The man with the gun, Albert, had a run in with another guy and soon there was chest bumping and pushing between the two when other men separated them. The bartender had called police and then thought all might work out as the differences between the two men had retreated to hard stares at one another. A waitress brought the man some hot noodle soup and left him with it. Moments later he simply got up with the bowl of soup in hand and began walking for the front door but stopped next to Albert's table and dumped the hot soup onto Albert's head creating a predicted outburst. Albert screamed as the hot soup was now burning his flesh and screamed as he threw a glass of cold water onto himself. Other patrons ran to his aid but he fought through them and pulled out his 'until then hidden revolver' as he moved towards the front door. When he opened the door, well, he encountered me. The rest is history.

Names, addresses, phone numbers, and hand written statements were collected from the witnesses. Albert was transported to the hospital for treatment of a broken and dislocated finger and burns. The man that had ran by me leaving as I was arriving had a last name of Randolf with a Bonney Lake address. He would be tracked down by detectives and arrested for felony assault.

No Running Away

Some people think they can run away with crime just because they were able to do it one time, two times, or even more than twice. They steal people's cars and other stuff; they deal drugs; or anything they can make easy money from. These are the kinds of people I loved catching back then – people who try to make a fool of us cops ... people who would rather get high than go to work and earn a decent living ... people who think they are invincible ... people who don't care about others. I wanted to teach these people the principle of "easy come, easy go". These next chapters are stories of those who thought they can run away, but there was no running away.

Muchmore stated that the body was that of a young Hispanic female, 15 years of age, nude, rolled up in a blanket, doused with gasoline and set afire – pretty standard stuff in a homicide where the killer or killers tried to hide any evidence that would lead police to them. Muchmore continued saying that the autopsy had found she had died of a drug overdose; cocaine, and that she had been sexually attacked.

Chapter 19

Predators

"Detective Frank Muchmore here, Granite County Sheriff's office, is this Sergeant Gill?" the voice asked.

"Might be" I responded, "Give me your department contact number and your extension, I'll get the Sergeant to call you back," I said to the voice on the other end of the line. He hesitated, then realized the paranoia of drug cops and rambled off the numbers, then hung up.

I was the supervisor of a narcotics unit based out of Puyallup Police Department, a three-man unit with an extra two tribal cops thrown into the mix. We worked some pretty good cases and about one in four cases would find its way to the Federal level for prosecution; not bad for a six-man unit.

I was working narcotics, and if some guy calls claiming to be a cop, you don't start talking shop with them until you verify who he is. Anyone could be calling (and I had learned years prior that drug dealers collect intelligence on cops that are working narcotics in "their area") having found my physical description, work hours, and a list of vehicles that I drove in the paper work of a drug dealer we had arrested during a search warrant. It was unnerving to say the least.

I quickly dialed the numbers Muchmore had provided and was greeted by a dispatcher from Granite County. I followed up with the extension and within minutes Detective Frank Muchmore answered the phone.

Muchmore told me how about a month earlier a farmer had called the sheriff's office to report he had found a dead body rolled in a blanket on a remote apple orchard. Deputies responded and verified the findings, and detectives were summoned to the scene.

Muchmore stated that the body was that of a young Hispanic female, 15 years of age, nude, rolled up in a blanket, doused with gasoline and set afire – pretty standard stuff in a homicide where the killer or killers tried to hide any evidence that would lead police to them. Muchmore continued saying that the autopsy had found she had died of a drug overdose; cocaine, and that she had been sexually attacked. More importantly, Muchmore told me who she was – another runaway from Granite County who had run from her family for whatever reason six weeks earlier and now she was dead.

"So what's this got to do with me?" I asked.

Muchmore stated, "We had no suspect so we reached out to the public, especially the Hispanic population and began getting phone call tips. One of those tips stated that a drug dealer by the name of Juan Mendoza was responsible for the homicide. We traced the phone call to a home located in your city and through our investigation found out that the caller was Mrs. Mendoza."

"Have you confirmed this with her?" I asked.

"Yes, we traveled to your town and have in fact talked to her," he continued. "She told us her husband was having an affair with a bartender that lived somewhere in Puyallup and she had learned of it and kicked him out of the house. She later found out that one night Juan and his drug dealing buddies had picked up a hitch hiker, our homicide victim then still alive, took her to a party and got her higher than hell and had their way with her. Somewhere in the process she died from the overdose."

We have also learned that Juan had left the party sometime after midnight and drove to his girlfriend's home in Puyallup. We learned that the party was somewhere in Des Moines, Washington. The following morning Juan's buddies drove to Puyallup and told Juan that the girl had died, probably of the dope she had been ingesting, and her body was now in the trunk of their car. They needed Juan's help in getting rid of the body.

"I know Juan Mendoza" I said.

"We know, you arrested him six years ago for dealing meth and cocaine," he said.

"Did you figure out the remainder of the story?" I asked.

"No! Nothing, we can't even find the charging documents or any reports after you guys got done with him," his frustration was apparent. "Do you know?" he asked.

"Yes, and this will piss you off" I answered. I told Muchmore the story of six years earlier.

My partner Pig and I learned of Mendoza's business from street snitches; but none would or could get close enough to him to help us build a case, so we watched and waited. Then one day we got lucky and spotted a car leaving Mendoza's mobile home on River Road in Puyallup and the vehicle got stopped by a motor cop for whatever reason and we heard the activity on the radio. As we arrived at the traffic stop we saw the young Hispanic driver wearing handcuffs and getting stuffed into the rear seat of a patrol car. After they took the kid away we contacted the motor officer. The driver had a suspended license and an arrest warrant out for him. My partner, Pig, soon learned the plates were from a similar vehicle, but this vehicle was stolen out of Seattle. The vehicle was secured in the Police impound and a search warrant was granted. In the vehicle we found three ounces of dope, two ounces of meth, and an ounce of cocaine. Once we presented this to the driver, we got him to roll over on Mendoza, and we opened up an investigation that led to his arrest and about two pounds of meth recovered following the search of his mobile home. We had Mendoza by the balls, until the Feds came knocking.

The Feds found out about our work and they were waiting for us the next day; Mendoza had not been shipped off to county yet and the Feds were at our door. They had been watching, even had offered to help us; but I wasn't a fan of the Feds, so they were told "no thanks" and we charged on. They did not come with soldiers this time but with generals who wanted to talk to our generals and work something out.

Apparently Mendoza has direct ties to a cartel in Mexico and the Feds wanted an in with the gang, and they viewed Mendoza as their key. We had no dog in the fight and soon Mendoza was transferred to their custody and it was the last I saw of him for a few years.

"So Detective Muchmore, you have a dead girl, probably homicide and you think I have the suspect in my town. I think I know what you're about to ask," I said.

"Correct, and yes Sergeant, we need your help," he quickly stated.

"What do you need and when do you need it?" I asked.

He rambled on about how the victim's mother had received an anonymous phone call, probably from Mrs. Mendoza, and the mother knew we had a suspect. Soon the mother complained to the press and now the race card was in play, white cops not investigating the death of a young Hispanic female.

Muchmore was frustrated and had reached out for help, and help he'd get. Mendoza was always on my list of "to do" assholes and he'd just got moved to number one. I told Muchmore I'd keep him posted and would get all my detectives on this. In the meantime he had to keep quiet and take it.

"Don't worry Muchmore," I said, "your skin will thicken."

I gathered my Detectives in the briefing room and explained the situation. I told them the story. Most knew of Mendoza, and now they all knew that there were no other priorities in our unit till he gets cuffed. All agreed and with that began their investigation.

Several days passed when I was met at the office by Wally, one of my drug detectives. Wally was clean cut and everyone in the valley knew him. He was a great, big, happy man that likes to talk and did so. I couldn't walk through a mall without someone recognizing Wally and a conversation would break out with Wally talking like a teenage girl. It was damn near ridiculous. Wally used to work in a very small town called Orting and to this day he is an icon there.

Wally had that look of excitement about him, "what you got?" I asked.

Wally asked me to follow him to an interview room where we entered, and there, before us, was a large Hispanic man covered in tattoos. A tattoo of "MS 13" got my attention. The mara salvatrucha, meaning Salvadorian crew, or gang, and M is the 13th letter of the alphabet. The "M" that the 13 represented was a way of showing respect for the Mexican Mafia. He was clearly a gang member of a very violent street gang that started in Los Angeles in the eighties. Wally introduced me to "Gordo", street name given to him, no doubt because of his size. Wally tells me he met Gordo years ago and helped his mother and younger brother through a rough time with food and money, small town cop stuff. Gordo had always offered his services to Wally if he needed it, with information and so forth, and promised never to do "his business" in Wally's town.

Then Wally said something that changed everything: Gordo knows Mendoza, and can do business with him. Inside I was jumping for joy, but Gordo would not see that in me. I looked him up and down, then turned to Wally, "let's talk" and we left the room leaving Gordo alone.

"What's the catch?" I asked.

"There is none boss, I asked if he would help and he agreed," Wally stated.

I had stepped into an adjourning room, and was watching Gordo through a one way window; he couldn't see us, but I was staring at him. After a few moments, Gordo slowly turned and was looking back at me, as though he knew I was there; he smiled then casually flipped me off.

"This fucker got game," I said, looking at Wally, whom was now grinning. "You know the rules, follow them explicitly, complete back ground check and make sure he passes all the department requirements for snitches, understand?"

"Consider it done," Wally replied.

"Sooner or later you gotta go to hell if you want to arrest the devil" I remarked and then said "get the big dog on this with you, Pig, understand?"

"Done," was his reply and he was out the door. I turned back to look at Gordo; I hate gangsters, but this one I need.

I returned to my office, picked up the phone, and called Detective Muchmore with the news and to also ask him to do a background on Gordo from the Granite County area. I wanted to make sure this wasn't a counter intel operation against our unit; I wanted this case clean, no slip ups.

The office was busy; there would be no goofing off, no practical jokes. We had a mission and it was a serious one. Detectives came to work early, ate lunch at their desk, and stayed late. Gordo had passed all requirements and was ready to make the first of his two reliability buys to become a confidential and reliable police informant required by the state of Washington. Things were coming together, and Mendoza had no clue we were about to pounce.

That evening detectives worked even later into the night and directed Gordo during two separate narcotic buys, both $100.00 baggies of walked on, watered down methamphetamine, sold by low level street dealers. Both dealers would walk away with our pre-recorded bills and we would allow them as required by our rules of engagement. These were easy deals that would be outlined in detailed reports and placed into the informant's packet to satisfy the court that Gordo was reliable and could thus be considered confidential. Gordo had earned the right to have only a number name for police reports and his true identity would be concealed from these reports.

I called Detective Muchmore and let him know that we were ready and the operation would start the next day. Warrants to record phone conversations with Mendoza was completed and signed by a judge. Warrants to apply trackers to Mendoza's vehicles had been secured and trackers had been installed the night before.

"What are the odds you guys can get a conversation about the killing recorded?" he asked.

"Not sure, 50-50, but we will try" I responded.

"I appreciate this sergeant, we are catching hell over here, we look bad and it's getting tough. There are protests in front of the Sheriff's Office and accusations flying" he whined.

"No problem, you'll owe us a few beers when it's done" I warned. With that, a few nervous laughs followed and the conversation ended.

The following day detectives met in the one way in, one way out, no windows briefing room early in the afternoon. A "meet and greet" operational plan had been developed and the plan approved from the top department brass. Gordo had not seen Mendoza for over six months so detectives believe that Gordo should not just show up and ask to buy dope. We didn't want to "hink" up Mendoza.

The plan called for two detectives to meet with Gordo in a secluded spot out of sight of the general public. Gordo would be thoroughly searched for weapons, drugs, and money as would his vehicle and given precise instruction as to what was expected of him. Gordo would then call Mendoza and tell him that he, Gordo, was in the area and was going to stop by to bullshit.

Gordo had told detectives this was usually how they got together and to Mendoza seem not out of the normal. He says they usually talk about business, dope quality and amounts, and of course women. He also told us they would drink some Mexican beer and it would be all over in an hour.

Gordo would be wired and the conversations recorded. He was told in no way was he to bring up the dead girl, only if Mendoza brought it up would he inquire. All other detectives would be placed in strategic locations around the park for surveillance.

I volunteered with another detective to climb onto the shit towers at the sewage treatment plant that offers a great view of the Mendoza's mobile home office. The problem is the weather will be hot and the smell of those towers is going to be nauseating. We would wear sewage treatment plant uniforms and appear to be working on the towers, but all the while watching, filming the activities playing out below us.

After everyone knew their jobs, the handlers called Gordo and set up a meeting. Detectives then departed and worked their way into their assigned surveillance areas and waited for the operation to unfold.

I got a call from the handlers and they had gotten a hold of Gordo and they were en-route to meet him; so far, so good. Early surveillance units had already spotted Mendoza conducting business as usual in the park. It is just a matter of time till the call would be made.

About 20 minutes later the handlers call out on the radio that they are ready to go.

"Make the call" I said over the radio.

Seconds later surveillance detectives stated they could see Mendoza answer his cell phone and have a short conversation with someone; Gordo?

Handlers announced over the radio that the meet and greet was a go and Gordo was on his way to the park. Several minutes later Gordo arrived and met with Mendoza. The two disappeared into the office then soon returned each having a beer to drink in the hot afternoon sun. I was a bit envious as the sweat ran down my back and the smell was sickening.

"How's the wire?" I asked.

"Good, all in Spanish, talking about business and women" responded the detective.

Great, I thought, city not going to like this translator bill – cost of business, and this was money well spent.

After about 45 minutes and another couple beers the men shook hands and parted. Gordo drove to a location to meet with the handlers and he and his vehicle would again be thoroughly searched. The handlers would then interview Gordo, gather the information about what they had talked about, and Gordo would be sent on his way. Surveillance detectives would slowly withdraw, making sure Gordo isn't being followed; and we would all meet back at the briefing room to analyze what had occurred and what had been said.

The handlers finally arrived at the briefing room and gave the team an update on what had happened. The meeting had gone good. The two had talked about women and the dope business. Gordo had complained that he felt he was getting walked on dope and the quality was poor.

Walked on dope is when a dealer/supplier mixes the dope with some other substance to increase the volume, but still sell it for regular price. It's a common practice, especially with lower level dealers and at times it happens at the higher level; but nonetheless the quality goes down as does the price and demand for weak dope.

Mendoza had bragged that his dope was pure, not tainted, and he was fetching $28,000.00 per pound. Gordo had told Mendoza that he was picking up in a couple of days and if the quality doesn't improve he would do business with Mendoza. Mendoza stated he would welcome doing business with Gordo. We learned that Mendoza took Gordo into a back room of the office and showed him about a pound of crystal meth. Gordo stated the shards in the bag were huge, best he had ever seen. Shortly thereafter the two men parted ways. There was no mention of the dead girl.

"Good start," I said. "Get the paperwork done and get the tape and pictures into evidence and let's plan our next move."

Next move was obvious. Wait a week or so then call Mendoza and complain about quality of the dope and order up from Mendoza. We had to be careful though. Mendoza had worked for DEA as a snitch and knew the route cops would take in working a snitch. The usual route is buying a small amount for a test, but I was worried that it might make Mendoza get suspicious. At $28,000.00 a pound, that would be impossible without DEA getting involved, and that was not an option. We met and had a meeting trying to come up with a clever idea to make buying less sound like we weren't the cops.

"Gordo, how much is your supplier charging you for a pound of meth when you're in the business?" I asked.

"$16,000.00," he responded.

"If you were to add an ounce of Mendoza's dope to your pound would that bring up the quality considerably?" I asked.

"I see where you're going with this, and it will work" he replied. Rob hadn't caught on yet, "what you talking about doing?"

"Mendoza already knows Gordo is unhappy with the supplier's dope and he knows Gordo is picking up soon. Next week we have Gordo call Mendoza and bitch about the crappy dope he just bought from his supplier. Ask Mendoza if he will sell him an ounce so he can mix it in with the pound he just bought to freshen it up. Get Mendoza to bite off on that then the next day we do it again. We wait three days, secure a search warrant then wait couple more days, call Mendoza and order up a pound. When Mendoza confirms he's got the dope we hit him with the warrant," I explained.

Glances bounce off everyone in the room.

"Well, what you think?" I asked.

"Think it will work," Pig said.

"Good, let's get on it, get the details down and get me an operation plan," I said.

After the meeting Pig got me aside.

"I'd feel better if Gordo could see the dope and we know for sure it's there when we hit Mendoza with the warrant."

"You have any ideas?" I asked.

"Not yet" Pig said.

"Let's think about it" I said, "see what we can come up with."

I called Muchmore and told him of the plan. He wanted to come over with his partner and help with the warrant service then get a shot at talking to Mendoza or some if not all his henchmen. I was pleased that Muchmore wanted to help out. I could keep my guys focused on the drug side of the case and Muchmore could work the homicide part.

Surveillance was conducted nearly around the clock. We needed to identify as many people involved with Mendoza as possible, especially those he parties with, in hopes of figuring out all the men that had been at the young girl's last dance. This was a daunting task for a small unit. I recruited two more cops. The first one was a fraud detective who had notorious skills wading through stacks of data looking for a shred of evidence that would help the case. Photographs of suspects, license plates, and any intel we developed she would dig into her computer looking for identities of those we had photographed. After I had told her what had happened to the 15 year old girl she needed no more motivation, as she too had a 12 year old daughter. The second one, the hacker, was simply a hacker. If it was an electronic device, phone or computer or what have you, he would get into it. Passwords and firewalls were merely speed bumps for him and whatever was in the hard drive would be exposed. I'd save him for the day of the search warrant service.

After a couple of weeks of intense surveillance we had Mendoza's quotidian lifestyle mapped out and several people, mostly customers, identified. However, there was one person that we have to yet identify, a young Mexican man that was almost daily with Mendoza. He never drove, did very little, but was joined at the hip with Mendoza. He had not been present during our first contact with Mendoza and Gordo, but we concluded that he was into Mendoza's business and most likely at the party. The man, we nicknamed shadow, would spend his nights at the business trailer where Mendoza conducted business and the same place where Gordon had seen Mendoza's methamphetamine.

Another odd thing was that detectives had filmed Mendoza wander off alone as he disappears into brushy areas, three spots in total in the trailer park. On one of these strolls Mendoza was photographed coming out of the bush with dirt on his left knee. What had he been doing?

Pig looked at the photograph and stated that Mendoza was stashing something in the brush areas, "probably money" Pig stated. "It's not uncommon for Hispanics to hide money and dope in the woods, I've seen it before" Pig stated. "They are masters at hiding dope and money" he stated.

Pig had once noticed some paint flakes on the floor of a bathroom under the cut out where the toilet paper dispenser had been placed. He had worked the entire dispenser loose from the wall and he found a string tied to the back of the dispenser. When he pulled the string from the wall it was attached to $86,000.00 in cash. Pig was a master at finding dope and money.

On one occasion detectives followed Mendoza and shadow, the unknown Mexican male, to a hardware store in the Puyallup area. One of the detectives noticed that a clerk was helping Mendoza with a few items and they chatted. After Mendoza left, the detective contacted the clerk about the transaction he just watched.

"Oh you want to know about Juan and his partner?" she asked the detective.

"Yes, what can you tell me about him?" he asked.

"Nice guy, flirtatious as heck though" she responded.

"What about his partner?" the detective asked.

"Nothing, he never speaks English and only speaks to Juan in Spanish and one time I noticed a gun on his right side, not unusual" she claimed.

The detective knew the clerk. She was his wife and thus this "interview" would not be disclosed. Later that night he told his wife of Mendoza and what he and his friends had done. Her response was quaint, "asshole, and I suppose I'm about to lose a good customer." Cops' wives, especially the ones that hang in there for the entire career, are a hardy bunch.

I called Muchmore and told him we were about to make two buys and if all went well a search warrant would be constructed. I would let him know how it goes and to keep his fingers crossed. Muchmore's tone was upbeat; he was optimistic and finally felt as though he was making progress.

The next day detectives met about noon at the police department. Pig provided me with an algorithm operations plan. Operation plans were basically blueprints to what was going to happen and how it would happen. Contingency plans were for emergencies and the unexpected occurrences.

Operation plans were Pig's forte'. If it was a high profile case, such as this or an undercover detective was to be used, I usually selected Pig to do the operations plan. After all, any guy that can supply you with hearing aid batteries in the middle of nowhere while on a SWAT operation is a guy that has everything thought out and well planned. His attention to detail astonished me. I had vowed years earlier that I would not do an undercover operation unless he was one, my handler, and two, had control of the operational planning.

I remembered that time when I got involved in a Mexican drug ring in the tri-cities area of Eastern Washington, the inland empire. During the operation Pig had somehow gotten separated from the rolling operation and it was pre-GPS days. I was unaware of his absence and charged ahead only to nearly be shot by a Kennewick police officer. When Pig arrived at the scene he couldn't apologize enough to me about getting separated but I understood that shit happens. On the other hand, he was spitting nails pissed off with the detective that had taken over the handler's job and had strayed from the operations plan.

I reviewed the plan and as always it was perfect in every way. I stopped by the Captain's office and gave him a copy. After he read through it he said he would run it by the chief.

"This is nothing more than a tug of war over the soul of a teenage girl," he remarked.

"Excuse me," I responded.

"You and your gang, Granite County cops, Mendoza and his crew, and a damn snitch that is just as bad as Mendoza, bunch of fucking predators."

"A girl has been killed so now we work for God" I responded.

"Okay," he said, "consider this signed and cleared, go get those sons of bitches" and he handed the operation plan back to me. I simply smiled and left.

"Green light" I said to Pig and Rob.

"That was quick" Pig said.

"Your work is 'perfecto', and as the Captain just put it, 'go get those sons of bitches,'" I added. They both left and went to their work areas and the plan began to unfold.

The handlers called Gordo and detectives were sent into the field for surveillance and once again I climbed a shit tower and enjoyed the stinking hot sun. I spotted Mendoza immediately, carrying on with his business, oblivious to our presence. I love a good ambush!

The handlers were with Gordo and stated they were ready to make the call. The stage was set and soon I saw Mendoza reach for his phone. Game on!

The conversation was short but successful. Mendoza put away his phone and disappeared into his business trailer. Shadow was with him.

"Yeah, go weigh out your dope" I mumbled.

The radio barked to life. The handlers confirmed that Gordo had made contact with Mendoza and Mendoza agreed to sell an ounce of dope to Gordo. Handlers stated that Gordo acted pissed off and told Mendoza that when this batch of dope is gone he wanted to do business with him. A good conversation was recorded. As was done previously, Gordo and his vehicle were searched for guns, dope, and money; finding none he is sent to Mendoza's office for the buy, with dope cops following, watching, and recording.

Detectives observe Gordo's arrival and soon Gordo and Mendoza are shaking hands. Mendoza points to shadow and makes introductions. Shadow has a name, Julio. The men continued to talk; a beer is introduced and they sat under the shade of a tree talking business and of course women. Mendoza asks about the bad dope and who Gordo is buying it from. Gordo plays it smart, tells Mendoza his source is a Mexican from the Aberdeen area and at first the dope was primo but has steadily gotten worse. Gordo tells Mendoza he has stopped buying from the asshole and needs a new source and soon. Mendoza offers up and the men strike a deal. Gordo tells Mendoza he will need between a pound to pound and a half a week. Mendoza agrees and asks when he wants to start. Gordo tells Mendoza that he has to fix the pale pound he still has, as it's shit as is, but he hopes the ounce will do it; if not another ounce would surely take care of the problem and his customers will be back. Mendoza simply says "let me know".

The men then disappear into Mendoza's office and the ounce is provided. Mendoza is paid $2000.00 in marked bills for his product and the men parted company. Julio never says a word.

Gordo is watched the entire time en-route back to their meeting location with his handlers, where he and his vehicle will once again be researched and debriefed.

A meeting followed shortly after the operation. Gordo stated that he personally saw three pounds of methamphetamine but stated there was more in another cupboard. Gordo stated that Julio had started to open the cupboard and Mendoza stopped him stating "not that stuff". Gordo thought that whatever amount was in the cupboard was probably already weighted out for a different customer. Gordo said he thought it was odd that Mendoza would have that much meth exposed, even to someone he trusted. Gordo went on and stated that he thought Julio is a body guard but saw no gun.

Gordo was excused and Detectives just sat and pondered, staring at the 50 inch monitor of a live feed camera trained on Mendoza's office.

"That's a lot of dope," I said breaking the silence.

They were thinking the same thing I was. We should be watching, following, and figure out where Mendoza gets his dope, probably smuggled up from some Californian or Mexico meth lab. That would require the Feds.

"Remember why we are here guys," I say again, breaking the silence.

"The girl," Pig said.

"Yeah the girl," Rob repeated.

"The girl," Wally said.

I glanced at the two tribal detectives, "you two, what you thinking?"

"The girl," they spoke simultaneously.

"I like this team, start on the warrant, let's write it now. Take turns watching this monitor, if no one shows up and dope stays, then we hit it; if someone leaves, we assume dope is gone, and then we buy again tomorrow and hit it with today's warrant if there is dope still there."

They said nothing and dove into the assignments.

"Detective Muchmore," he answers.

"Gill, Puyallup."

"Look, we just got an ounce out of Mendoza but there was more than three pounds still in the office."

"Tell me you're hitting the place sergeant."

"We're working on the warrant."

"Were on the way, be there in two hours."

"Look, it's a gamble, we are watching the place, if the dope leaves we won't hit it tonight but wait to verify if more dope has arrived tomorrow, then hit him if there is dope there," I said to Muchmore.

"Has Mendoza said anything about the girl?" Muchmore asked

"Nothing, he's too smart to say anything about the girl. He has a body guard; the guy is constantly with him, young, will not want to spend the next 20 years in a federal prison. He is neck deep in the dope dealing and we think he just might talk," I replied.

"We'll be there as soon as possible," Muchmore concluded.

So close yet so far. A lot can go wrong, I thought to myself and I know I'll be questioned about not getting the feds involved. They had their chance and blew it.

Several hours had passed and I was near the trailer park, watching and waiting with couple of my other detectives. No movement, nothing going on, and sunset was close. We had never seen Mendoza deal after dark and now I wanted the dark to arrive, quickly.

It wasn't the dark that arrived, but a small Honda, and Mendoza arrived just behind him. The two men got out and entered Mendoza's office with Julio in tow.

"Damn it," I shouted inside my car.

"Did they have anything with them when they went inside?" I probed.

"Can't see them very well, didn't look like it," Rob responded.

I asked Carlos if he could get his piece of shit Nissan Stanza into the park, closer, without being noticed. Carlos is a tribal detective, looks Hispanic and looks like a shit head, seriously. Carlos had long wavy jet black hair, scruffy beard, heavily muscled and covered in tattoos. He began moving closer.

"Try to see what they are carrying when they come out," I said to Carlos.

"Do my best sergeant," he responded.

I called Pig on his cell phone. "Status" was all I said.

"I just got to Stanley and Seaports, a high end restaurant, waiting for the judge."

"Waiting?" I responded.

"He's eating dinner with his family and doesn't want to be bothered during dinner, so I'm sitting in the waiting room."

"Un-believable, call when it's signed," was all I could say.

"They're coming back out," Carlos said over the radio.

"Are they carrying anything?" I asked.

Moments passed by then Carlos answered up, "Guy getting into the Honda has a small gym bag."

The wind in my sails now escaped and I had to make a decision. We could seal this down and hope the warrant gets signed; we do have probable cause for Mendoza and Julio, or we could exercise some patience.

"Ok, you guys stay with the Honda, follow it. I want to know where that guy sleeps and any intel will be of great value; I'll stay with Mendoza and Julio," I said, making my decision.

The detectives slowly moved out of their surveillance spots and the last I heard of them they were N/B on 167, heading towards Seattle. Dark settled in.

I sat and watched Mendoza and Julio standing in the parking lot in front of the office. I would have loved to have heard that conversation. Julio then got into the Escalade and Mendoza wandered off on foot. Julio sat in the passenger seat, quietly waiting and Mendoza slipped into some brush, one of the three spots he usually goes to. After several minutes passed, he emerged and was brushing off his hands. He just hid some money, I was positive.

I could feel the buzzing of my phone in my pocket.

"Muchmore, anxious fellow," I thought to myself.

"Yeah?"

"Muchmore here, about 10 minutes out, where do you want to meet?" he asked.

"PD, know where it's at?"

"Yup, I've been by there before."

"Park out back, I'll meet you there."

With that the conversation ended and I reluctantly left Mendoza's trailer park and made my way to the PD. When I arrived Muchmore and his partner were already there. Muchmore was in his mid-forties, balding, mid-drift pudge that so many cops get and his partner was young and quiet. I liked the quiet part. After introduction we began talking about the case and it was soon interrupted, phone buzzing away.

"Carlos, what's up?"

"Sgt., you aren't going to believe where we followed this guy to".

"Go ahead."

"Des Moines; an apartment in Des Moines."

"Stay put, watch, record; you know the routine."

"Got it; later."

"Good news Muchmore, we may have just found your crime scene, the apartment in Des Moines" I informed him.

"Excellent, are you guys still hitting Mendoza tonight then?" he asked.

"No, all or some of the dope just got to an apartment in Des Moines so we are going to do it all over tomorrow" I responded.

"You two got a hotel yet?" I asked.

"No, any recommendations?" he asked.

"Several nice ones on South Hill; take your pick, we are going to work another two or three hours then call it a night and will be back in around noon tomorrow. We'll meet here, get on the same page and go from there" I told him.

"Sounds like a plan, see you then."

We continued into the night for several more hours gaining nothing but intel from the Des Moines apartment. Several cars came and went; all Mexican males and more work for my fraud detective. We had a signed search warrant in hand with 10 days to serve it.

As planned we all met at the police department at about noon the next day. Muchmore and his counterpart were clearly overdressed.

"If you two are going to be working with us you all need to lose the sport jackets and ties; hope you brought some street clothes," I explained.

"Just trying to make a good first impression," Muchmore said with a smile.

"Not impressed," I said not smiling.

We decided to stick to the plan and contact Mendoza again: complain that we needed a little more dope to refresh the badly watered down pound, hope he goes for it, and hope we see dope. Pig stated that he would like to put a video wire on Gordo, to watch and see for himself what was in the mobile office. Pig thought that Gordo might be embellishing the contents of the mobile, he just had a feeling. I'm good with that but I was unaware that we had a video wire.

"We don't have a video wire," I stated.

"Yeah we do, wait here," Pig fired back.

Within a couple of minutes Pig returned with a small black bag. Setting it on the table he slowly unzipped the bag and opened it like a small book. Inside was all the components of a video wire – sender, small camera that looked like a button, wire antenna that would send it to a small recorder, and viewing screen – the works.

"Should I be worried about where this came from, my Velcro covered friend?" I asked Pig.

"I borrowed it," he stated.

"Spell 'borrow' for me, and of course, your interpretation of the word." I asked.

No answer. It is well known that Pig is covered in Velcro, and if you leave a better equipment than his' lying around, it would somehow stick to Pig as he leaves your office. Here at the police department we were onto him and he didn't make off with much, but the feds were absolutely helpless around him. They'd leave something out and Pig would put it away, in with his collection of self-issued high tech equipment. I usually ignored his covert activities because many times I would be a recipient of his "used equipment" that he had just traded up for. And of course Pig loved these very moments when he could proudly display his miss acquired piece of equipment knowing full well we wanted and needed to use it, thus making us all part of a massive conspiracy to covering up the knowledge of misplaced "stuff".

Pig also knew that since my miserable run in with DEA administration 'nitwits' years earlier, I would suffer a lifelong mistrust of them and a general aversion to their rules. In other words, he knew I did not give a rat's ass and had a steal them blind policy in effect 24 hours, 7 days a week.

"Let's attach this thing to Gordo, I can watch and record the entire ordeal and hopefully see how much dope is in the place," Pig said.

"How's the sender attached to Gordo?" I asked.

"Tape," was his one word answer.

"You just going to shove it between the folds of Gordo's fat; tape it there and hope it sticks? It's going to get "from-under-cheese all over it," I claimed.

"I'll clean it later," Pig said.

"Ok, make sure it works and that it will hold," I said.

"You guys are grossing me out," Muchmore whined.

"Welcome to the life of dope cops," I said as I looked at him.

"We can use the same operations plan as yesterday; just change the dates, no info about the video wire, as I don't want to explain that to a Captain yet, and update the rescue version of the plan in case something goes wrong, ok?" I ordered.

"Don't worry about the video wire sergeant, just tell him we borrowed it," Pig said.

"I used that excuse 100 times and I think he's getting suspicious," I fired back. "Oh and put the Granite County guys in the plan, Muchmore with me and his partner with the rescue team" I suggested.

The Granite County boys left to change clothes and the remainder of us went to our respective corners to begin work on today's adventure.

A couple hours later the handlers called Gordo and met him in a non-disclosed location for the usual groping and searching of his vehicle. The remainder of us had been on the trailer court watching Mendoza and Julio. Mendoza had just picked up his phone and after a short conversation summoned Julio to meet him. A brief discussion and the two climbed into Mendoza's pearl white Cadillac Escalade and left traveling towards Tacoma. We followed like a pack of stalking wolves.

I contacted Wally and told him to sit tight as Mendoza had just left and we were tailing him heading for Tacoma. Mendoza made it to Southbound I-5, then Eastbound 512 and took the Steel Street exit. We turned Southbound on the Spanaway Loop road and drove by the notorious coffee shop where four police officers had been assassinated couple years earlier.

We then found ourselves still southbound but now breaking off onto the Roy Y and heading into banjo country. My guys backed off but kept ever so vigilant. As the parade pass thru Roy, Mendoza turned onto a country road now eastbound. Our first vehicle and second vehicle continued south and the next detective turned in behind Mendoza and I followed. There were three cars on the road, two cops and Mendoza. Lack of traffic is problematic. We came to an intersection and the detective in front of me turned left leaving Mendoza directly in front of me. I gave him lots of room. I knew that my guys would quickly U turn and drive like mad bastards to get back into the tail and the turn out procession would start all over. We had done this a hundred times and never got caught.

Soon I saw Mendoza's brake lights come on and he turned onto a gravel driveway that disappeared into the woods. As I drove by the driveway, I noticed that the flag on the mail box had been replaced to show a Mexican flag. Perfecto!

I called Pig, "you familiar with this area or address?"

We did some big cases out there when I was with the task force, lot of Mexicans and dope."

"I got the feeling Mendoza is picking up a load."

"I think you're right" Pig responded.

"Why don't we have Gordo call Mendoza, tell him he has possible buyer for the dirty pound but wants to add another ounce for good measure, and also have him order up a pound and half to be picked up tonight," I said.

"Might work; be interesting to see if Mendoza answers up and what he says while he is here at the supplier house, if that's what this place is," Pig answered.

I called Wally and relayed the plan. "Have Gordo do it now," is how I finished the conversation. Now we just wait and find out what is said, if anything.

The minutes drag by. I stared at my phone, waiting. I don't think it was through the first buzz, it was Wally.

"Mendoza bit off on it" he said.

"Exactly what did Mendoza say?" I asked.

"He said he is going for the deal and will have the dope," Wally responded.

"Quit fucking with me," I responded.

There was a laugh and then Wally stated Mendoza said, "I was just about ready to leave; good thing you called, I'll be back in half an hour, meet me then." Wally was still laughing as he hung up.

Bingo, I thought and I shared the conversation with Pig and the others. We do a lose tail back and we hit him today.

I sent Pig and Carlos back as soon as Mendoza showed from the driveway. They drove like madmen to get back to the trailer park. I wanted Carlos in close for a view at what was coming out of Mendoza's rig and Pig would be his cover. We were stretched thin.

The tail back was un-eventful and it was just a nice drive back on a hot afternoon in August. I watched Mendoza turn into his trailer park and I disappeared for my shit tower and sewer company uniform.

"Why do we have to put these things on?" Muchmore asked.

We will be out in the open, gotta dress like the rest, don't want to stand out in a crowd" I responded. I hadn't told him about the lovely and yes, lingering smell I was about to introduce him to.

"Holy shit, this stinks bad," Muchmore began bitching. "If I'd known how bad this was I should have sent the kid up here," he stated.

I just grinned and listened to his bitching. Act like you're working, as I switched the cameras on. Pig called, Carlos spotted Mendoza get out and then Julio got a large gym bag from the back of the Escalade under the tonneau cover. Julio carried it into the mobile office and Mendoza followed closing the door.

I called the handlers; they were ready and sent Gordo to Mendoza as they followed. Ten minutes later Gordo showed up in his usual way. Introductions were made and the three went inside the mobile office.

"How's the camera working Pig?" I asked.

"Good, a little fuzzy but I can see and all looks ok," he responded.

We listened and watched. Gordo told Mendoza the bull shit story about a dumbass white guy that was going to buy the crappy dope. Gordo acted jovial about doing business with Mendoza and said he can get his customers back and then some. Gordo gave Mendoza $1800.00 in marked cash that had been just hours earlier in a safe in my office. The ounce was a shy ounce thus the reduced cost. Gordo told Mendoza he would be back in the evening for the remainder.

Then all hell broke loose!

As Gordo opened his vehicle door and began to climb into it, the sender of the video camera came loose and popped out from Gordo's fat folds like a baby throwing up bad milk. And Mendoza saw it and knew immediately what it was, a DEA camera, probably the same one he once wore.

The surveillance crew probably couldn't see it but Muchmore and I had a front row seat. Mendoza jumped Gordo and Julio piled on. They were hitting him and now Gordo, no slouch in a fight, began landing his shots. Pig's newly acquired camera sender dangled onto the ground with the antenna wire tangled somewhere in Gordo's shirt with the camera button. It did not survive the fight.

The detectives raced to the park as quickly as I told them to rescue the informant. It was clear that Mendoza and Julio were trying to pull Gordo into the trailer. It was a daunting task since the rather large man didn't want to go. In seconds detectives took control of the situation and all three men lay sprawled on the hot afternoon pavement. Even Gordo laid there, wires and sender coming from under his shirt. He would be the first led away, searched and statements taken as to what had been said and what had occurred.

Mendoza and Julio would be separated, cuffed, and searched, and the warrant would be served.

Muchmore and I climbed down off the tower, changed out of our borrowed uniforms and drove to the scene.

"You guys stink," Pig greeted us.

"You and your camera idea," I smiled as I said it.

"Well, Gordo got a little sweaty while waiting for us to get back to town and when he climbed into the car the folds simply could not hang on any longer and spit the sender out after defeating the tape," Pig explained.

"I know, I saw it," I responded. "How's Gordo?" I asked.

"He's fine, said they were trying to drag him into the trailer. Mendoza was going to shoot him in there," Pig responded.

"Got that on tape?" I asked.

"Yep," was his one word response.

One of my detectives drove Muchmore, his partner, and Julio to the office for an interview. I wanted a dog in the room to take notes about the dope; Muchmore could keep the notes on the homicide if Julio wanted to talk.

We spent a great deal of time inside Mendoza's mobile office. We found a loaded Beretta 9mm pistol, six and half pounds of methamphetamine, and a small amount of money. $1800.00 of it was our buy money that Gordo had used for the buy of meth just before the fight outside.

We began checking the three bushy spots that Mendoza would secretly wander off to and in all we found buried and hidden water cooler jugs, like the ones you can buy at sporting goods stores or hardware. We unscrewed the tops of the coolers and found money, one had $28,000.00 cash, another had $11,000.00 and yet another had $6000.00, and a couple ounces of cocaine.

Mendoza exchanged glares with me; there would be no love lost here, we had an intense dislike for one another since the first show down I had with him when he was cornered under another mobile home. He did however keep asking to speak to "Mr. Pigman", desperate to work out a deal. Pig told him he had had his chance and blew it, this one he was going to ride out. We said nothing about the homicide investigation that would be for Muchmore's pleasure.

We went to his half million dollar home and spoke to his wife and told her what had happened. She showed no pity for him and his destiny. I considered seizing the home but there were children involved and elected not to move in that direction. Making people homeless is bad press and she was going to have a hard time making ends meet. She was unemployed, as was her dope selling husband, never had a job but had a half million dollar home. America gotta love it, and oh the opportunities.

I did seize his vehicles, a rather nice truck and of course his fancy Cadillac Escalade. We learned that he owned 17 properties in the park; we didn't hesitate and seized them for the city.

Our assessment of Julio, Mendoza's shadow, was correct. He was a body guard; first job, snuck across the border like so many do, and basically worked his way up the dope ladder to earn a protection job for Mendoza. Julio had no interest in going to prison for years on end and coming out a middle aged man. He said they were going to pull Gordo into the trailer and Mendoza was going to shoot him.

Julio confirmed that there had been a party with a runaway girl but the girl had ingested the dope on her own, with a little nudging, and dope was supplied by Mendoza. Julio got sketchy on the rape but admitted to improper behavior.

Granite County was happy. They had a conclusion, and a good story on why they appeared to be doing nothing, and they had been, waiting for us to do it. Granite County prosecutor office dragged their feet on the case. It was weak to say the least, but the dope angle was strong.

Mendoza got 26 years for his drug activities in a federal prison; Julio got six and half years. Granite County bailed on the prosecution of Mendoza after he was sentenced to the 26 years saying simply that they couldn't get more time and the case was probably un-provable.

Several months later I parked my newly acquired Cadillac Escalade in the back lot of the police department. Mendoza had been erased from the vehicle and it now contained all my SWAT gear and other condiments that I travel with. It already smelled of cigar.

When I got to my office Wally was sitting at my desk staring out my window.

"You ok?" I asked. He turned and got out of my chair and stood looking at me.

"They killed him," he said.

"Killed who?" having my full attention.

"Gordo went to Mexico, a town named Nacimento de los Negros and he was found executed, single shot to the back of his head," Wally said.

"I told him over and over not to go to Mexico," I said; "so did you."

"I know sergeant, I know, just feel bad for his mom" Wally said, and with that turned and wandered off.

I got into my government issued Escalade and began the drive home but took a detour, a small one. I drove the bright shiny Cadillac into Mendoza's park. I drove slowly, up and down every damn road in the park and I let them all see who was driving Mendoza's much valued car.

Captain was right, just a bunch of predators. The girl's soul was set free and I suppose God was happy.

Nacimentos de los Negros simply means "birthplace of darkness".

There is no county in the state of Washington named Granite. I didn't want to associate this with a certain county. The county was in Eastern Washington and that's as close as I'll get. Thanks for understanding. The phase "we work for god" was something I got from a homicide training class. That phrase belongs to retired NYPD Lt. Cmdr Vernon J. Gerberth. Whenever a person is murdered the cops that investigate the case say "we work for god". Gerberth is an excellent cop and teacher.

I began thinking of ways to make this new adventure go smoother and ways we could film these transactions. We should have a warehouse for these cars to be delivered to. We could put up cameras and record the transactions! That would keep us out of the court rooms and prying questions. *So much to be learned,* I thought to myself; but this was our first car case and we will learn and get better. It was the way we were. I had no idea that in a couple of short years a Pierce County Prosecutor speaking at a Police Chief and Sheriff convention would state "if you want to know how to do a car sting, ask Puyallup's SIU cops, they're the best at it."

Chapter 20

Failures of Fathers
Sins of Their Sons

"Did you see that?" I asked.

"Yep, got a customer," Pig responded. "They're circling around and stopping, checking the area," Pig continued.

"That didn't take long, 'tis the season" Rob tossed in.

"Anybody get the plate yet?" I asked.

"Running it, out of Graham, female registered owner," Pig came back.

"Ok, hunker down, they're checking the lot for cops" I announced.

I opened my cooler next to the lounge seat I had concealed in the back of the soccer mom van and placed my half eaten sandwich back on ice, time to work.

It was mid-December. Christmas shopping was at a fever pitch and so were the thieves, out in numbers to spoil it for normal everyday citizens just trying to make ends meet and raise happy families. People would go into the malls, load up on "stuff", return to their cars and have a careless moment and leave the new merchandized protected by only the glass of cars doors. We had always expected this to happen but for some odd reason this one lot was getting killed this year. We had already run a successful operation that netted a man and woman team that had made breaking into cars as routinely as you and I going to work every day. But the rash of thefts had not stopped, so we were back again with a different bait car and a different set. Bad guys trade "what happened to them" with the other bad guys in an effort to evade the police so it forces cops to get creative. We were on a roll and now had another customer at our bait car.

This area was lined by 39th Ave to the North, 43rd Ave to the South; Meridian to the East; and Best Buy, Ross, and several other retail stores to the West. The lot was peppered with restaurants. Traffic on Meridian was a nightmare so the access road to and from this parking lot was shortcut gold between 39th and 43rd and for some reason more than its fair share of assholes cut through here. If a shopper leaves valuables exposed in their car while they ate lunch or dinner, a thief would surely strike.

We had a small fleet of cars that had been seized from their former drug dealer owners and we used them for rolling around town and running dope deals or set them up as a bait car. Today it was a white Honda Civic. We had found a prime parking spot near the entrance off 39th into the lot and up against the shortcut runway that was heavily traveled. In the back seat was a large flat screen, correction, large flat screen box that we had gotten from Best

Buy. Retailers are always helpful in matters such as this and never disappointed us.

We had parked the car so that when anyone drove by, could see the car interior and the flat screen box inside. Irresistible and we were rarely disappointed; but we could never leave it unattended or it would cost us a broken window every time. On this particular evening, we had waited about 20 minutes when we had a customer.

They just sat, lights out, slumped down in the seats, and looked at each and every car they could see. They'd already found their prize, they just want to make sure no cops were attached to it. Soon the car lights came on and they moved in directly next to the passenger side of the bait car and shut off their lights again. Pig and Rob were in the lot, hidden, and I was in the mini van parked directly in front of the bait car putting the suspect car within 10 feet of me.

I had another sip from my well creamed coffee as I watched, and waited. The male passenger climbed from the interior of the car, and as he did he pulled up his hoody, concealing his shaved head. He simply walked over to the bait car and tried the door handle. It was locked.

Damn it, I said to myself, *I told those guys to leave it unlocked, windows are $200.00 a pop and the Captain had taken notice of the bill, several of them.*

I put my coffee down and climbed out of my comfortable chair to the floor next to the side door, where I'd launch my attack when the time came. The passenger looked again around the lot and removed something from his pants' pocket. I told Pig and Rob to get ready; he was going to break the window. He stepped to the passenger door window of the two-door Honda and with absolutely no violent motion at all held a closed fist to the window, in a second, the window shattered. Window punch, slick!

"He broke out the window, get him," I announced on the radio. *Why bother*, I thought to myself, *Pig and Rob already had it under control.*

Pig blocked the suspect car and Rob tackled the passenger as he pulled the weighted box from the bait car. By the time I got there it was pretty much over, but for the cussing.

I removed the female driver from the car and immediately noticed she was pregnant. She was handcuffed nonetheless.

"How far along are you?" I asked.

"Six months," she said. Not that I gave a damn but a pregnant woman is tougher to get into jail.

With the two occupants separated and sitting in the back seats of two patrol cars we began our systematic approach to searching the vehicle. The usual pile of crap; but after a few minutes we figured out that not only were they thieves, they had a forgery/fraud operation running out of their car. The trunk was the storage unit for the two, mostly small valuable items taken from cars and people's homes.

We ran the two and found previous convictions for burglary, auto theft, and of course UPCS, unlawful possession of a controlled substance, meth. Now the woman is pregnant and society will have another drug addicted newborn to house and feed, and the cycle continues.

The passenger, the man that broke into the bait car was named Jordan. Checking, I quickly learned of his father's name and did a background on dad. It showed burglary and motor vehicle theft ... same crime as son, just not as many times. It was a usual pattern cops see all the time – failures as fathers usually add up to be sins of their sons, and daughters.

We impounded the car; we would need a search warrant to properly search it so off it went to the secured impoundment lot. The two were transferred to the police department for interviews and booking.

Pig would do the interviews and see what else we could learn. The gal's name was Dora and the baby we learned would be a boy.

Pig began with Jordan. He was a short man but stocky. His blond hair was cut short and spoke with an odd accent. We found out that Jordan's parents were Russians. As Pig talked to Jordan we found out that he was tied into several criminal groups that worked the Puyallup Pierce County area, mostly stealing cars. Jordan stated they steal from mailboxes and try to pass those check bank card company's end to customers.

"Every once in a while we get lucky" Jordan stated.

Pig and Jordan talked for couple hours but Jordan wasn't very interested in working off his crimes. He said he had been to prison before and could do it again.

I butted in at this point, "what about your wife and son?"

He had a puzzled look to him, clearly he hadn't thought about that angle.

"She didn't have anything to do with this," he protested.

"Bullshit and you know it, she is an easy mark," shooting back.

"You guys would prosecute her?" he asked.

"Why not? She earned it," Pig said with calm, convincing tone.

He reacted to this, clearly upsetting to him. The room was quiet, Jordan was thinking.

I had a copy of Jordan's rap sheet and one of his dad's. I held up dad's sheet and began reading the crimes off for Jordan to hear easily.

"Burglary, burglary, vehicle theft, theft and it goes on and on," I said to Jordan.

"I'm no angel, I already know that," he said.

"I wasn't reading your rap sheet; that was your dad's."

Quiet, not a word; we just stared at each other.

"And if I'm still working 20 years from now I'll read yours to your son that will be seated where you are now. The failure as a father results in sins of the son, he will turn out just like you and your dad" piling it on and it had the desired effect.

Total silence, staring at each other and I would not blink. He did, and dropped his head.

"I'm going to give you a little time to think about it, your choice. If you work with us over time I can make this stuff disappear, if you want to tell me to fuck off, fine, I book you and your family into jail and prosecute the hell out of all of you" I said sternly. "You have a chance to break the cycle. Think about it."

Pig and I got up and left the room.

"Well? Think it will work?" I asked Pig.

"It was the only play we had left," Pig stated.

"I think he will go for it; definitely on the ropes," I said.

We gave him about 15 minutes then we went back inside to see what Jordan wanted to do.

"Can I talk to my wife?" Jordan asked.

"Detectives will be in the room while she is here, ok?" I told him.

"Ok," he answered.

Rob went to the holding cell and found Dora and brought her to the room. Now seated together, Jordan told Dora he could work off these crimes by working with us.

"That'll make you a snitch, you sure?" she asked.

"Detective, can you read that rap sheet off again, the same one?" Jordan asked.

"Burglary, burglary, auto theft, theft and it goes on and on," I responded.

"Now if you would, read mine," Jordan asked.

"Burglary, theft, auto theft, UPCS and it continues" I said.

"The first one was my dad's; the second one was mine, and I don't want this life for our son" Jordan said quietly to his wife.

I could see the tears welting up in her eyes. Jordan had hit the mark and played the moment well.

"What's going to happen to us if we fix this?" Dora asked.

"If Jordan follows the rules, both of you stay clean and Jordan brings good players, I can make these charges disappear, but you both must stay clean," making my point with tone.

I continued, "We are still going to serve a search warrant on your car, what we find we hold, and if you two try any bullshit I'll come after you with a vengeance, understand?" again, making my point clear.

"Ok, I'm in, Jordan says, let's get started" he said.

And with that, we began. Dora was returned to holding, fed, and tucked in for the night. Jordan goes through the confidential informant paperwork, all the while telling us of an auto theft ring he knows of and can get us in if we want to start there.

"Works for me" I told Pig.

Jordan supplies names and how the ring operates. They steal cars then sell the parts or sell the entire car if they find a buyer that knows how to give the cars new identity or ship them out of state.

"When they have buyers, we lose cars", I said to Pig.

"How do they steal the cars?" Pig asked.

"Whatever it takes – shaver keys, hot wire, and defeating alarms is not a problem," Jordan said.

Pig gave me a quick glance. "Where do these guys live?" Pig asked.

"One lives in Tacoma, the other two in Puyallup, in one of the trailer parks along River Road," Jordan replied.

"Shocking," I made a smartass comment.

"I can call them and tell them I found a buyer, wants cars to ship outta town to California, something like that," Jordan continued.

"We need to do a background on these guys, see if they're worth the effort," Pig told Jordan.

"They're bad asses," Jordan commented.

"Stay in here, we'll get back with you in a bit," Pig said and we left with the names of three "bad asses", so to speak.

Austin Meeks, Billy Walker, and Jason Sword were the names supplied to us. Doing background checks on them revealed they were career criminals. All three have been to prison. Sword did time for first degree assault; and Meeker and Walker only had a predilection towards casual violence, but all three were car thieves and burglars. They had very long rap sheets and I was impressed by the bunch. Good trade, I thought to myself.

"What do you guys think"? I asked of my men.

"This is a good trade" Rob spoke up.

"I agree" said Pig.

"Let's get this thing started then," I ordered and we opened our first car case.

We pulled up detailed arrest records making sure these three knew none of us and they didn't. Their photos were posted in the briefing room along with their backgrounds.

Meeks and Walker live in Puyallup and Sword lives in Tacoma. We went back in with Jordan and asked him how long has it been since he has seen these guys and learned it's been three or four months. We decided that Jordan can call Meeks and find out if they have any cars they want to move or if they are even in business. It was basically to get his foot in the door and tell Meeks that he has met a high volume buyer moving the cars out of state. We decided to try that and see what he says.

We went back and talked to Jordan and he liked our plan; thought it will work. We handed Jordan his phone and told him to do his thing and that we'll be listening. Jordan searched his phone for the number and hit send.

"Hey, Jordan here, what's up?"

"How ya doing, heard you got stopped by the cops."

"Which time?" Jordan asks.

"Tonight, by Best Buy, on the hill," Meeks responded.

"Ya, got busted for neg driving, then the assholes write me tickets for being suspended and no insurance, fuck it man, I hate the cops."

"Ya, I hear ya, what's up, what you need?"

"You still boosting cars? Got a buyer," Jordan claimed.

"Whenever I need one, who's the buyer?"

"I met him about a week ago, I can only bring him shaver cars because I haven't got the hot wire thing down and working alone is a bitch."

"So, you hung out by cops tonight and you call me looking for cars? I don't know about this."

"Just got a ticket is all and besides, some of the shit you and I have done, kidding?"

"Meet me in an hour, bring this dude with you and you're going to have to prove to me you're not working with the cops, ok?"

"Where?"

"18th and River."

"See you in an hour," and Jordan hung up.

"Can you guys be ready in an hour?" Jordan asks.

"Don't worry about it, we'll be ready," Pig says.

We leave and formulate a plan, kind of like drawing up a play in the dirt at a football game. We get Kevin, young kid but hell of a liar and quick thinker, to do the UC on this opening act. I don't know what this guy is going to do to make Jordan convince him we aren't the cops but we have to be ready. Kevin was at the time an officer for Orting Police Department, a small town to our East; and we had used Kevin before in undercover cameo roles and usually just a phone call away and lived close.

"Get couple sets of eyes on 18th and River. Service station there so we need be there now before Meeks gets there and surveillance crews will also be rescue. Pig, get this on paper so we are working within department SOP." As I finished, the guys were already up and running. Damn good crew.

I got a hold of Kevin and ask him if he wants to do the UC on this thing and he quickly agrees.

"Look, I don't know what Meeks is going to throw at you but be ready, might be simple or he might want you to smoke a bowl, that's not happening. If he presents a bowl, turn to Jordan and say, "I thought this guy was a pro, not doing business with a pot head and leave, ok?" I asked of him.

"Got it," was his reply; I had faith in him, just young.

I did a quick review of the operation plan; perfect as usual. Kevin was loaded with $500.00 cash in case Meeks shows up with a car and off we go. Surveillance units have seen nothing of Meeks and Kevin arrived driving Jordan in a very nice Chevrolet pickup truck. They backed into a spot off to the side of the store and waited. After about five minutes Rob spotted Meeks coming out of a trailer court, about two blocks from the service station, and walking towards Kevin and Jordan.

He appeared to be alone and when he arrived in the service station lot quickly spotted Jordan in the Chevrolet pickup truck. As he arrived at the window, greetings were made. There was much talk but we had no wire so I had no idea what was being said. They talked about five or so minutes then I saw Meeks reached through the window and handed something to my detective. Meeks pushed away from the door and left towards the trailer park. Detectives followed Meeks to the park, found his trailer, and watched him go in.

Detectives retreated to the police department to figure out what had just occurred and what our next move would be. Once gathered in the one way in, one way out room with no windows it is Kevin's turned to tell the remainder of us what happened.

Meeks stated that about a week ago he broke into the Earth Rite company yard in Sumner and one of the items he stole was a single key to one of the company's trucks. If we want to do business with Meeks and friends then we had to steal and deliver this truck before morning.

I looked at my watch, 2200 hrs; I got plan.

"Rob, get me a representative of Earth Rite Company. Sumner PD will have it and I'll call him or her as soon as you get it to me. If I can get them to play along we'll get the truck, Kevin will sell it to me at 18th and River Road in front of this idiot Meeks and I'll leave for Tacoma. You two guys follow me and make sure I have no one tailing. Kevin, you then feed Meeks some clever bullshit about how easy that was and what does he have in return for us then give him your UC phone number. While you're talking to him I'll call you and bitch you out for grabbing a bright green truck with writing all over it that shouldn't be out after midnight. You take that verbal bashing in front of Meeks and make excuses so he knows you're talking to me, the guy that just got the truck. When Meeks asks you who I am, just tell him I'm the boss. Got it?" I asked.

Pig grinned with easy excitement and approval of my clever, get in the fucking door plan, and all turned and hastened to their duty. Pig as usual would design the operations plan and things would click like a finely tuned machine. I just needed Earth Rite Company to step to the plate.

"Here's the number Sergeant" Rob said as he handed me the note. Estridge and a Sumner prefix.

"Hello?" the voice said.

"I'm looking for Mr. Estridge, might you be he?" I asked.

"Yes, this is Estridge, who are you?" he asked.

"Detective Sergeant Gill, Puyallup Police Department, was your business broken into about a week and a half ago?"

"Yes it was; did you find out who did it?"

"Yes, did you lose any keys?"

"Yes, one key to one of my trucks."

I relayed the story in full to Estridge and told him I desperately needed to steal his truck, so to speak.

"So you want to meet me at the business and I let you take a truck?" he asked.

"Basically, I'll bring Sumner police marked cars and Puyallup Police marked cars so you'll know we are cops and your truck will be safe and most likely returned within the week," I responded.

"I'll meet you at 2300 at the business," Estridge said.

"Great and thanks in advance," I said.

"No, sergeant, thank you," he said.

All were at scramble pace but that was when these guys were at their best, type A's get it done attitudes. Meeks and his bunch would have no chance.

Soon we finished all that needed to be done. We gathered in the dark parking lot and went over the plan one more time so all knew their role. A marked Puyallup car joined us and we left for Sumner Police Department. We re-gathered in their parking lot and soon a marked Sumner car joined us. Our next stop was Earth Rite on Middle Valley Road. We arrived five minutes early as did the owner, Estridge.

I climbed out of my Escalade and walked towards Estridge – tall mid-fifties, broad shouldered man. He noticed me immediately and as I reached for a hand shake I introduced myself as sergeant Gill. I simply handed him my wallet badge for his inspection.

"I would never have thought that you were a cop by simply looking at you," he said.

"I get that a lot," I responded.

After his inspection he looked about and was comfortable that we were who we said we were and he asked to see the key. I handed it to him and he inspected it.

"Ah yes, it's for that pickup truck over there," pointing to a bright green pickup truck with the company's logo painted all over it. I looked about the parking lot and noticed many similar painted trucks and figured we could return the truck easily within a few days at the most.

Estridge opened the gate and the truck was "stolen" by Tina, one of my detectives. I gave Estridge a business card with my number and my Captain's number on it in case he wanted to contact us. With that I thanked him for his cooperation and away we went.

We followed back roads into Puyallup, careful about exposing the truck anywhere that street people might see it. We hid the truck at a city underground parking garage and left the lot guarded for a short time.

If we called too soon we would look overly anxious and it was only 2330 hrs. A call to Meeks would be better placed at 0200 hrs or a little later. There was plenty to do, some of which would include a group meeting thinking of anything we had not already thought of. By 0120 hrs all that needed to be done was done, some done twice, and the guys were getting antsy.

"Okay guys, gather up briefing room; five minutes," was my order.

Pig was ready, pretty much all I needed to hear. In less than three minutes all involved had found a chair in the briefing room. I went over the plan; it was a basic dog and pony show to get us into the ring and I was good with the plan.

"Okay, here is what we are doing. Jordan will drop in a call to Meeks and tell him we got the truck and are on the way to 18th and River Road, the service station. After about 10 minutes Kevin will drive the Earth Rite truck into the service station from 18th followed by Jordan driving his private car. Both will park on the west side of the service station store. If Meeks isn't already there they'll wait. We wait till Meeks shows up and about a minute later Rob will enter the lot and drop me off. I'll grab the key from Kevin and then I'll grab the Earth Rite Company truck. After a quick inspection of the lights I'll jump in it and drive off westbound on River Road with Rob following me. Pig will be in the control van at Cars R Us lot across the street. He will mark the cues and be the director; any questions?" I asked. "Good, everyone else is surveillance and rescue, and fill-in on Pig's request. Surveillance guys get to your positions," I ordered; and with that people began to scramble.

"What do you think, Pig, think it'll go?" I asked.

"We'll know soon," he responded "and if it does we are going to be busy."

"I got a feeling we'll be bringing in the auto theft task force in if this takes off; need more people with badges," I commented.

"I'm already starting to figure out where to store the cars," he said.

"City shops for now, covered in tarps," I responded.

I received a call and learned all the surveillance units were in place and there was no sign of Meeks.

"I think it's time to make the call, let's go to the interview room," I said.

We filed into the room one by one: Pig, Rob, Kevin, and I where Jordan awaited us.

"You ready?" asked Pig.

Jordan nodded affirmative.

"Call Meeks, tell him you guys got the truck and have it already sold and they are meeting the buyer soon at the service station, 18th and River Road. Tell him you're about 10 minutes out and if he wants proof, be there and he can see for himself. Be serious with your tone, make a believer out of him, make him want to show up," Pig instructed.

"Got it," Jordan said and picked up his phone.

"We got it, too easy, we have it sold already so if you want to see your proof we will be at the 18th and River in about 10 minutes," Jordan said into the phone.

"You want what? It was only a key and you gave it to us," Jordan responded.

"Let's talk about it when we meet, ok?" The call ended.

"He wants $50.00, part of the truck payment for the key he gave us," Jordan said.

"You tell that son of bitch if he wants to play that game then you get $50.00 for every car he sells to the buyer you're bringing to the table," Pig said with great aggression.

"We don't let tail wag the dog in these matters Jordan; don't worry, Kevin will deal with him," I assured Jordan. "Let's roll, time's wasting," I said.

With that we made our way on foot to the underground parking garage. Jordan found that detectives had moved his car to the garage and he was given the keys.

"Do anything squirrelly and I turn these guys loose on you," reminding him of our deal.

"Don't worry Sergeant; I got a chance, not screwing this up," Jordan assured me.

Kevin led us out, followed by Jordan. We hesitated a bit not rushing to the scene before Meeks gets there. We waited, listening to the radio for a moment then drove slowly to the area, listening to the stage become life and the actors make their appearance.

Kevin arrives driving the "stolen" Earth Rite truck followed closely by Jordan. Both men park their vehicles and Kevin gets out of the truck and into Jordan's car. They sit and wait. We hear over the radio that one of our detectives spots Meeks walking out of the trailer park towards the meeting. As he entered the lot he looked at the Earth Rite truck and then went to the passenger side of Jordan's car where Kevin was seated. A conversation was on-going and I was sure Kevin was filling Meeks in on "you aren't getting $50.00 out of us" routine.

"Probably time to start heading that way and make our appearance," I said to Rob.

"Yep" was his answer and we drove to the parking lot turned stage. Just before arriving, Pig called us on the radio and said "your timing is perfect" as he noticed us coming down the street.

We pulled in and stopped in front of Jordan's car. I got out and contacted Kevin standing next to Meeks, but I gave Meeks no recognition.

"Got the key?" I asked of Kevin.

Kevin handed me the key and pointed at the truck.

"No shit, looks like it has a neon light on it saying stolen. Bright green, Earth Rite written all over it and probably not something that is out this late."

"I'm taking this one directly to the garage," I said acting irritated.

As I turned to walk to the Earth Rite truck I heard Meeks ask Kevin who I was and heard Kevin's answer, "the boss". I heard nothing after that.

I got into the truck and left west bound on River Road with Rob following closely. It was up to Kevin to finish the show and put the fine touches on owning Meeks. I drove quickly to the city shops and found a place to hide the Earth Rite truck and quickly rejoined Rob. I was anxious to hear what was going on.

"They're still talking, nothing changed. This could be good," Rob said.

Soon Pig announced that Meeks was leaving after shaking Kevin's hand. That was a good sign Kevin had done his job and sold us into the ring.

All detectives met in the briefing room anxious to hear what was talked about in the dark of the parking lot, hoping our ruse had worked.

Kevin had entered with an evil grin, one that told me we had succeeded with our plan. Meeks says he will get us a car soon, this morning, and will call when he has it. He told me he has two friends that he usually works with and will contact them. He wanted to know more about our operation and I didn't say much, basically ship the cars out of state and provide them with new identities.

"Great, so you think we should hang out or take a break and stay close in case Meeks calls?" Pig asked.

I was still thinking, planning ahead.

"Take a break, stay close and ready; no drinking," I said.

With that detectives began leaving, disappearing into the dark but all closely held together by cell phones.

"Can I stay in your spare room, grab a nap?" I asked Pig.

"You always have a place if you need it," was his response.

"I'm trying to figure out what to do with Jordan and Dora," I said.

"I think the rap sheet gig you pulled hit home, I'd let them go home after a stern warning, and to call us if Meeks calls him," Pig responded.

"Works for me," and with that I left for the jail.

"Need to spring Jordan and his girlfriend Dora," I said to one of the jailers. "Have you kept them isolated?"

"Yes sir, like they haven't even been here," the guard replied.

"I like you despite what everyone says about you," I mentioned to the guard.

"My wife talking bad about me again?" he asked.

"No I think it was your girlfriend," commenting back.

"Forgot about her, yep probably was her," he rolled with my smartass remarks not even trying to fend me off.

I was once again reunited with Jordan and Dora.

"Your car is in the parking garage and the cameras in the lobby are turned off. You two are free to go for now. No screwing this up. If Meeks calls you tell him you haven't seen or talked to any of us since tonight, then call me or Pig, understand?"

"Yes Sergeant, thanks for the chance," Jordan said.

"You can thank me by staying clean and taking care of your family," I responded. With that they left, disappeared into the dark; now it was my turn.

I rode with Pig to his house and found "my room". I have stayed in my room on long missions using his spare guest room to nap between operations. I peeled all my badges, wallets, and weapons from the various hiding spots where I kept them concealed, kicked off my Harley boots and flopped back onto the bed. I was tired but sleep would elude me. I could not stop thinking about scenarios that might occur during the operation.

Up until recently we had nothing but a bunch of narcotic cops but the administration had changed our mission and name. No longer were we narcotic cops only, we were now SIU, Special Investigations Unit, and were tasked with a proactive attack on thieves and dopers.

It was one thing to buy dope, all different animal-finding car thieves and then tricking them into selling the stolen cars to us; but we were off to a good start.

I had drifted off to sleep when I was awakened by the buzzing of my phone. It was Kevin.

"Meeks has a car for us," Kevin spoke.

I glanced at my watch, 0330, "took him a mere hour and half," I responded.

"He has staged it behind some shrubs next to the golf cart business near Tacoma on River Road, stated the key is a shaver and that the engine is off but the key is not all the way turned off making it an easy start," Kevin continued.

"Very customer service like of him," I mentioned. "Call the tribal guys and I'll get Pig and Rob; meet at department ASAP."

I gathered all my battle trinkets and when I opened the door Pig walked by heading for the garage.

"I never fell asleep, just knew we would be back to work; heard your phone, knew what it meant, I'm ready," Pig said.

We arrived back at the department and were soon met by the other detectives in the briefing room. We came up with a quick plan: Kevin and I would drive to the location of the stolen car; I will get it started and leave Westbound towards Tacoma; the car will be moved onto southbound interstate 5 to highway 512 then eastbound back to South Hill Puyallup and the city shops.

"At the ramp where I get onto interstate 5, Pig, Rob, and Kevin, you guys peel off and keep an eye on the on ramp and make sure I'm not being followed. When you're sure I'm not being followed, Kevin, you call Meeks and find out where he wants to meet and get paid, strongly suggest 18th and River Road. Pig and Rob, make sure Kevin is sent home with no marks, ok?" I finished my speech.

"Want me to start an operation plan?" Pig asked.

"No time, we'll get it done first thing in the morning," I responded.

"I'll get $300.00 copied up for buy money," Rob said and away he went.

Once again we met up in the parking lot and did a down and dirty review of the plan so all are on the same page. Kevin and I left and headed to the area through a little freeway town, Fife. The other detectives would find clever ways to melt into the surrounding of where the stolen car is located and would await our arrival.

Kevin was flying. We needed to appear to be coming from Tacoma as we had already told them that our shop was there. Coming from Puyallup would be strange and would make it tough to answer any questions brought up about it. We were unsure if Meeks or any of his bunches would be at the car but we had to play it as if they would be there.

"Shit" was all Kevin said. Then I saw it, a Fife cop pulling us over for the speed we were driving at. He was young, not known to me or Kevin. As he began his routine, I badged him.

"I'm Detective Sergeant Gill with Puyallup Police Department and we must get to Tacoma. We are in the process of buying a stolen car. We gotta go," I said with authority.

He looked confused then said "I'll call my sergeant and he can sort this out."

"What's the name of your sergeant?" I asked.

"McKinney," the officer said.

"Okay, here is my card, give it to Jeff. He knows me and what I do; we are leaving," I again told him using a voice of a supervisor that is getting irritated. Sgt. McKinney's first name is Jeff.

"Gotta go." I motioned to Kevin to go.

We sped off leaving the youngster standing next to nothing. I looked back and saw the kid turning off his emergency lights and turning his car around. Within a few minutes we turned onto eastbound River Road and were heading back towards Puyallup. Kevin was again up and flying and the speed cameras that lined River Road in the S curves of the road lit up taking pictures of our license plates.

"You did change out your plates with those ones I gave you, right?" I asked.

"Yep," he replied.

Months earlier Pig and I weaseled through a bunch of license plates from a WSP inspection garage. The plates we got were older plates; looked just fine, but if anyone ran the plates they would simply come back with "no computer record" meaning the plates had been purged from the system. This action was prompted because we were getting tired of writing memos explaining red light camera tickets or like this, speeding cameras. Some over educated sergeant had complained to another over educated captain we were breaking traffic laws. I was summoned to explain the tickets to the captain.

"Drive it like you stole it," was my response when he asked about the tickets. He looked confused with my comment.

"Damn, you should have been a detective and learned police work before they promoted you," I thought to myself; they call that the Peter Principle.

"Look captain, we follow stolen cars. They just stole the car. Do you really think they give a shit about traffic laws? We have to keep up with them and hopefully find out where they take them and sometimes we break the damn law doing so. If you don't want us to follow stolen cars and bad guys then let me know. Get it "okayed" by the Chief and we will stop doing our job," I said with irritation.

He just stared at me for a moment then said, "get out".

The next day Pig and I came up with the plates from WSP.

"There's the golf cart business and that is the hedge I assume," Kevin said.

"There's the car, behind the hedge," I announced.

It was a nineties Honda Civic, red in color. I climbed into the vehicle and found the key exactly how Meeks said it would be. It took a little bit of wiggling and I started the car with the shaver key, my first. I quickly backed the car out of the spot and turned westbound on River Road towards Tacoma and interstate 5. As I got to the on ramp I saw three cars peel off, one came to a stop and the other two continued slowly moving. The tribal guys now had my back and we drove quickly to the Puyallup City shops via highway 512. I was anxious about what was going on at 18th and River Road. Arriving at the shops I learned from tribal that the deal had gone well with Meeks and that all involved had made it back to the police department and Meeks had returned to his trailer with $300.00 in his pocket.

Tribal, Paul and Paul; yes they have the same first name and wild ass last names so we call them tribal, gave me a ride back to the department and we had a short meeting. Kevin stated that he has already talked to his other two guys and they will be out working tomorrow night and told me they would be in touch.

"Tina, can you call the prosecutor's office tomorrow and find out how many cars we need from each of these guys for maximum time in jail and when we hit that mark we will shut this down?" I asked.

"No problem," was her response.

There is a points system used for time in prison. The number of points depends upon the crime. There are more points, for instance, for armed robbery than auto theft. In Sword's case he had already more convictions for auto theft and burglary than did Meeks or Walker; therefore Sword would require fewer cars than Meeks and Walker to max out on time in prison.

"Kevin, keep that UC phone close to ya, don't miss a call," I told him.

We decided that coming in around 1900 hrs is a good time to meet; we all knew we would be up late.

Morning had already arrived and the break of the sun was lighting up the early sky as I left for home. My sleep was going to be restless; I was worried about our new mission, and we were venturing into uncharted waters so to speak. *1900 hrs came way too fast*, I thought to myself, as I entered the back of the police department. All the usual suspects were there fluently speaking bullshit. Pig was busy working on operations plan staying to himself, and Tina was working on her latest fraud case.

"What did you learn with the prosecutor today?" I asked of Tina.

"Austin Meeks needs to steal six cars, five now after last night; Billy Walker needs six cars; and Jason Sword only needs four since he's a frequent flyer of the judicial system, won't take much to get him back into prison," she responded.

"Thanks," and with that I went to my office. "Gee, we only need 16 stolen cars, how hard can that be?" sarcastically thinking to myself.

Tina was a tall slender gal. Of all my SIU detectives she was clearly the smartest and meanest. She had the same work ethic as Pig and the two often clashed in the field then settled it in a domestic violence fashion after the operation. Even though she was late thirties she wore braces, clearly a target for those brave souls that wanted to mess with her, but few did. I made a mistake one time and said something stupid about the braces. A week later Tina wandered into my office acting busy, looking over a report then quickly left. Within seconds I realized she had left behind a nauseating silent fart that nearly gagged me. I staggered to her cubicle to file a complaint and there she sat grinning at me.

"Next time you mention my braces I will pull the door to your office shut and you'll be stuck in there with it," she said.

I re-thought what I was going to say then turned silently around shaking my head and grinned. I walked around the outside of the building till my office could be occupied again.

I began thinking of ways to make this new adventure go smoother and ways we could film these transactions. We should have a warehouse for these cars to be delivered to. We could put up cameras and record the transactions! That would keep us out of the court rooms and prying questions. *So much to be learned*, I thought to myself; but this was our first car case and we will learn and get better. It was the way we were. I had no idea that in a couple of short years a Pierce County Prosecutor speaking at a Police Chief and Sherriff convention would state "if you want to know how to do a car sting, ask Puyallup's SIU cops, they're the best at it."

I looked up the fathers of Billy Walker and Jason Sword. It was amazing! All of their rap sheets look the same: auto theft and burglary dominated the men's background and now their sons were making them proud.

"Just got a call," said Pig shoving his head into my office. "They have two cars stashed for us in Puyallup," he continued.

"Ok, I'll call the task force and see if we can borrow a couple guys and let's get the operation plan completed," I said and with that we hit the ground running.

Kevin learned that Meeks and Walker were waiting to meet with us at 18th and River Road when we are ready. Pig was ready with the operation plan and we all met in the briefing room. We had obtained two task force cops that looked like they belonged in prison. The plan was for Kevin and I to meet Walker and Meeks and have them ride with us showing us the cars and where they were parked. After we inspected the cars they would be paid and we would move to the next car. Since Kevin and I would be wired, our conversation recorded, Pig would hear where the cars were parked and direct pick up cops to get the cars. Pick up cops would work in teams of two: one driving the stolen car, the other following. The cars would be eventually driven to the city shops and stored, but tonight we would hide them in a concealed lot next to Fife P.D. The entire time Kevin and I were with Meeks and Walker we would be followed and watched for by the last three detectives I had available. We were stretched thin.

Everyone was on board and the operation started. Kevin and I drove to 18th and River Road. I told Kevin to go inside the store and watch the parking lot monitor near the clerk's desk, and when Meeks and Walker get to the car I'll get Meeks to get in the front seat with me. I don't want both those assholes sitting behind us. We left the back lot of the police department and drove to 18th and River Road. Kevin called Meeks and told him we were there waiting. Meeks stated they would be on the way. Kevin got out and disappeared into the store.

As I watched and waited I had nervous thoughts; we need more men with guns. This could get out of control. Soon there were Meeks and his friend, Walker I assumed. As they walked up to the car I said "hop in". Meeks piled into the front seat and Walker into the back seat, behind me. This made me nervous but about that time Kevin arrived and climbed into the back seat.

"Where to?" I said, looking at Meeks. Meeks held out his right hand, introductions, and an important matter for criminals working together.

"Austin," he said.

I shook back, "Gill".

Kevin and Walker performed the same ritual in the back seat and we were off heading for Tacoma. While driving I asked about the two cars they had gotten: how they got them, where they got them. Of course their answers were all being recorded. We drove to Tacoma's eastside and on some quiet side street parked in the dark was a Honda prelude. I pulled up next to the car. Kevin jumped out and shut his door. He "inspected" the car and when he got to the far side of it he knelt down and gave his location over the wire. If Pig didn't get the location, one of the following three detectives would figure it out, and soon the pick-up cops would grab the car and drive it to Fife for temporary storage.

The second car was not far from the first. We located it behind an office building accessed by an alley. This one was an Acura, newer model. I was impressed. Again, Kevin hopped out and went through his bullshit routine and we were soon off and running. When we began to drive back to Tacoma, Walker's cell phone chimed up.

"What's up?" he said. He was listening intently and he tapped Meeks on the shoulder and gave him a turn-round sign in the air with his index finger. As I turned my car around, Walker hung up. "It was Sword, he's got a Toyota truck and has it hidden near a marina next to Skinheads Bar and Restaurant on the tide flats.

"Good," I thought to myself. "Get to meet this asshole."

I was well aware of the area we were heading to. I had lived on a yacht for several years at this marina. Our kids were suffering boomer rang issues. They leave home for couple months then return, so we simply sold the house out from under them. Tough love I guess, but it worked; they now make more money a year than I do.

Arriving, we found Sword and the stolen truck. As I spoke to Sword, introduction and such, I noticed one of my detectives parked in the parking lot of Skinheads Bar and Restaurant watching us. *Good cop*, I silently thought. The three men were paid for their services and all wanted a ride back to Meeks' place. *Why not?* I thought. And it was a delight to watch Walker slide over next to Kevin and Sword jam himself into the seat behind me. Kevin had the eugh-ee look to him and I smiled ever so slightly. Meeks rode shotgun with me in the front seat. As I drove from the area I noticed the pick-up cops pass by heading for the marina and the stolen truck.

The conversation was light on the way back to Puyallup. My ford Taurus was packed with criminals and cops and for the time being we would get along, but soon we would be at war.

"Which mobile is yours?" I asked Meeks, even though I already knew which one. He directed me to his mobile and they all got out and went inside.

As I backed out I mentioned "the next three cars stolen will be from Puyallup".

"Yep" was Kevin's reply.

The three stolen vehicles found their way to the city shops for storage and reports were being written. It was about 0300 hrs and most of the reports had been completed when Kevin ran into my office.

"Meeks just called, they got three more cars and they have them at the trailer court, 18 and River Road," he said.

"Damn," get the guys, meeting three minutes briefing room," I responded.

Kevin ran off and made notifications and in minutes everyone but Pig and I had assembled in the briefing room.

I got to Pig first. "My office, quick," I said. "We are in over our heads here, we need more help, got to figure out a way to slow these guys up, got any?" I asked Pig.

We silently looked at each other then he spoke. "Tell them we are full and taking a load to California, be gone for three days. That would buy us three days to re-plan and re-load."

"Like it," I answered. "Let's get to the briefing room," I said.

When we walked in I noticed some tired faces, but men and one lady ready to charge on. After a brief discussion we decided that I would drive Kevin and tribal Paul to the trailer court. We would pay the three for the cars and tell them we are full and taking a load to California so we would be gone for three days. That would buy us time. Paul and Kevin would drive out two of the cars and down the road a ways. We would switch out Kevin with Tina and I would bring Kevin back for the third car. Everyone else would be surveillance.

The operation went without a hitch – smooth, safe, and successful. We bought three more stolen cars and bought three days to catch up.

My people found a whole new gear and sped up even more. They were excited with the new challenge and this was the first time Puyallup Police Department had ever done anything like this. I often referred to my people as the "best of the 311th". The Police Department's address is 311 West Pioneer, thus the phrase best of the 311th. I didn't make up the phrase, but used it often.

We no longer had two detectives from the task force; we had the entire damn task force. We had impressed the two task force detectives and they had brought all their friends, more men and women with guns. We even got the Washington State Patrol (WSP) on board. They had heard of our adventure and offered their plane for surveillance. The plane was simply cool. Best part, it had infrared cameras that could and would film us at night as we made our rounds buying stolen cars. They could easily mark the cars' location for pick up cops. The plan was coming together beautifully. It was a rehearsal for the next couple years of work we'd be known for, the best at what we did: car stings.

Pig was in a bubble bath of planning. He loved this and all the tools he had to work with. There was nothing being left to doubt. The three days of planning flew by. Everything was in place and everyone was rested, ready and anxious to get going. On the third day I had Kevin call Meeks to tell him we were back and ready if he had anything.

"They already have three staged; been waiting our arrival," Kevin told me.

"Wow, busy bees," I responded.

"Told Meeks we will be in touch soon," Kevin said.

"Good, lets meet back here at 2000 hrs, get things rolling then," I said and with that most detectives left for a short RR at home.

Pig and I drove near 18th and River Road and hid in a dark, out of the way spot. We got out of our car and disappeared into the night, sneaking on foot to the trailer court Meeks lived in. We both figured if they have three stolen cars already, they probably put them in the park. Humans are creatures of habit. We found the three stolen cars parked in the same spots they had before with the first three stolen cars we had gotten from them just several days earlier.

We made our way back to Pig's car. I went with Pig to his home for a cold drink and some small talk. Pig has a room in his house, a vain room. Most men have them, a room with the achievements of your life and past. Pig was no different. His room contained pictures of his adventures in DEA task force, pictures of him and me during SWAT training, and pictures of us on police bicycles. A spattering of life saving medals, merit medals, recognized achievements, badges that he had worn in Sumner and Puyallup police departments. His walls were well covered, a man proud of his past. I had a very similar room.

We spoke about how our most recent case had electrified the administration.

"They're scared , yes excited but they sit in their think tanks elated about the work we are doing but all the while hoping we don't get the department into trouble," I said.

Pig then nodded in agreement then said "Let's eat; found a new restaurant with a cute waitress," he claimed.

We made our way out of his home and soon we are seated in a restaurant with a cute waitress. It didn't take long for us to eat. Cops eat fast; becomes a habit after years of patrol work. You eat fast cause you just know you're going to get interrupted by someone needing something. Now, we just eat fast because we are used to it.

2000 hrs roll around and the building is full of detectives and a couple WSP pilots. Briefing will start at 2015 hrs and a phone call to Meeks will be made after that. Briefing took a while, many tasks and many people working together that had never worked together before but they'll get through it. Kevin found a lonely spot and called Meeks.

"Nothing, no answer" Kevin said.

"Try again in 10," I told him.

Ten minutes passed by and again another call was made to Meeks; again no answer.

"It's 2030 hrs; bet they are out stealing cars," Pig said.

"If they are we are going to be busy all night," Rob said.

Then Kevin's phone jumps to life "it's him" Kevin announces making a dash for a quiet room followed by Pig and I.

"What's up my man?" Kevin said. "How many? Impressive!" he added. "Where you at now?" Kevin asked. "Look man all we can take is nine at a time, so stop when you get there and we'll pick you up; just call and tell us where you're at."

With that the phone call is over. They have seven total, Walker and Sword are working some movie theater on South Hill trying to get two more. I told them to stop at 9; which gives Meeks a total of 6, Walker a total of 6, and Sword will have 4.

"They are clearly working together," Kevin said.

"Okay, let's get this to the guys in the briefing room," I said. "Ok, listen up, things just got interesting. They currently have seven cars waiting for us. Walker and Sword are out working the South Hill for two more. Meeks says he will call us when they have all nine stolen cars. Kevin and I are going to grab Meeks, Walker, and Sword with surveillance following us. During the break Pig and I found three of their stolen cars back at the Meeks trailer court. If Meeks takes us there we will just ignore those three, can recover them later. Pig, you and Tina use my van and pay attention to the wire. We will keep you updated then you two direct the pick up teams. Since we only have four pick up teams we will grab the first four cars they show us tonight, just not the ones at the trailer court. Surveillance crew will continue to follow us, and let Pig and Tina know where the remaining two cars are located once Meeks and his buddies lead us to them. WSP plane crew can also mark the locations of the cars and can film the entire event. Coordinate everything through Pig and Tina," wrapping up my presentation of Pig's work.

"After we locate all the stolen cars we will drive to the warehouse area north of Puyallup, the Snowden warehouse. On its north side there is a drive up ramp with a roll up door. I'll pull up to the door. Kevin will get out to unlock the door and open it. He will then realize that he doesn't have his keys. He will motion to me that he needs keys. Then I'll turn off the car, get out and we basically "beat feet" out of there. Surveillance teams then become a take-down team and take Meeks, Walker, and Sword into custody. It's a slam dunk," finishing my speech with enthusiasm. The plan got scrutinized, but after a few matters of confusion were sorted out, all were on board.

The pilots left to get airborne as it was clear that these bad guys work hard and fast. I got Pig and Tina aside.

"Tina, if there is a problem with getting the take down team in place at the warehouse call me on my cell phone. Talk to me like you're my wife or girlfriend; they'll probably hear your voice, but you calling me means you all need more time to get the takedown team in place and I'll find a clever way to slow up our arrival. The last thing I want to do is show up and the team isn't ready," I told her.

"Got it" was her response.

I found Kevin and we had a quick discussion about seating arrangements for tonight's operation.

"I don't think there is a way to get us separated. Sit crooked in the front seat while watching and talking to them," I told Kevin.

"Yeah, I don't like it either but it's tough one to get around," Kevin said.

"Oh and Kevin, when they call you back tell them "the boss" will not have any money on him tonight, he will pay you at the warehouse afterwards. I don't want them to think I'm holding three grand in cash," I said.

"Good idea and that will set up the take down perfectly," Kevin responded.

I held out my right hand to shake his hand and tell Kevin good luck, and he does the same for me. Kevin is more than another cop to me, he is my nephew.

By 2200 hrs all is ready. We have gathered in the briefing room and nervously await the call from Meeks. Somewhere outside is the WSP plane, circling and also waiting; and somewhere out there in the dark of the night three men are stealing cars. Meeks called us at 2220 hrs.

"Look we are going to pick you guys up, you show us where the cars are at then we'll take you to our warehouse and pay you there, ok?" Kevin told Meeks.

"We're good with that," Meeks responded.

"See you in 15," Kevin said ending the call.

Our nervousness was replaced with driven purpose and the room quickly emptied as Detectives moved to their assigned locations. Kevin and I climbed into our Ford Taurus and began the short drive to Meeks' trailer with an entourage following us. Arriving, we found Meeks, Walker, and Sword standing outside Meek's trailer smoking cigarettes. Following introductions, Meeks pointed out the three stolen cars stashed nearby. Kevin walked over to look at them and gave their license plates out over the air to Pig and Tina listening to his wire. I made small talk with the three.

"Well, Meeks got to hand it to you; you were right when you said you and your guys would out work my two guys. All my guys have done is pick up your cars," giving Meeks and his bunch a pep talk.

"Told ya," Meeks said smiling.

Kevin returned to the group and said "They're good ones."

We get into my Taurus and I asked where to. We spend the next forty five minutes driving from one location to another and the same routine plays out. Meeks directs us to yet another stolen car, Kevin gets out, does a bullshit inspection and we leave to find the next stolen car. As we find our sixth and final car Kevin climbs in and says "all good".

"Let's get these guys paid," I said as I slipped the transmission into drive.

We made our way along back roads and streets heading to north Puyallup and the warehouse. My phone rang; it's Tina.

"Hey babe stop and pick up a dozen eggs before you come home okay?" she said.

"Okay," I respond and hung up. Tina just told me they need 10 minutes to get homecoming ready for the three idiots in the back seat. I found a "7-11" store, parked off to the side, and turned off my head lights. I pulled out a small short cigar and asked for a lighter. Surprising me, Sword whips out a lighter and tosses it to me. I take my time lighting it and the first few puffs were that of a man smoking a fine Cuban cigar.

"Needed that," I said. "Look, I'm going to show you guys our warehouse and how we operate" telling the three. "I trust you. You don't tell anyone of this, especially your god damn girlfriends, understand?" and the three nod in compliance. "If anyone of us gets jammed up by the cops we keep our mouth shut; you'll have a job when you get out of jail, agreed?" I said. Again all nodded in compliance. "I only want to make two loads a month, don't want to get any attention but that will pay you guys an easy two grand each, just stay quiet and work carefully," I continued.

I glanced at my watch. *Been twelve minutes since I talked to Tina, they should be ready,* I thought to myself. Better be ready I'm running out of bullshit topics for the three musketeers in the back seat.

I turned on the headlights, slipped the car in reverse, and began to back out. I couldn't help but notice the three giving "high fives" to one another in the back seat.

"Dumbasses," I thought to myself.

I drove slow; speed limit no more, no less. I could see the number of cars behind me, all cops, all ready. When I pulled into the warehouse area I traveled to the North side of the Snowden and the ramp where this case would violently end. As I drove up the ramp I stopped, put the car in park, and Kevin jumped out and walked to the lock searching his pants and pockets for keys. He looked at me and motioned that he didn't have his keys. I turned off the car, stepped out, and shut the car door. As I approached him we made eye contact, a slight grin appeared on his face matching the one on my face and then I said "run".

We both spun running for the rails that lined the ramp and we both cleared them and landed on the asphalt of the parking lot four feet below. I whirled around hitting the lock button on the key fob delaying any attempt for the three stooges to get out of the Taurus. Cops appeared out of nowhere and converged on the Taurus and its three, up until now un-suspecting occupants. I stopped running, turned around to look at the mealy. I again hit the button on the key fob, unlocking the doors.

Sword came out fighting, kind of expected that of him. Meeks and Walker tried to resist but they were well outmatched. Sword got his ass kicked but it was the only way he was going to go, with a fight. Kevin found me watching and he displayed a huge grin.

"That was fun, let's do it again," he said.

"How about next time, we actually have a warehouse and do it right?" I responded.

Kevin and I walked over to the scene. By now Meeks and Walker laid face down on the pavement and Sword joined them; he was bleeding of course. We waited till three marked police cars showed up and transported them to jail. As Detectives stood the men up I looked at Sword's facial injuries, minor but he was sporting a goose egg bump.

"Have fire check him at the jail," I said to one of the officers.

"I'm killing you once I get out mother fucker," Sword said to me.

"Whatever, but you'll have to get in line bigger, tougher, smarter men than those already in front of you," I responded.

He spat on the asphalt, glaring at me as he got stuffed into the back of the police car.

Reports were written, stolen cars reunited with their owner with tips on how to keep their cars from being stolen. The department administration was elated over the operation and wanted more.

A couple weeks passed by and the front office called my desk.

"There's a man in the lobby that wants to speak to you," she said. "He doesn't look happy."

I arrived in the lobby and met a man with the last name of Walker; dad.

"You tricked my son you asshole," was his opening statement.

"Wait here Walker, I want to share something with you," I said.

I turned around and returned to my office. I found two rap sheets; both had the last name of Walker on them, but two different Walkers. I returned to the lobby and dad. In the lobby there was a counter and I laid the rap sheets on the counter, side by side.

"Have a look Mr. Walker," speaking to him.

Really there were basically no differences in the rap sheets except the first names and the dates. Walker studied both the sheets then glared at me.

"What's this supposed to mean?" he stated.

"You failed as a father and now your son is paying for it," I responded.

I was waiting for the incoming fist or something but nothing occurred. He continued to glare at me as the truth set in. I gathered up the papers before us. We had the front office staffs' full attention by now, not sure how this was going to play out. After a few tense moments Walker simply turned and walked out of the lobby.

Sometimes the truth hurts.

Early the next morning, we all met at the police department to begin building a chop shop that would have serious consequences for all that did business there. Since Rob and I have carpenter skills we would work on the garages and Pig, well he had other skills. As I have mentioned in another story, Pig had a way of collecting stuff. We needed a camera system and that is Pig's job. We needed a wire and sound system, again, it's Pig's job. We needed an alarm system, yup, it's definitely Pig's job. We badly needed props, and only Pig can do the best job in that. As Rob and I got our tools together and a list of items we needed from the hardware store, Pig found the keys to a large truck.

Chapter 21

Bulldog

I was in Rob's office when my cell phone rang. It was the patrol sergeant who was working.

"Gill, what do you need?" I answered.

"We just got a call of a possible chop shop at the Brookdale Apartments. You guys interested in checking it out?" he asked.

"On the way," I responded.

"Contact the manager, she is cop friendly and tired of all the bullshit going on in those apartments," the sergeant said, and with that he hung up.

"Rob, possible chop shop at the Brookdale's; let's go check it out," I told him, and we left the office after gathering needed items.

The Brookdale Apartments is one of Puyallup's armpit arenas and a government subsidized hell hole-housing project which attracted nothing but the finest people. Criminals of all types lived here or couch-surfed in one of their friend's apartment – sex offenders, thieves, thugs, gangsters, and dope dealers, all in one spot. There were actually good people peppered among them that were fighting to get out of their predicament; hiding behind sheetrock walls, concealing from criminals lurking nearby, next door. It was a cop's hunting ground, but cops too must be weary when hunting within the confines of this battlefield.

Arriving at the manager's office, we were greeted by a couple young ladies that worked for the apartments and they quickly wanted to know our business. Rob and I had shed anything that would identify us as the police.

"We have an appointment with the manager, something about repairs," I told them.

A voice from behind said, "I'm the manager, don't recall any appointments today."

As Rob and I turned around we found a middle-aged woman standing in an open door to a private office bearing the name plate "Manager". She quickly assessed us, and then said "oh yeah, step into my office please."

As we walked into the office I couldn't help but notice how she looked "roughed up" but also tough. She shut the door and made her way to her desk and chair.

"Take a seat, detectives," surprising us with the accuracy of her assessment.

"Really, are we that obvious?" I asked.

"No, actually it would have been my last thought, but the patrol sergeant mentioned a couple scary looking detectives would be stopping by," she answered, settling my nerves.

She told us that a tenant had stopped paying rent on a garage unit and after not hearing from the tenant she had the lock cut from the garage door and inside they had found the remains to a stripped car and motorcycle.

"Considering the vast amount of criminals living here, I assumed the worst and called the police," finishing her overview of the situation.

"Let's take a look," I said, and soon we were walking among the buildings working to the east side of the complex and several long rows of single car garages.

Each row held six garages and directly behind and attached were six more single car garages – all under one roof and all unconnected inside. That made for a total of 12 garages, under one roof, with 12 garage doors; 12 separate, yet connected garages. She led us to garage number 43 and quickly slung up the garage door revealing the contents. Car and motorcycle parts lay cluttered around the chassis of a stripped car. Rob quickly dove in and started searching for VIN numbers that would expose the truth about the vehicles, their owner's name, and if the vehicle was stolen. VIN simply means "vehicle identification numbers" and all motor vehicles are to have them; some out in the open for all to read and then there are those that have been hidden. Rob was born with a little grease monkey gene and he was handy to have around in these types of matters. I asked the manager, Jennifer, about the activity that was going on in the apartment complex. Jennifer spilled out her frustrations and fears and what it was like working with criminals and liberal government officials that forced the apartment complex to accept such garbage.

"You know, one day I came to work in the morning and found taped to the front doors of the office a picture of my 10 year old son walking up my driveway to my home, and under the picture were simply the words 'know where you live,'" she told me. "My husband is in the Middle East fighting for these sons of bitches that suck off the tax payers' tits and I'm afraid for what they could and might do."

Her words and tone of her voice made me realize my first assessment of her to be correct "a roughed up woman". By now Rob had rejoined us and said the car and motorcycle was not reported stolen and was registered to a Joseph Benning.

"He is the tenant that rented the garage," Jennifer said.

"How far are you willing to go to help us help you?" I asked her.

"Can you call in an air strike?" she asked with a sober face. I grinned and thought *"I like her."*

"Let my partner and I talk and we'll get back to you," I said. Then I asked "What do the pink locks mean that are posted on garages 42, 44, 45, and 46?"

"Those are vacant garages," she answered.

"Thanks, we'll be in touch," I stated.

Jennifer shut the door to 43 and walked off back towards her office. I watched her walk off. My mind was whirling. I had an idea that until now only read about, but decided before my career was over I wanted to try it. I turned to look at Rob and he simply said "store front". *"Like minds think alike"* I was thinking of him as I smiled.

"Let's get Pig and brainstorm this and see what we can come up with," I told him.

"Agreed" was all he said and we made our way back to the van we had left near the office. As we got to the van I returned to Jennifer's office.

"I need one of your cards, and could you put your cell number on it?" I asked of her.

"Sure," she responded then completed the card and handed it to me.

"We will be in touch," I said. She smiled and I left.

As we drove to the police department Rob and I began talking. We discussed setting up a fake chop shop that would be completely wired for video and sound.

"We could set up shop and have car thieves deliver cars to us," I mentioned. We could even use it to collect burglary items that had been stolen, basically an illegal pawn shop," I continued.

"You know if this gets done and we get it up and running we will be swamped, we simply don't have enough people to do this," Rob said.

"You're right," I said to him. "Let's give it some thought, see what we can come up with," I continued.

Neither of us spoke the remainder of the ride to the office; just two men deep in thought. As we stepped into the elevator that leads to the second floor and our offices, it hit me.

"Do you remember what happened during our first car case?" I asked Rob.

"Yeah, we got swamped," he responded.

"Of course we did, then we invited two task force detectives to join us and they did, and the following night we had the entire task force and the State Patrol show up.

Remember?" I asked Rob.

"You want me to contact the task force to see if they would help?" Rob said.

"No," I responded then stole a line out of a movie called "Field of Dreams". "Build it and they will come," I smiled as I said it to Rob.

"That's the problem; we build it and they will come, we just won't be able to handle it," Rob said a bit frustrated with me.

"Not the bad guys, my German-built friend. We build it, tell the task force cops of it, and they will come, to help," driving my verbal tipped spear home.

"Love the way you think, sergeant," Rob responded.

We stepped off the elevator and headed to our offices.

"I'll hunt Pig down, let's meet in the briefing room and keep quiet about this," I told Rob. "It will frighten people, especially the administration," I continued.

I stuck my head into Pig's office, "Hey big guy we are meeting in the briefing room, got an idea," I told Pig.

"What you two been doing?" Pig asked.

Then I just turned around as I walked and quickly glanced at Pig and said, "A field of dreams."

Pig and I entered the room where Rob was seated and waiting. With the door closed the three of us began working on our idea and planning; basically brainstorming the biggest, most aggressive campaign of our careers.

After sharing the idea with Pig and all the possible things we could run out of our little store he asked "you two really think it's wise we do this in the middle of "that" set of apartments? That's bad guys' ground zero," he stated.

"That is what makes it perfect," Rob responded.

"Look Pig, we do this right under their collective noses, in their backyard so to speak, it's the last place cops would set up something like this they'd think," I picked up where Rob had let off. "We are good enough to do this," I said looking at Pig and Rob.

"Take me up there; I need to visualize this before I can go any further," Pig demanded.

"Before we go, one thing needs to be clear: we say nothing of this to anyone, not yet. When the plan is completed I will present it to the admin, they will have questions and we will want to have the answers."

"Agreed," says Pig and we leave the police department.

I made a quick phone call to Jennifer and learned she is at home but has a master key for all the pink locks on the garages. Having already done a complete background on Jennifer we know she is a good person with absolutely no criminal history. We will be up front with her as to our plans. We need her involved and already figured she wouldn't hesitate.

We arrived at her home and as we arrived on the front porch Jennifer opens it to greet us.

"Please come in," she said.

Pig introduced himself and we laid out our plan to her. We didn't have to wait long for her answer.

"You men are going to be busy? Here is a copy to the master key for anything pink. And do you gentlemen need an apartment to relax in while running this thing?"

"Thanks for the key and we will think about the apartment; but for now, thank you" I said as she handed over the key. "Oh and by the way, by this time tomorrow we will have cameras posted outside, watching-recording anything or anybody that approaches your home in the cul-de-sac."

"Much appreciated," Jennifer said.

We bid farewell and made our way to ground zero. Arriving, we parked out front of garage 44. *"Good number"*, I thought to myself, my badge number. We unlocked the door and swung it open revealing a garage, completely void of anything but a three foot wide shelf running across the back. We then opened garages 45 and 46: 45 and 46 are the same as 44, closed off with one shelf and room for one large vehicle.

"How are we going to make this work?" Pig asked.

"Let me make a call," I said as I pulled out my cell phone, hit re-dial for Jennifer.

"Hello?" Jennifer answered.

"Do you care if we connect 44, 45, and 46 with inside walk thru doors we can cut into the wall?" I asked.

"I really don't give a damn what you guys do; have your way with it," she answered.

"Thanks," and I hung up.

"Here's a thought: we cut walk thru door between 44 and 45 then another walkway door thru 45 and 46, all lined up so you can look down the "hall" into all the rooms. It will provide a great camera shot at anyone walking through those doors. Great for identification," I finished saying with some enthusiasm. Pig doesn't say anything, just raised a brow.

"What about a room for camera monitoring, radio control, and alarm monitor?" Rob asked.

We went back outside and started looking for more pink locks and we found them. We opened garage 42 and it's the same as the others except for one thing: on the shelf in the corner there is a big red stuffed bulldog, something won at the fair and now left behind because of its size. It was huge.

When Rob saw it sitting there he simply said, "Well, we just got one thing done, the name of this operation should be bulldog."

Pig and I smiled at Rob, "like it" Pig mentioned.

We walked around the east end of the garages to the back side and another six garages. Only one pink lock left and it was on the very last garage at the far east end, directly kitty corner of garage 46. Opening garage 52, we found it completely empty and the same shelf as the others. We quickly shut down all the doors and drove back to the police department.

Having just gotten a visual of the building, we outlined it on a grease board and began laying out a blueprint of what we want and what will work. We decided to turn garage 52 into a wire room. We would construct a hidden 2 foot space at the back of the garage then rebuild the back wall, concealing it. We would then sound proof the area where the wire operator would be posted. In the hidden room would be alarm system for the other garages we would use to include the wire room, a camera monitor, and radio and charging system. There will be a comfortable chair and table for the wire operator to relax between operations, a 5 gallon bucket for bathroom facilities, and a C clamp. Since there was no way to lock the garage with the operator in it he would simply C clamp the door shut, thus effectively locking it. Garages 44, 45, and 46 would be the shop or store front and undercover cops would work with their clientele. Two walk thru door openings would be constructed and all would be under camera and wired for sound.

Early the next morning, we all met at the police department to begin building a chop shop that would have serious consequences for all that did business there. Since Rob and I have carpenter skills we would work on the garages and Pig, well he had other skills. As I have mentioned in another story, Pig had a way of collecting stuff. We needed a camera system and that is Pig's job. We needed a wire and sound system, again, it's Pig's job. We needed an alarm system, yup, it's definitely Pig's job. We badly needed props, and only Pig can do the best job in that. As Rob and I got our tools together and a list of items we needed from the hardware store, Pig found the keys to a large truck.

Prior to leaving, Pig found me and asked, "Are there rules specific to my duty that you might want to advise me on, sergeant?"

"Would it do any good?" I responded.

"Probably not," Pig answered.

"Then go be yourself," I told him and out the door he left.

Knowing him, the feds would be his first stop and victims; the auto theft task force his second stop; and all police department property rooms in between.

On the trip up to the Brookdale's I asked Rob if he wants to be one of the under covers in this operation.

"What about you?" he responded.

"I'm getting too old for this stuff, making mistakes that I would have never made before," I responded.

Silence for several minutes followed and then Rob said "I would love it; I think I can handle it."

"I knew you could, even way back 17 years ago when I first started training you, and you have turned out to better than I ever thought of you," I quietly mentioned to him.

Silence, his mind was whirling but mine was at ease. It was a pass the torch moment and he was clutching the torch. It was in capable hands.

Arriving, we stashed our large framed holstered firearms under the front seat of the truck and placed smaller pocket pistols into our pockets. We would never be unarmed, especially on this stage. We opened garage number 46, backed our truck slightly in so we would not be easily seen working, and quietly began cutting in the doors that inter connected the garages, 46, 45, and 44. Shelves were then installed, those plastic cheap ones that I had stolen from my own garage. More shelves of wood were built for small speakers, not ones that would actually work but ones that would conceal pin cameras that Pig would "acquire" from one of his "sources". Posters of scantily clad females were pinned to the sheetrock walls. "House rules" were hand written onto one of the walls in garage 46 that read like this.

HOUSE RULES

1) Use it, put it away.
2) Make a mess, clean it up.
3) Break it, buy it.

4) Drink it, replace it.

5) Get arrested, you don't know shit!

6) If your girl is hot, have her bring a freind!

We purposely misspelled friend, seemed appropriate.

Running low on carpenter work for garages 44, 45, and 46, we closed the door to 46 and drove around behind and unlocked 52. After opening the door we began to build the secret room. We had to be careful with this work and could not be seen doing it. We kept the garage door half closed as we worked cutting, fitting, and wiring the wire room. It was late afternoon when we heard a truck park outside of garage 52. Checking, we found it was Pig arriving with his day of bounty hunting treasures. As I watched Pig slide out of the cab to his truck I noticed that grin that told me I probably should be worried. I wasn't disappointed.

"What have you got for us?" I asked with some concern.

"Some of my best work," he smiled as he opened the rear canopy cover, "mother lode," he bragged.

Inside I don't see the miss match of his usual gatherings but items that were neatly placed into large black pelican hard shelled cases that had large latches and places for locks to be used. I quickly reached up and shut the canopy door.

"Rob, move our truck. Pig, back your get away truck into the garage so we can have a proper peek at your stuff," I said.

As they finished moving vehicles around, Pig had the truck backed into the garage and now we could examine the contents. I grabbed the biggest plastic box and slid it out onto the tailgate. Opening I found cameras, lots of cameras. Pinhole cameras and other cameras that can be controlled by a joy stick from afar and a receiver system that would not only power up the system but record all cameras when in use. Also in the back of the truck was a brand new portable alarm system known as a Varda. The alarm was wireless but the camera system was not. Also in the truck were car parts: bumper, fenders, and a damn fiberglass engine hood for a Honda and a complete dash from yet another Honda! Suddenly I got the feeling I wished I wasn't his damn sergeant.

"Damn Pig, I gotta ask and I'm not so sure I want to hear your answers," I said to him. "Where did this stuff come from and who are we hiding it from?" was my first question.

"Well I found the Varda system on your chair in your office, must have arrived via mail this afternoon. The camera system is Tacoma's, and the car parts came from the auto theft task force" he finished.

"Perfect timing on the Varda system," I mentioned. "I had got authority to order it weeks earlier and did so. We wore the older Varda system out and seriously needed a new one." "So ... I'm a little worried you managed to make off with the camera system from Tacoma P.D." I pried further.

"Actually I got it from a tech guy I know, had to tell him we had something big in the works and he would be involved as soon as we got it up and running. He practically threw the stuff at me," Pig said with a grin.

"It's late in the day, let's start fresh tomorrow; put your truck in one of the alarm garages at the shops, we'll pick you up," I said, and with that we closed up the garages and left.

Rob and I began to discuss how we were going to run camera wires through the attic of the garages.

"Let's get young Jedi up here, time he moves to the big leagues," I suggested.

"Agree," Rob said.

Young Jedi is the name we gave to a young explorer that followed us around when we allowed him. He was 19 and smart with the unusual mix of common sense that eluded most very smart people. He would make a great cop in the future, and did so, I learned after my retirement.

We arrived back at the police department, finished a couple of small tasks that needed attending to, and agreed to meet at the department early the next day. *Much to do,* we all agreed. I could see their excitement growing; they had bit off on the idea and now their personality of "drive" moved them forward with determination for success. As I slipped my Escalade into drive my cell phone rang. I knew the phone number; it was Sergeant Piper, supervisor of the auto theft task force.

"I'm hearing rumors, Puyallup is up to no good," he said with a chuckle.

I smiled and thought to myself *"build it and they will come,"* hell it wasn't even done being built and they were already scratching at the door. I relayed the plan to Piper and asked that he keep it under his hat till we have it built and he agreed.

"How about I send a couple of techs to you in the morning, can help get the wire room finished and I'll have other guys find tools and we have an engine puller we can use as props inside the shop," he added.

"Much appreciated," I said, ending the conversation.

The following day closed with much success. The wire room was completed, cameras were up and running; and more props arrived to decorate our stage. Oil was spilled on floors where cars would have leaked the fluid, and more posters of scantily clad women were posted on the walls. Another poster, one that would not draw the attention of male clients was placed on the wall of garage 45. It was a movie poster advertisement of Pirates of the Caribbean star, Johnny Depp. Rob had cleverly placed a pinhole camera in one of the beads that hung from his hair. He told me there was a camera in the "hair" of Johnny Depp and then challenged me to find it. I couldn't see that damn thing to save my ass. Finally Rob pointed it out to me. *"Damn"* was all I could say as I looked at it in amazement.

"Now look up sergeant," Rob said grinning and again challenging me.

"Find the camera," was all he said.

I looked up into the rafters and spotted the Honda dash that Pig had brought the day before. Inside the dash was concealed a camera, the kind that moves with a joy stick.

"Hot damn, you guys are good," I said in astonishment.

"Now look down," Rob said.

On the floor was a small spot of spilled red paint. I looked at the floor in all three garages and found three more red paint spills.

"Those are markers. They give locators to undercover detectives for suspects when they take money from the detectives for the stolen cars they delivered," Rob said proudly.

"We've thought of everything," smiling as he finished his presentation.

"I'm impressed," I said. Rob was beaming with pride that he had outdone most of my clever moments, and I didn't mind.

My cell phone rang, it was Piper.

"Hey we just got to the city limits, we have a butt load of tools and an engine puller and four of my guys that can't contain themselves. They want to see what you guys are up to," he said.

"Make sure you all skin down, no badges or anything that say cop, okay?" I responded.

"No problem. By the way, where are we going?" Piper asked.

"We will open garage 44 when you get here, back in; we are at the Brookdale apartment complex, east side midway back," I responded.

There was a slight hesitation with his response, "that takes some serious balls to put this in that complex," he said.

"Wait till you see it; amazing and perfect," I finished our conversation. "Hey Pig, get ready to open door to 44, they're coming, they will back in."

"Who's coming?" he asked, having not heard my prior conversation with Piper.

"Piper and his high rollers from the task force," I responded. "We built it and now they are coming," I continued.

As they arrived, the door to garage 44 opened and the large windowless van backed into the garage. The side doors opened and soon Piper and four of his big dogs are admiring our work. Rob, Pig, Jedi, and two task force techs began showing off their work. Eleven driven men began wandering inside garages 44, 45, and 46 looking at all that had been accomplished. Rob played his 'find the camera' game with our new guests; it was a hit of course. The group moved individually or in two man units to garage 52 and once all eleven men were inside garage 52 the door was shut and the C clamp was installed, thus locking the door.

"This is the wire room," I boasted. Quiet hesitation filled the room with glancing, doubtful looks.

"A table, a chair, and a five gallon home depot bucket?" Piper said in a questioning tone.

"Oh, yeah, the bucket is your shitter, carrying out the torcher just a wee bit longer," I said. "Pig, do the honors" I followed up.

Pig pulled out a switch blade, flipped it open, and carefully slid the blade into a crack between the back walls, made up of sheets of pressboard. Rob helped him slide the four by eight foot piece out, revealing the wire room. A 50 inch flat screen television displaying six camera angles in garages 44, 45, and 46 now lay exposed to gathering of men. As the five task force detectives began checking our work, Piper summed it up by saying "cool".

"What has your administration said about all these?" Piper asked.

"They know nothing of it," I said. "Thought I'd bring it up after you guys bought on," I continued.

"Count us in and if they don't approve we can run it with you and your team under our flag," Piper said pretty much closing the deal. Bulldog was a "go"!

The next morning, after my SIU team left for Bulldog, I found my captain in his office.

"Need to talk, got something to run by you," I said.

"What you have?" he asked.

I told him of the concept and it was cutting edge police work that has only been tried in police departments of California. I explained its design and how we would use it. He listened intently and asked, "So when do you want to start this and where?"

I love moments like this, and so I eagerly responded, "It's already set and ready to go!"

"Where is it? I want to see this," he demanded.

"Get out of those clothes and meet me back here. We will need to put a hat on you and keep you out of view the best we can. You have spent far too much time in front of a TV camera," I responded.

"I'll be back in an hour," he said and immediately left the office, leaving me seated at his desk.

At the time I wasn't sure if that was a good or bad sign. An hour or so later he came to my office. "Ready to go," he said.

I gave him the once over and found his appearance barely acceptable.

"I got a truck we can drive and when we get there wait till there is an open door then go directly inside, don't get caught outside," I told him.

"Not a problem," he responded and we made our way to the parking lot away from the police department.

When we got to the truck he asked: "How long you guys been working on this?"

"I've been thinking about it for months and about two weeks ago an opportunity presented itself and away we went."

"I knew you guys were up to something; gone all the time and quiet," he said.

I could tell by the tone in his voice that he was excited. Soon we were within a half mile of the apartment complex known as the Brookdale's.

"So this is not in a business area?" he asked.

"No, that's the best part," I responded.

In a few moments my left turn blinker was on, and we turned into the eastern entrance of the Brookdale's.

"Are you fucking kidding me? This is hell hole and you're going to do that here?" he said with great astonishment.

"Just wait, don't pull your skirt over your head just yet captain," I said grinning.

I called Pig and told him I'm arriving with the captain.

"Get a door open for us," I said and hang up. I parallel parked in front of 44, 45, and 46 and the captain got out and walked briskly through the open door of 45, and the door was shut. Not a word was said as he looked at the three garages with amazement on his face.

"Un-fucking-real," I heard him mention.

"Can I take some photos? Chief and assist chief need to see this."

I grinned as I heard the captain ask me for permission.

"Sure, just keep them under wraps," I responded.

My SIU guys were glancing at each other smiling; this plan is coming together. Rob played the "find the camera routine" act he has gotten down to a science and the captain was as impressed with it as I was.

"Where do you monitor the cameras?" he asked.

"Pig, get the door" I said, and 45 opened and the captain hopped in my truck.

"Meet you and Rob at the wire room," I said closing the truck door.

I simply slipped the rig into reverse and backed around the building and stopped in front of garage 52. Pig and Rob were already arriving from the other direction. Opening the door, we all stepped inside and used the C clamp to lock the door behind us.

Captain's response was predictable, same as Piper's the day before.

"Take a picture of that wall, the back one," I said as I pointed at the wall.

Captain did as he was told; raised the camera, and the shutter went snap. I nodded to Pig and Rob watching the Captain and me. And with that signal they turned and walked to the back wall. Pig removed his switch blade and it snapped open. Captain made a quick glance at me about the knife and I gave that "I don't give shit" look back. As the knife returned to Pig's pocket, the two of them slid open the four by eight foot piece of pressboard, revealing the contents.

"Not only have I never seen anything like this, I haven't heard of anything like it," the captain said as he stood there looking at the screen and controls before him. More pictures were taken by the captain and we left the room and got the captain out of ground zero.

"This is cutting edge," the captain mentioned.

"Cutting edge for this area but other police agencies have done it down south; I read about it, we have a solid plan," I said.

"I'm a little worried about the location," he said. "What has the management said, or do they even know what you're doing?" the captain asked.

"The manager is in on it, loves it, and we did a background on her and she is clean as a whistle," I responded.

"Have you invited the task force?" the captain asked. "You'll need help."

"Yes, they're excited out of their skulls to get started," I responded.

Nothing more was said till we pulled into the distant parking lot from the police department.

"I'm still worried about the location," the captain said.

"Look captain, I got the best people working for me. The task force and all their skill revved up and ready to go, all trying to figure out where the hell we are going to put all the damn stolen cars and stolen stuff we get," I said. "This location is the last place these sons of bitches will think would be located by cops. It's perfect," I finished saying trying to fend off the incoming tips of fear spears.

"I'll recommend to the chief that this operation goes forward, but it will be his call in the end," the captain said just before he closed the door.

I hadn't told him that the task force would run with it if our chief chickens out. That would give my administration a way out from this and they'd toss the ball to the task force and my guys would be their wingmen. My people deserve better because they are, "better".

My phone rang and it was Pig.

"What you doing?" he asked.

"Kissing some undeserving ass, why?" I responded.

"Bullshit, you not the ass kisser type; we are ready to open business," he responded.

"Everything is a go?" I asked of him.

"Everything is perfect," he replied.

"I'll let the task force know and let the games begin," I finished the conversation.

"Hey Piper, it's Gill, chop shop is ready," I said.

"Let's meet out here in the morning, all of us and brainstorm the hell out of this. The prosecutor will be here as well as the representative of WATPA, Washington Auto Theft Prevention Authority. We need the liaison between us and the insurance companies so they can drag their feet on pay outs to customers that may lose their car to us," Piper said.

"Good thinking. Prosecutor is a good idea and I had not even thought about WATPA," I said to Piper basically ending the conversation.

Pig, Rob, and the remainder of my group arrived back at the station. I noticed a bit of a spring in their step. I'd seen it before – the excitement of cops ready for a big case fringed with danger and close-calls, and this case would prove not to disappoint them.

The following morning we met at the Puyallup Police Department and converged in the offices of the auto theft task force in Lakewood. We entered through a coded door in a strip mall of businesses. As we entered we saw open offices with desk, since they use an open concept for office space with no private area. To the left were enclosed offices for supervisors and a clerk that manages money, property, and reports. Further down the hall were planning rooms and more offices for undercover officers to work out of. These rooms can be quickly sound isolated in case they receive a call from a bad guy. Further down the hall you make a right turn through a door that opens into a large room containing several large grease boards, a television permanently channeled to ESPN, and a large table lined with chairs. This is the war room. Another door leads to a storage room containing all their high tech equipment and radios, and one more door leads to a 4-door garage with enough room to park six cars and several motorcycles out of sight of the general public. All rent, some salaries, and overhead are paid for by WAPTA. Insurance companies have a big interest in curbing auto theft and they pay for it.

Most of the task force was already seated as Puyallup's SIU entered the war room. Bullshit was flying and greetings were made.

Conversation turned to the Bulldog garages and the work that has been done out there. Also in the room was a bald headed man dressed in a suit and wreaked of insurance, a representative of WATPA, and a lawyer, not any lawyer, a deputy prosecutor for the superior courts of the state of Washington. She was a tall, attractive woman that had the drive and determination shared by cops: catch bad guys and put them in jail for as long as possible. A surprise struck me when I noticed some King County auto theft task force enter the war room and took their seats. *"Build it and they will come"* played once again in my head and I smiled slightly to myself. Introductions were made and soon Rob and Pig took center stage and began to draw out the garages and showed the camera angles and how to best use them. This was Rob's and Pig's area of expertise and they did not disappoint me. Their presentation was flawless. Any questions thrown at them were answered.

I noticed the WATPA representative paid close attention to Rob and Pig, something that I learned would pay off down the road. It was King County's first look at the Bulldog garages; until now they only heard rumors and they were impressed. No one in the room had ever worked anything like it and the attitude and enthusiasm was building. Assignments were offered and volunteers snapped them up. The undercover officers were identified, one of them was Rob and the other two were from the task force. They were a solid group led by a small framed Irishman that I will call Irish. The last was a big guy who looked Russian and was a very intense man. I will call him Russ. It was a good mix —Irish reminded me of a Jack Russell Terrier, Russ was a money man and intimidator, and Rob was a quiet grease monkey who later became quite the property negotiator for fenced items from burglaries. The stage was set, roles given to the actors, support crews identified, and our very own special prosecutor ready to handle the legal battles that followed.

Shana, the prosecutor, began to speak and stated that when we identify a suspect we are to get the suspect's name and record back to her office. The points system would be figured out and how many cars we needed from the person; and at some point we would find a reason to stop doing business with them. How we would stop doing business with them would be up to our powers of creativity.

"Anyone got anything to add?" Piper asked.

No one said anything.

"Get to work then," he ordered and people started moving.

I knew what was going through their heads; it would be a race to get the first customer to the garage and it wouldn't take long. In fact it was about two days later when Rob and Pig had found a snitch that could introduce players to the garage; and Irish and Russ had found a high roller snitch that could introduce a herd of suspects to the Bulldog garage. Two days later we were off and running.

The parking lot of the bakery on South Hill was peppered with detectives as was the side roads leading to and from the bakery. A guy named Cromwell had heard from the street of a group running a chop shop somewhere in Puyallup and was buying up stolen cars. He wanted in and agreed to meet us at the bakery. Cromwell met with Irish and Russ, the three men shook hands and a light conversation broke out. The subject soon got turned to business and Cromwell point blank asked if Irish was into buying stolen cars.

"If they're decent cars, yes we are," Irish answered.

"Is that Mustang in the parking lot decent enough for you?" Cromwell asked nodding at a shiny newer model Ford Mustang in the parking lot of the bakery.

Irish glanced at Russ and nodded. Russ got up and walked outside the bakery and made a quick trip around the Ford then as he was walking back to the bakery gave a thumb's up reply to Irish.

"I'll give you $500.00 for it," Irish said to Cromwell.

"I want at least $600," responded Cromwell.

"Irish looked at Russ and asked "is it worth $600?"

Russ replied with a "yeah" and Bulldog's first car was purchased. Detectives had been listening to the conversation over a wire that Irish was wearing and by now the plates on the Ford had been ran and sure enough found the car had been stolen four days earlier from the Edgewood area just north of Puyallup. Russ and Irish stood and shook Cromwell's hand.

"Next time, bring it to our garage, I'll tell you where it's at when you have another car," Irish said.

Cromwell agreed and stated "see you soon," and the three parted company.

Russ got into the Mustang, found the flat tipped screwdriver, and used it to start the Ford as the ignition had been popped. All it took to start was simply to insert the screwdriver into the starter switch and turn it on. Irish followed behind Russ and the two of them were followed by two other detectives. Cromwell was on the phone and waiting outside the bakery. Several minutes passed by and soon a small Honda arrived with two males in it. Cromwell got into the Honda and the three men left. They were not alone but had seven detectives following them. A registration check found the car was owned by a guy named Duncan. Duncan, like Cromwell, had an impressive rap sheet that included car theft, possession of stolen property, burglary, and of course a spattering of narcotic violations. Cromwell had an outstanding misdemeanor warrant for his arrest. As I listened I reminded myself to run their parents when I got back to my office. It had become an obsession of mine that proved time and time again of the failures of parents.

Detectives followed the three to a large movie theater complex that had a large amount of cars in the parking lot. Every detective knew what was going to happen next.

"Rob, take Jedi and go to bulldog. Get the place up and running, get a hold of Russ and Irish, bring them up to speed, and have Jedi run the wire room. These guys are going to rip off one or two cars and we need to be ready," I said over the radio.

"Got it," Rob replied and they fell out of the follow.

As predicted, the Honda stopped and Cromwell and another guy got out. They dispersed into the maze of cars and detective split into two teams. They watched while being undetected and slick. Cromwell struck first and in seconds was in a red Ford Ranger. He could be seen working on the ignition area of the truck. The other guy had found a Honda Prelude and was also working the ignition of the vehicle. Soon both vehicles had been started and Cromwell led off with the two Hondas following from the parking lot. I couldn't help but notice that Cromwell was on his phone as he drove by, probably calling Irish. I later learned I had guessed right. Three of the follow detectives broke off and drove like mad bastards back to the Brookdale's and set up outside surveillance. The three vehicles were followed through traffic and back roads to escape police. Little did they know that the police were already watching, filming, and following them discreetly.

Eventually we arrived at the Brookdale apartments. Cromwell slowly and cautiously led the group to garages 44, 45, and 46. He got out and knocked on 46. Russ greeted him.

"That didn't take long," Russ said.

"Did say I'd see you soon," Cromwell replied. "Got two more for you, that truck and this Honda" he continued.

"Put the truck in here and I'll open 45 for the Honda," Russ told him.

Introductions were made once the rigs were put away and all the doors to the shop shut. All the while the group was being filmed and recorded.

Cromwell introduced his friends as Duncan and Justin. The three bragged about how good of car thieves they were and how many cars they had stolen in the past. Justin couldn't keep his eyes off the girlie posters and Duncan rummaged around and even spent several moments looking at Johnny Depp. Rob was busy "inspecting" the two cars. Rob didn't say much but had on a set of old greasy coveralls, filthy hands, and dirty rags sticking out of his rear pocket. It made for a great show on our little stage of bullshit.

Cromwell made his way to 44 and saw the mustang he had sold earlier. Good move on Irish's part for thinking of using the mustang, now prop, for the latest buy. Russ pulled out a roll of money and began laying out eight $100.00 dollar bills on the hood of the truck in 46.

Cromwell protested saying, "We need at least 900 for the two."

"Go ahead, the truck is worth it," said Irish.

Russ added one more 100 dollar bill and Cromwell picked up three of the bills. Duncan got three and then Justin picked up the last three – all caught on color camera.

Soon the conversation dwindled and the three left the garages and back into the Honda and out of the apartment complex with six detectives following. Duncan dropped off Cromwell first, and then Justin. Now detectives would follow Duncan to his apartment and we would know where to find them when the time came.

All detectives involved gathered at the auto theft task force offices, reviewed the day's events, and watched the movie captured inside of garages 44, 45, and 46. The prosecutor, Shana, had been given the names of the three and soon she called back and stated that Cromwell needed only two more cars and Duncan and Justin each needed four more cars before maxing out.

I noticed a new face at the table.

"Who's he?" I asked Piper.

"We stole him from records division. He will track of everything we do, make sure all detectives submit reports for their part in the operation, and keep files on all the suspects."

"Great idea" I thought to myself. My attention was brought back to the group when I heard a roar of laughter break out.

"Play it again; play it again," said Kelly.

The tape was re-run and you could hear Irish say "I gotta get some hair products," then runs his hands through his short red hair. He was having a conversation with three bad guys and that rolls out of his mouth.

"What's that all about?" I asked Rob.

"Well, just before you guys got there Russ and I bet Irish he couldn't get that line in during a conversation with the bad guys; now we owe Irish a beer."

"So during an undercover operation you goof balls decided that playing a "bet you can't say that" game gets introduced," I grinned as I said it to Rob.

Rob just smiled and watched the re-run again, and again laughter broke out.

I opened my computer and ran a check on Justin. I was surprised to find out he was raised in a wealthy home on the ridge overlooking the Puyallup valley. The view from that ridge was said to be a million dollar view as were the homes that lined it. The view was stunning. A person on the deck of one of those homes could see beautiful Mount Rainer in the distance, city of Orting, Sumner, much of Puyallup, and all the way to the north to Auburn in King county. If you lived there you had money and all the happiness money was supposed to bring. So why was Justin stealing cars and living in a shit-hole apartment? I pried further and soon the pieces of the puzzle began to fall together. Justin was the youngest of four kids therefore the reins of parental control had slackened. I had noticed that there are wealthy people who sometimes buy out their parental responsibility by using their money. They give the kid two or three hundred bucks on the weekend and tell them "go have fun" and kids usually do. Justin eventually got caught with oxycontin and his parents pulled on the reigns. Now Justin only responded to the reigns of oxycontin. The next thing that happens is the kid, Justin, fails at school, gets kicked out, and well if you aren't going to make something of yourself, get the fuck out of our house parenting routine. Since Justin can no longer finance his habit, he then takes up selling oxycontin tablets to finance his new cheaper form of oxy, heroin. At 19 he was stealing cars and selling them to the cops. Justin wasn't the first kid I'd seen this happen to. Over the last years as a policeman I saw this occur hundreds of times. It was an extremely sad failing of our culture. Replace love and attention with money and you will see bad things happen.

I recall working narcotics years earlier and during an investigation I arrested a 20 year old kid for selling heroin. During the interview he laid out his life to me, just like Justin's. When he finished telling the entire story I asked him a simple question "what's next?" and his answer I will take to my grave. He simply said "death". He was 20 and that was his plan, death. Two years later he was killed in a robbery attempt that went bad.

Rob's phone rang and when he answered it I knew something important was being relayed to him.

"Sergeant that was one of my snitches with some good information," Rob said. "He knows three people that are kicking the crap out of us with residential burglaries and their house is full of stolen crap. Apparently the three are having trouble moving it, he wants to meet us," Rob continued.

"Don't be shy, set it up," I responded.

Rob turned back to his phone and removed himself from the room to call his snitch back. He returned while I was talking to Piper and Pig.

"In an hour at 176th and Meridian, snitch will be there. He told me that he has to go pick one of the bad guys up from a meeting with the guy's parole officer," Rob said.

"Piper, can I steal couple guys from you?" I asked.

"Not a problem, take French and Kelly," Piper responded.

Rob, Pig, French, and Kelly followed me to another room; I had a workable idea.

"Okay guys got an idea, I'm going to make a run to the Home Depot store in Puyallup and grab some high end power tools from the manager there, and he will cooperate. Rob you're doing the undercover. The tools I get we put in the snitch's trunk. The snitch tells the guy he is meeting with you because you buy stolen stuff which he has shoplifted and you buy the stuff right there in front of the bad guy. Let him see you do it and hope he bites. Got it?" I finished. "Pig, use one of the Bulldog operation plan forms, fill in the blanks, write a quick description of what we are doing, and let's roll," I finalized my plan. "French, run this guy and make sure he is all that the snitch says he is and let's make this happen," I finished as I walked out the door.

I hustled my way to Home Depot and contacted the manager.

"Hi Jerry, need a favor," I said. I told Jerry the fast forward version of what I was doing and promised anything he gives me he will get back before close of business. Jerry then without so much as a question grabbed a shopping cart and said, "Let's go".

I've known Jerry for several years. I first met him while I was in patrol when he needed help with shop lifters, then later when I worked general detectives recovering stolen property belonging to the store. Jerry had always told me that if ever I need something, "just ask". He quickly filled the cart with some high end tools and out the front door I went. I made a swing by the police department and checked out a couple hundred dollars in buy money and called Rob. He said they are at 176th and Meridian and waiting for the snitch.

"On the way," I said and left the department en-route to the 176th and Meridian.

As I arrived, I found four detectives and a snitch concealed behind the Fred Meyer Store located there.

"French, this guy the snitch is telling us about, is he worth it?" I immediately asked.

"Oh hell yes, and the two he is working with are just as bad, we want these three," French replied.

"Your trunk is empty?" I asked the snitch.

"I think so, I'll open and check it," he said.

We then grabbed the three power tools from the back of my Escalade and put them in the trunk of the snitch's car and closed the lid.

"Does the snitch know what to do?" I asked.

"Yes, I've briefed him," Rob responded.

"Where is the snitch picking the guy up at?" was my next question.

"Just down the road near Walmart," Rob replied.

I handed the $200.00 dollars in buy money to Rob, "pay him $100.00 for the tools and he can keep the money and then just load them in your car. Make sure the bad guy sees you do it," I again told Rob.

"I got this sergeant, ease it up," Rob growled at me. That's when I realized I was acting like an over protective parent. Rob can do this.

Pig and I left to find the parole office and suitable places for surveillance and photographs. We settled in and began watching. Soon Pig spotted a guy come out of the parole office and immediately dove into his phone. After a short conversation Rob called us on the radio and said the snitch just got a call and is en-route with French and Kelly following. Rob said he is going to wait five minutes then leave to do the meet. Within minutes we saw the snitch pulled into the parking lot and picked up his "friend". He then drove to a secluded area of the Walmart parking lot and parked. Five minutes later Rob arrived and quickly located the snitch. Rob pulled up driver's door to driver's door, stopped, engaged in a short conversation, and pulled forward lining up his trunk to the snitch's trunk. Now all three men are out of the cars looking at the tools in the snitch's trunk. Soon I saw money being handed to the snitch from Rob and the three men transferred the tools to the back seat of Rob's car. Some more talk occurred between the three then I saw what I wanted to see, hand shake between Rob and bad guy. Rob left and we followed him all the way to the police department. I tried to call Rob but he was not answering his phone and I was sure it was to torment me. I later learned that it was a correct assumption.

We arrived back at the police department and gathered in the briefing room with no windows.

"So how'd it go?" I asked.

"Good, he got my phone number, said he and friends have lots of stuff and are constantly getting more," Rob replied.

"Do you guys know their names yet?" I asked.

"James Borders is the guy we met today and his co-workers are Skylar Sanders and Misty Chapman," Pig said.

"A girl is working with them?" I commented.

"She is Skylar's girlfriend," Pig told me. "According to the snitch she drives and serves as the look out while the other two bust into a home. They've been averaging two homes a day throughout the Puyallup, Sumner, Fife, and Edgewood area."

"We can't bring them to Bulldog then," I said quietly.

Pig and Rob were quick to pounce. "Why?" they asked.

"They will swamp us and the more we buy the more motivated they will be to break into more homes and sooner or later they will get into a house and someone will be there and all hell will break loose. Plus if we have to take them off in a week we jeopardize the Bulldog garages. I'll run this past Shana and see what she thinks but I don't think we should bring them to Bulldog," I finished.

Glancing looks about the room and there was an air of agreement that we probably shouldn't bring these three to Bulldog but we are definitely going to get them.

I then called Shana and informed her of what we had gotten ourselves into with the three burglars. She was excited but was worried for the same reasons I was and we would open ourselves to liability if we just kept buying stuff for the sake of keeping Bulldog open.

I returned to the briefing room and confirmed with the guys that Shana agrees we are not bringing these three into Bulldog and so we'll just do them in a parking lot that offers good filming angles.

"I'm going to bring the captain up to speed on today's activities and we need to get reports completed before we leave. This is a hell of a start," I told the group.

Before I went to the captain's office I stopped by mine first. I put the names of James Borders, Skylar Sanders, and Misty Chapman into the data base. Borders had a troubling background as did his dad; I figured. Skylar had the best shot at life of all three. He came from money, and the three bedroom house that all three lived in belonged to his parents and they allowed him, Misty, and James to stay there rent free. His childhood had been bought off and now mom and dad lived elsewhere in probably a very nice place. Misty had a troubling, abusive past and at one point in life passed out on her baby, killing the infant. In other words she was a mess and oxy and heroin were all their drugs of choice. I often wondered what parents were worse: the thugs and criminals that found stupid women to bear their children, or the bright adults that had education, made tons of money through their business or high paying jobs, and then bought off their responsibilities of parenthood simply because they were so busy to be a part of the young lives that they had sired. I decided there are no winners or losers except the children. This is a sad reality.

The captain was briefed, the reports written, and exhausted detectives left for home. I had one stop to make before calling it a day. I stopped at Home Depot and returned the "stolen property" to Jerry and thanked him for his cooperation.

We elected to simply skip going to the police department and to start our day at the task force office and brief them to our burglary angle to Bulldog. We didn't have a chance. Irish's phone began ringing and he jumped and ran for a silent room yelling back at us that it was Duncan calling. The remainder of us just sat, made small talk, and waited to see what was developing down the hall. Irish returned talking like a magpie to Russ.

"It was Duncan, he wanted to know if we were open for business today and I told him we'd be at the shop later today if he had something," Irish told us.

"Let's go sit on his house and watch him work," Piper said.

With that we vacated the building screaming towards Duncan's apartment, hopefully catch him before he leaves. First arriving detectives found Duncan's car still parked in the apartment complex lot so detectives took up positions around the area and waited. About 45 minutes later Duncan emerged from his apartment with Justin in tow. The two men climbed into Duncan's Honda and we were off tailing the two as they set out for another profitable day. We followed them South till they arrived at 176th then they turned west bound onto 176th. They made a turn just prior to Pacific Highway and landed in a neighborhood riddled with mobile and manufactured homes, and let's just say property maintenance was not a neighborhood priority.

Pig called me and said, "we are close to where our burglars live do you realize that?"

"Yeah, noticed that I could almost see the back side of their house about two miles back," I responded.

"Quite the neighborhood," Pig said, and I agreed.

Duncan pulled onto a 'gravel and garbage' filled front yard. Both men made their way to the front door, and knocked. Moments later they disappeared inside and detectives were left to watch, wait, and think.

Surveillance is about as boring as it comes. Sometimes detective must get creative when Mother Nature calls. Pig has a clever way of relieving himself even in crowded conditions. Basically he stands in the open driver's door with his right foot still in his rig, left arm draped over the top of the driver's door holding a cell phone to his ear, left foot planted back and on the ground, and his right hand aiming his junk to the ground. Someone passing by doesn't notice anything but a big guy on his phone. I've tried this technique, but frankly speaking it's a bit un-nerving to me so I do the cowardly thing, bail from my rig and dart into the woods. However, if I'm trapped in a parking lot I carry empty Gatorade bottles and just do it behind the blacked out windows of whatever rig I'm driving. All detectives working dope, or in this case, cars, carry with them usually three days' worth of food and water. During the Y-2-K paranoid days, guys including me carried sleeping bags, tents, and gallons of water, plus a week's supply of rations along with extra guns and ridiculous amounts of ammo in their rigs.

About 20 minutes passed by when Duncan, Justin, and two women left the shack they call home and climbed into Duncan's car. The females sat together in the back of the vehicle. By now we had several names associated with the address the women had been at, but we needed pictures of the gals to confirm their identity. We followed the foursome north on Pacific highway towards Tacoma. Detectives talked amongst each over radio on a secured channel debating the location the car would go. Most believed they were headed to the Tacoma Mall and the vast parking lots that skirted the massive mall. When the Honda turned west onto 72nd street the game of guessing turned with them. There was no clear cohesive guess of any one location; the guessing had a spread that would match a shotgun blast pattern on a map of Tacoma. Soon our presumptions came to a stop as the vehicle turned right into a large parking lot at 72nd street and Interstate 5. The parking lots located here supported numerous restaurants, fitness gym, and a large sporting goods store. The four slowly drove up and down each isle looking. Detectives peppered the area and silently without being spotted, watched, and filmed. Soon the vehicle came to a stop and both women got out, directly in front of where Pig had backed in. A gold colored Honda had caught their eye and that would be their prize. As one of the gals stood at the back of the car, the other boldly walked up to the driver door, slipped in a shaver key, and began wiggling it. In seconds the door opened and eight seconds later the backup lights came on. As the gold Honda moved in reverse from the parking spot, it stopped long enough for the passenger to climb in and soon both ladies were driving from the parking lot. Four detectives followed.

Duncan and Tyler soon fell in behind the ladies as they merged onto south bound Interstate 5 with all detectives following.

"Rob, you and Jedi bust ass to bulldog and get things ready, French and Kelly go with them, get set up and ready, we will be there soon," I said over the radio.

Soon I saw the detectives slid into the fast lane and their speed increased. They disappeared off the front of the follow, not drawing any attention to themselves.

Piper got on the radio and said, "If the ladies break away from the two men take what's left of your SIU guys and stay with them, we'll stay with the men."

"Sounds good," I responded.

Soon we exited Interstate 5 and now we were east bound on highway 512 towards Puyallup's South Hill. It would appear as though we were heading to Bulldog, but when the two Hondas exited onto Pacific highway and turned south on Pacific we began to wonder what their plan was. Soon the ladies turned right and entered onto the PLU campus. The streets and parking lots located at Pacific Lutheran University College were packed with cars of its students, faculty, and staff. It was a happy hunting ground for a car thief.

I heard over the radio that Piper and his crew has followed the two guys also onto the PLU campus but on the far side away from us and now occupants of both cars were searching, slowly driving among the cars in the lots and lanes. Soon the Honda came to a stop next to a parked Honda. The driver jumped out and immediately was at the driver's door of the green Honda and passenger slid over into the seat of the gold Honda and closed the door. Soon the gal was in the green Honda and as before it backed out of the parking stall.

I contacted Piper by radio and told him our girls had just scored another Honda. I learned that Justin was in the process of stealing a Ford Ranger truck.

I called Rob and let him know we have three cars on the way, "get ready, we still haven't figured out who the women are and they are better at stealing cars than the two guys," I warned him.

"We are ready and waiting, Russ and Irish just arrived; I will let them know," he said then hung up.

We followed the gals back out onto Pacific highway, north to highway 512 then east bound back towards Puyallup's South Hill. We learned Piper and his crew were about two miles behind us with the stolen Ford Ranger. The gals exited onto 9th Ave Southwest inside the city limits of Puyallup and this exit gave them access to the parking lots of South Hill Mall. The ladies entered the parking lot and found spots to park their stolen cars then they got out and were away from the stolen cars smoking a couple cigarettes. They were waiting for Duncan and Justin to arrive. It didn't take long and soon all four were standing away from the stolen vehicles smoking cigarettes and talking. Not long after Duncan took out his phone and made a call. It was a brief call and the four continued smoking and talking. After about five minutes they separated, got into their newly acquired vehicles, and left the lot. Justin led the gals with Duncan bringing up the rear. Only three detectives remained with the suspects, watching and now following them out of the lot en-route to bulldog. The phone call Duncan had made had been to Irish telling him he and friends had three more cars to be delivered. Within minutes the four arrived at Bulldog and Duncan knocked on garage 46. Soon the doors to 44, 45, and 46 opened and the three stolen cars disappeared into the garages and the doors were shut.

The conversation, transaction, and movements inside the garage were now being recorded by operators in the locked down wire room, and rescue teams were poised outside in case something went wrong inside. The constant updates from the wire room made it clear the detectives inside were in full control and everything was going good. After about 15 minutes the door to 46 opened and the four walked out. The door was immediately shut. The four climbed into Duncan's Honda and they were followed by a skeleton crew of detectives. Everyone waited and listened to the follow crew and after about 20 minutes they reported that the four had arrived back at the gal's house and were all inside. Almost immediately the three doors of the garages opened and the three stolen vehicles were backed out by Rob, Irish, and Russ. They shut and locked their garage doors and they were led out of the complex and followed by detectives. The vehicles were moved a short distance from the apartment complex and placed into a fenced and alarmed facility at the city shops. The license plates were removed and the vehicles covered in brown tarps. Once the cars were put away and Bulldog was locked and alarmed, all detectives involved retreat back to the auto theft task force for a debriefing.

Irish spoke first and stated that the two females are roommates and lived out near Spanaway. Becky is one of the gal's names and she says she got both the cars going. Lyn came alone to drive one and make a little money on the side.

"Took her eight seconds from the time she opened the door till backup lights came on," Pig said.

"So much for gone in sixty seconds," another detective remarked.

It drew some laughter, making fun of a movie with the title of "Gone in Sixty Seconds".

"A lady with talent," was a follow up remark by yet another detective.

"How much did it cost us?" Piper asked.

"They wanted 1200 and we settled it at 1100 and they split it on the spot, all on camera," Irish responded.

During the debrief I flipped on my computer and pumped the names of Becky Layman and Lyn Ridell into the data base for a back ground. Becky didn't have a chance from her day of birth, horrific! She had been raised by damn animals, not parents! I didn't find much on Lyn, actually not a whole lot, not what I expected, but then again she needed the money and didn't have the skills or nerve to steal the cars. But something was going on considering the company she was keeping.

Becky's and Lyn's names were provided to Shana and we learned that Becky only needed three cars having an abundant arrest record for theft, especially cars, and Lyn only had a misdemeanor record of shoplifting. We would use her as a witness and strip her of her newly acquired felony charges if she agreed and cooperated.

"You heard from Borders yet?" I asked Rob.

"No, nothing," he responded.

"I had hoped he would have made a call by now" I thought to myself. Maybe I was overconfident and we had not been as convincing as we thought we had been. The day would be short and successful considering we got three stolen cars. Then on queue Rob's phone sprang to life.

"Borders," he said as he disappeared down the hall with me in tow.

"What's up?" Rob answered.

As he listened he glanced at me and gave me thumbs up.

"What caliber?" I heard Rob ask and I knew then they have a gun to sell.

"I'll take the gun and I'll look at the other stuff and take what I want," Rob said.

I heard Borders still talking but not able to make out the word for word so I was on edge.

"Give me couple hours to finish up on a job I'm on and I'll call you," Rob said into the phone.

The conversation, Rob told me, was that they hit a house that day and got a gun, computers, and a new flat screen along with some jewelry. They wanted to sell that along with some they already had.

"I bought some time so we can work out the details," Rob said and we moved back down the hallway when my phone rang. It was Jennifer, the apartment manager.

"How you doing"? I answered the phone.

"Doing good. Hey, whatever you guys are doing has caught the attention of two of my better tenants," she said.

"They came into my office to advise me that whatever you guys are doing out of those garages is bad; they think you are up to no good," she continued.

"I didn't see that coming," I remarked.

"Told them I'd look into it," she said, "don't want them to call the police on you guys or that could be an uncomfortable situation," she said finishing it.

"Give me some time to think on it and I'll get back to you," I said to her and with that our conversation ended.

Rob had already returned to the war room and relayed his conversation with Borders to the group. As Pig and the group began planning the meet with Borders, I got Piper off to the side.

"Got a little problem and I got a solution but need to make you aware of this," I told Piper.

I relayed to Piper what Jennifer had told me. Till that time only the administration knew of Bulldog. If someone called the cops, well cops not knowing of the operation, and they show up, a problem could occur and Bulldog would be compromised.

"I think I need to tell my patrol division of this operation and give them instructions on what to do if they get a call to Bulldog," I told Piper.

"You trust them?" he asked.

"97% of them, but there are some haters and lazy fucks in the ranks," I responded.

"Gotta do what we gotta do," he said, and with that I began making notes as to instructions for a police response.

"You come up with a plan yet?" I asked Pig.

"We are meeting them at 176th Street east and 22nd Avenue in Spanaway. There is a gas station with a convenience store located there and kiddy corner to that is a Pierce County fire station. The fire department has a training room along 22nd Avenue that will give us an excellent location for filming the parking lot," Pig answered.

"Good, how's Rob?" I inquired.

"He's cool, calm, and collected, a little of you has rubbed off onto him," Pig smiled saying it.

"I gotta let patrol division in on Bulldog," I told Pig.

"Why?" he asked.

"Couple neighbors complained to management that they think we are up to no good, manager says she can hold them off but afraid they will eventually call police," I explained to him.

"Damn, that's a fucking curve ball," Pig responded.

"Yeah, I'll deal with it through the Captain and go from there," I told him.

Detectives moved from the offices with a solid plan and began to pepper themselves into the folds of life at 176th and 22nd to watch Rob perform. Several of us badged our way into the fire department located there and found a well-windowed room that gave us front row seats to Rob's stage and a good camera angle to record the event. We were ready to go. While watching we noticed a white Toyota Camry pull into the lot and park nosed into the West side of the building and then a large four wheel drive truck parks next to it. Detectives can see a male and female in the Toyota and one male in the truck but also noticed they have their door windows down and are talking. Detectives confirmed that the people in the vehicles being watched with spotting scopes were Misty Chapman and Skylar Sanders in the Toyota and James Borders in the truck from previous arrest mug shots. Rob was notified that the suspects have arrived and simply responded, "On the way."

As Rob arrived he nosed into the rear of the suspect's vehicle with his passenger side of the truck next to a fence. We wanted to film the suspects taking property out of their cars and placing it in the back of Rob's truck – just another clever nail in the coffin, and it worked to perfection. We watched and filmed as Rob greeted Borders first, then Sanders, and Chapman. Borders had long scraggly hair and a dirty look to him. Sander's head was shaved and rough looking, and Chapman was a small gal with long blond hair that looked as though she had been ridden hard and then re-ridden a couple more times. Life has not been good for her or to her. The four talked for a bit then Rob's attention was moved to the back of the truck and trunk of car for inspection of the merchandise.

Detectives that knew pawn shop owners had been contacted and we had been given tips on the worth of some of the stuff we might encounter and the information we had learned proved to be a wonderful tool for Rob. I watched intently as Rob moved and spoke with confidence among the three thieves. He had a commanding presence on his stage and with Pig running the behind scene action, we were clicking along like a finely tuned clock.

Soon we watched and filmed the three happy thieves taking items from the backs of their vehicles and placing them into the back of Rob's truck. Once done, we watched and filmed money exchange from Rob to the three, more hand-shakes, and soon Rob was leaving the parking lot. He had two detectives tailing him and the remainder of us would follow Borders, Sanders, and Chapman. It didn't take long. They simply went home, just a mile and half away. We stayed and watched just in case they did something unexpected but we figured they had their money, had some dope, and were doing what dopers do, get high. After several hours we withdrew from the surveillance operation and met back at the task force offices. By the time we arrived, Rob and other detectives had already figured out where the property had been stolen, two homes: one in Edgewood and one in Puyallup, both were hit earlier today and reports were still being written by officers of those jurisdictions.

"Did they say anything to you about where this stuff came from?" I asked Rob.

"Told me they got it today and said they have more at their place and would begin mixing it in with the new stuff," Rob replied.

"We need to watch them leave their house with this stuff so we can get a search warrant for the house," I mentioned to Rob.

"I think they came directly from the burglaries today," Rob said.

"We will have to use patience; we need that house," I told Rob.

He agreed and we began thinking of ways to make them leave the house to meet with us, and of course we will be watching the house from now on.

Detectives wrote reports, put away recovered property, and finally they got out of the office dragging their ass. I stopped by my Captain's home and gave him a quick briefing as to our day and made my way home. I began thinking to myself that it's only been a week and a half since we opened for business and already surpassed anything we have done in the past.

"*Six weeks,*" I said to myself. If we last six weeks without this thing caving in or cops getting burnt out, I'll be surprised.

The next morning we met at Puyallup and caught up on department business and basically showed our faces. I met with the Captain and told patrol division of our operation. I figured some, if not all, knew what was going on but that they were missing some details.

"I think it's an officer safety issue in case we get called up there, things could go sideways quick," I told the Captain and he agreed.

I constructed a memo that basically outlines Bulldog: how we operate, where we operate, and what our goal is. I also included instructions as to a police response. "Call us" before you show up was my message.

"From now on," I also told them "we will notify dispatch to send a message over your computers in your cars that we have an operation going on, and if you get called to Brookdale's for any reason let us know and we will just figure it out, as it plays out."

The memo was sent to all patrol sergeants so they could get the word out to their officers. I knew the memo would cause a stir and I fully knew which two sergeants would be a problem and it would lead to a heated topic at a sergeant's monthly meeting; but that fight was several weeks away and we'd all be loading our battle guns for that showdown.

"Hey, do you remember that snitch by the name of Jordan on our first car case?" Rob asked me as he wandered into my office.

"Sure do, is he and his old lady staying clean and out of trouble?" I asked.

"Sounds like it, he just called, said he got into a couple guys that have a stolen Honda stashed along River Road in a trailer park looking to sell parts off it. He says they stole it yesterday out of downtown Fred Meyer lot," Rob told me.

"Can he get us a meet with these guys?" I asked.

"He says he can," Rob responded.

By then I was checking my computer for a motor vehicle theft from the day before and sure enough found one reported stolen around 3 pm from downtown Fred Meyer.

"A 96 Honda," I said as I showed the report to Rob.

"That may just be the one," Rob responded.

"Get Jordan down here; I'll get hold of the task force," I told Rob as I picked up the phone.

About an hour later I heard that Jordan was in the interview room and I elected to stop by and say hi.

"How you been Jordan, and your family, are they well?" I asked.

"Yes sergeant they are and my son is growing like a weed," Jordan proudly said then added, "I got a job and we are living with her grandmother till we can afford a place." We spoke nothing more of his private life, we didn't need to.

Rob and Pig arrived and soon Jordan was dialing up our newest target, Tyler.

"Jordy here, you still have that Honda?" Jordan asked.

There is a response on the other end of the line and I can't make it out but Rob was almost cheek to cheek with Jordan listening.

"Don't sell it to those guys, this guy already told me it's worth 400 for a 96," Jordan said.

There was more talk and then I saw a slight smile came to Rob's face and a quick glance at Pig and I followed with a wink.

"Yeah he's got a truck, what's the code for the lock?" Jordan said into the phone.

"Okay, as soon as I get a hold of him we'll be over," Jordan said as he hung up.

Jordan relayed the conversation and Rob confirmed it. We learned that Tyler had verbally sold the 96 Honda to some other guys for 300 but he hasn't taken it to them yet. Tyler had a couple of buddies that he ran with and about an hour ago a guy named Collin showed up at Tyler's trailer with another Honda that he grabbed from a K-Mart parking lot in Puyallup. Collin was still at Tyler's trailer and asked that we grab Collin's bicycle from the K-Mart lot. He said it is locked to a light standard and gave the combination.

"So they have two cars?" I asked.

"Yeah," Jordan said.

"We have a bit of a problem with the task force, most of them are off training today and that includes Irish and Russ, so we need another undercover," I said.

"Was Tyler going to deliver the Honda to someone else?" Pig asked.

"Yes, some guys that have a garage up on Canyon Road," Jordan said.

"We have three guys coming from the task force and we have two ways to play this. First way is I drive the blacked out Honda with two task force guys over to Tyler's trailer following Rob who's driving the truck. While Rob gets the deal done with Tyler and Collin, the task force guys grab the two Hondas and we beat feet. Second way is have Tyler and Collin drive the Honda to the Casino and meet Rob. They do the deal there and when Tyler and Collin leave we simply recover the cars and bring them back to the shops. What you guys think?" I asked. It was pretty much unanimous, meet Tyler and Collin at the trailer, do the deal there.

"Get it on paper and let's get going," I said and we began with tasks that needed completion.

I didn't want the bad guys bringing the cars to Bulldog. I didn't want Rob alone inside the garages with these two idiots and we simply didn't have enough people to do it right.

Motivated men don't take long to get the required tasks completed and soon we were ready to make a call.

"Hey Jordy here, you guys still at your place?" Jordan said to Tyler. "I got a hold of the guy and he is bringing some of his guys to get the cars, 15 minutes away. "Yeah, he'll get the bike. Can I just tell him where you live? It's tough for me to get out," Jordan asked. "Okay, great, they'll be there soon, you owe me a little on this deal," Jordan finished and the conversation was over.

"How much have they given you for this?" Pig asked.

"50 bucks, cheap fucks," Jordan said.

"You're getting 300 from us," Pig said.

"Much appreciated," Jordan responded.

Jordan was paid and he left the building. Surveillance units left and went to find a spot to watch and take photos; not easy in a trailer park but we've done this before. Rob, Kelly, Martin and I headed for the shops to get the undercover truck and blacked out Honda we are going to use for the deal. French and Kelly are Lakewood cops and look rough around the edges, but Martin is a Washington State Patrol guy and let's just say that he looks like he should be in an institution with bars. We arrived and soon we were ready to go. We went over the plan one more time to be sure everything is straight. Rob led us out and we followed.

"Are you guys confident with shaver keys?" I asked Kelly and Martin.

"Don't worry, we got this," Martin said.

Soon we arrived at the K-Mart parking lot and began searching for the bike. Rob found it, combo lock was unlocked and the bike was tossed recklessly into the back of the truck. It was a short drive to Tyler's trailer. I don't think another word was spoken till we arrived in front of the trailer. Rob got out, greeted Tyler and Collin, and a quick assessment of the cars was made. Soon they were handing money between the three and this was a signal for Kelly and Martin to get out of my Honda and into the two stolen Hondas. In seconds the two stolen cars were running and ready to go. Suddenly Tyler jogged to the Honda with Martin in it and said something through the window to Martin. Martin looked around the dash and floorboards and soon I saw the trunk lid popped open. Tyler got a computer bag from the trunk and then shut the lid and tapped on the trunk lid. He jogged back to Rob and the three shook hands and Rob got into his truck. As Rob began to drive off, the two stolen Hondas pulled out of their parking spaces and moved in behind Rob and convoy was off, cradling the two stolen cars. I reached down under my seat, grabbed to my radio, and flipped it on. Rob was already on the air instructing the surveillance crews to stay with Tyler, Collins, and their truck.

"The laptop they just took out of the trunk of the stolen Honda is en-route to the garage off Canyon road, another chop shop. He says the laptop is stolen," Rob told us.

"Pig, this is all yours till we catch up," I said over the radio.

"Not a problem," he responded.

As we drove the convoy of stolen cars to the shops I listened to Pig and two other SIU guys following Tyler and Collin towards Canyon road.

We arrived at the city shops and got the stolen cars parked inside the fenced and alarmed facility. No time to remove plates and cover them with tarps. Bulldog had competition on Canyon Road and we would eliminate any competition. As soon as the city shops were locked I called Pig.

"Where you guys at?" I asked.

"We are in the 12200 block of Canyon Road, a house or should I say compound by the looks of it. There is a solid wood six foot fence with a six foot sliding gate and two strands of barbed wire running the top of the entire fence which completely surrounds the house and large garage. This place screams we are criminals, stay the fuck away," Pig answered.

"We just left the city shops, about 10 minutes out," I said closing our conversation.

I next dialed up Piper and it went straight to his voice mail; thought he must still be in training. We were on our own from there. Arriving, I met with Pig in a local Starbucks and he filled me in.

I learned the guys followed Tyler and Collin to this address and when they were in the left turn lane a guy slid open the front gate just enough for Tyler to get his truck through then quickly closed it. While it was open one of the detectives spotted a green Honda civic parked off to the side of the driveway but could not make out the plate. There were other cars at the location but they simply can't be seen. Detectives waited in the area to watch Tyler and Collin leave and hopefully get a better look at the green Honda inside. We didn't have to wait long and soon the gate slid open. Detectives could see the Honda but the guy sliding the gate had stopped holding the gate open and he blocked the license plate from our view. The gate was shut and locked and we elected to follow Tyler and Collin back to Tyler's trailer. The remainder of the shift was uneventful. We re-gathered at the police department for a debriefing before we called it a day.

"Hey sergeant, when Tyler calls me with another car how about I tell him we have a full load and are heading south and can't buy it now? Bet they will take it to the Canyon Road shop. We have to watch it like hawks then if they do, we get a search warrant for the property," Pig said.

"Nice, I like it," I replied. "Everyone is good with that?" I asked.

No one said anything. I think they were simply too tired to care and the paperwork hadn't even been started for the two cars we had gotten.

"Let's finish the paper and get out of here," I said as I left the room.

It was getting late and the paper was trickling into my office as my detectives completed it when I got a call from Piper.

"Piper here, what you guys been up to, heard you got some cars and found a chop shop?"

"That pretty well sums it up," I replied.

I relayed to him the day and now the night's tasks and our plans to let next stolen car from Tyler or one of his friends "walk", hoping they take it to the Canyon Road chop shop giving us an open door to the property via search warrant.

"Did Irish get any calls today?" I asked of Piper.

"Duncan, he called twice and we blew him off, left a message about doing business so we think he has a car," Piper told me.

"Tell me we are doing him tomorrow, we are beat," I responded to Piper.

"So are we, we are calling it quits for tonight," Piper answered.

"Good, we'll be at your office around ten tomorrow morning," I told him and we hung up.

Ten in the morning had come way too soon, I thought to myself as I coded into the front doors of the task force followed by the usual suspects. We gathered with the remainder of players for that day's event in the war room. Suddenly two phones began ringing and chirping and two men reached for their phones, Rob and Irish. I jumped with Rob and got to a quiet room as did Irish and Russ. Men in two separate phones plotting out their task and each one not knowing what the other was planning while the remainder of men and women simply waited in the war room where today's wild start would be sorted out. Rob's conversation was over quick but he had built in a window of time, a small window he had found a way to hold the stolen car at Tyler's. Soon Irish and Russ entered the war room and they relayed their story to us.

"It was Justin, they have three cars ready, stashed about and want to get them to the shops today," Irish said. "Told him I had a hangover but would call him when I got my shit together," Irish added.

"What you guys get Rob?" Piper asked.

"Tyler holding a stolen car; wants to sell it to us, told him we might be loaded and that I will call him within the hour and let him know for sure, he seemed good with that," Rob said.

We had enough detectives to do two operations at the same time. Four detectives would go to Tyler's location and find the stolen car he has staged there and the remainder would do the Bulldog operation and buy the three other stolen cars. If everything went as planned we would have three more stolen cars and a search warrant to be served on a chop shop by the afternoon. I'm a firm believer in "Murphy's Law", what can go wrong will, but today Murphy wasn't around and by 3 pm we had purchased three cars from Justin's little group of thieves, Becky and two new guys, Grayson and Brody. Four detectives had followed Tyler, driving yet another stolen Honda, and Collin, driving Tyler's truck to the house off Canyon Road where they left the stolen Honda. A search warrant had been written and soon detectives would serve it on Canyon Road, thus eliminating any competition for Bulldog.

After putting away the three cars from the Bulldog operation, all detectives converged on the Canyon Road address. Padlocks were cut, doors battered down, and soon three more car thieves were in custody. Police recovered four stolen cars in various forms of dismantling. We also found the stolen computer that had led us to the chop shop. A small team of police went to Tyler's trailer off River Road and he and Collin were also arrested. We wanted everything associated with the Canyon Road chop shop eliminated and since they had no ties with Bulldog would not pose a threat to the operation and we would continue to purchase stolen cars the Bulldog way. By one in the morning detectives had pretty much served, searched, seized, put away, and completed most reports. A weary bunch of men and women slipped away into the night to families that had dozed off awaiting their arrival home.

When I arrived at my office the following morning, I didn't even bother to look into the backgrounds of the five new people that we had gotten involved with the previous day. I already knew what I would find and I was in no mood to start my day with disappointment.

Over the next month we ran Bulldog and soon had collected more cars and more names of people that stole the cars, delivered the stolen cars, and every one of them had a drug problem and had a bad upbringing. Then one day we met a young guy by the name of Dylan. Dylan had been introduced to Rob during a property buy at 176th and 22nd by Borders, Sanders, and Chapman. Dylan brought with him the usual type items stolen in burglaries that included a remote controlled airplane. A quick check of the data base and we learned Dylan is a 360 guy, steals everything and anything and his family was just an up standing bunch. Detectives contacted the victim of the burglary where the remote control airplane had been stolen and learned that not only had Dylan cleaned him out but had used the victims' van to haul off all the goods. Detectives started doing surveillance on Dylan's house that was located one mile from the Canyon Road chop shop we had busted only weeks earlier. A quarter mile down the road was a grocery store where detectives would take breaks or eat when I spotted a guy on a Schwinn Paramount. Paramounts at the time were Schwinn's top of the line bicycle and the guy riding it clearly had no idea what he was doing. I did a quick data base check and found that a Schwinn Paramount had been stolen only days earlier in a burglary of a Puyallup home. We continued to watch the guy riding the bike then he rode off and ended up at Dylan's house. A quick check and we found out that the guy is Gavin, Dylan's older brother. We continued doing surveillance when detectives learned of a vacant lot behind Tyler's rented house that gave detectives a view of the back yard area and spotted the stolen van taken in the burglary. A search warrant was secured. While waiting to serve the warrant the following morning, detectives watched Tyler arrived home driving a stolen 2008 Kia Spectra, followed by his girlfriend and Tyler's dad! Talk about some quality father-son time!

During the service of the search warrant, Dylan, Gavin, and dad elected not to go with the pre-planned program and in a violent 30 seconds got their collective asses kicked. Dylan was armed with a loaded stolen stainless steel 9 mm semi-automatic handgun in a shoulder holster. Hours later during the interviews of the three, dad was more than willing to throw his sons under the bus claiming they were out of control and he had just arrived there to try to talk them out of their lifestyle. Dylan refused to talk to detectives but Gavin had no problem tossing dad under the bus claiming "he does the same thing as us, sometimes helps." Checking dad's background, we learned Gavin was telling the truth.

It took detectives all day to get all the stolen property from the home. We even called two victims to come get their stuff after it had been processed because there was so much of it. Both victims were delighted as they felt they would never see their stolen items again. By day's end three relatives went to jail, two stolen vehicles recovered, and approximately 600 stolen items collected and some returned.

Summer had arrived and with it vacation time. It was beginning to get tough to open Bulldog when most people were gone on vacation. The prosecutor, Shana, wanted the burglary portion of Bulldog shut down. She had reviewed the reports and took notice when Dylan had been caught with a stolen shoulder holstered firearm and now she just read the report of how Skylar had called Rob while he was doing a burglary standing in the victim's house asking if he, Rob, wanted to buy an Xbox system he was looking at.

Detectives were nervous too and we turned most of our attention to Skylar, Misty, and James and getting them off the streets but we also wanted to search their house. Finally we got a break. Skylar had called Rob about meeting up as he and others had some property to sell. Skylar told him he couldn't meet till later that day around 3 pm. This bought us time, valuable time to get to the back of the graveyard that border their home and gave us a view of it. Two detectives in camo disappeared into the woods and found a view of the home and hunkered down for a long wait. Both cars were in the driveway out front so there was a good chance that Skylar, Misty, and James were inside the home. At approximately 1445 hrs the garage door opened and out came the three loading items into the back of the car and truck. Photos were taken and soon the door to the garage was shut and the three took off to meet with Rob. We now had the means to secure a search warrant and would do so and bring the three to justice. The burglary portion of Bulldog was coming to a close.

Early morning the following day, the doors were battered down as we had done so often and the three were taken into custody. None were willing to talk to us but we didn't need their cooperation. I did get a call from Skylar's parents. They acted shocked! Their son was using drugs? Their son was stealing from homes? Their son was arrested by the police? All I could think about was how "out of touch" they had become of their son's life and his activities. If they had just visited they would have known but they didn't bother and chose to keep their heads in the sand. Ignorance is bliss. Honestly though, the parents had chosen that path years earlier when they opted out of his life.

Detectives were burning out; hell I was even burning out. The prosecutor was totally fried and she agreed that Bulldog had run its course. We had quit buying from some of the bad guys. We have gotten enough cars from them already, yet they were questioning why we weren't buying anymore. What we usually told them was that we needed to run low key as we were drawing too much attention to ourselves. But then they would learn that we had bought a car from one of their friends. It was surely time to pull the pin.

The prosecutor provided 21 arrest warrants and with that detectives and patrol officers went to work rounding up the 21. Not one of them contested their arrest and eventually the lawyers worked out the sentencing. Some got maximum sentence, others got less, but all were convicted.

Now a new daunting problem existed: returning the 3000 pieces of jewelry, computers, televisions, I-pads, guns, and just about everything that could be stolen from a person's home. The nine cars we had gotten from Tyler and Collin and the other Canyon Road chop shop had already been returned, as did Dylan's two stolen cars he got caught with, but 26 cars we had actually purchased in the Bulldog garage now needed to be returned. The police administrations of all departments involved were salivating and could barely stand themselves and wanted desperately to make a press release. I had heard of debates on which department would take credit for Bulldog but it was sired, raised, and built on Puyallup turf, therefore Puyallup's administration would launch the media circus.

Detectives knew all too well that media was going to try and find a negative angle for good police work and we had outguessed them. We knew they would work their asses off looking for an upset victim because some of the cars we have had for over six weeks and surely that would generate a controversy.

A captain got in front of a television camera and made a press release about how great Bulldog had worked out and what detectives from multiple departments had done, working in harmony as a team combating crime. The press was invited to the city shops where all 26 cars had been parked in a group with the tarps removed. Victims overwhelmed our call center. "Did the cops find my mother's lost locket?", "did they get my car?" they'd ask.

Detectives began calling victims that had been identified. We would meet the victims at a remote spot away from the city shops, tell them what we had done and that we had had their car the entire time because we needed to protect the undercover detectives. We would gauge their response and pleasantly learned that 25 owners were not only supportive but volunteered to go onto camera and tell viewers they were pleased the police were working for them. One was pissed off. We left him at the remote spot, slipped into the media frenzy at the city shops, and simply drove his car to him. I gave him my business card and the name of my captain for him to make a complaint to but it was the last I heard of him.

Detectives had gathered at the city shops and watched the three major news outlets of the Puget Sound area pounce on the owners of the cars. "Are you upset that the police had your car so long?" they would ask. Not one victim, not one citizen complained to the press. Just the opposite; they praised us, loved our work, and it spoiled the media angle. They had no choice but to report the truth. One man told the press that he had to buy a car to replace the one that was stolen so now he has an extra car. The press pounced on him.

"Are you mad at the cops, after all they made you buy another car?" they asked him.

"I got a kid that just turned 16, I'll let him buy it from me," he said smiling.

Having failed to twist the story into a media generated lie that would have turned the cops into bad guys, the press got their un-glorified and un-modified story and left.

Detectives began calling burglary victims and set up a Saturday for all of us to meet at the city shops. We opened our entire garage, all four garage doors, and set up tables and grouped the 3000 items atop and around the tables and tried to keep items that were purchased together, thinking most of that stuff would belong to the same victim. Many of the items had already found their owners with help of detectives that had identified the victims through police reports. Those items that had yet been returned were set aside waiting for the owners to verify that detectives had guessed correctly. When I stepped back and looked at the enormity of the filled garages it looked like an out of control swap meet.

As the victims of the burglaries began to assemble, we closed the garage doors and waited till all that had made arrangement to come to the shops came. Most had copies of their police report and for those that did not have a copy a detective would provide one. Once everyone was present one of my detectives gathered them around and simply told them that they would be on the "honor" system and we had full confidence that they would only identify items that had been stolen from them. If they found something of theirs they needed to contact a detective and a more thorough inspection of the item could be made. With that we opened all the garage doors and went about the business of reuniting the stolen property with the owner. This event devoured most of the day and by the time the last victim left there were about 80 items still unclaimed. Most the items were trinkets and jewelry but there was one shotgun and one small flat screen. I noticed a locket on the table that appeared to be an antique. Opening it I found what I believed to be two initials and a last name with what I believed to be a date of birth. I then dove into my computer and quickly realized I was in over my head and summoned the young Jedi for assistance. I showed him the locket, the name and DOB and said "find the owner" and he pulled his seat up to my computer and got to work.

About 15 minutes passed by when I heard Jedi say "hey sergeant, found the owner," and I approached him. "Here are the victim's name and her phone number," he said pointing to the screen.

"That's not the name in the locket," I said.

"No the name and date of birth in the locket are that of this woman's grandmother," he said smiling.

"I don't even want to know how you figured that out," I said as I dialed the phone.

"Hello, Detective Sergeant Gill here, Puyallup Police Department, have you been the victim of a crime recently?" I asked.

She responded by saying "yes, about a year ago a box of jewelry was stolen from my car in Tacoma," the voice of an older lady replied.

I gave the woman our address and asked if she could meet us here as soon as possible and inspect the items we still had and she agreed. About half hour later she arrived and I explained what we had done and now we were trying to find owners to what we had left. I took her to the only table left with items and asked her if she saw anything familiar. Almost immediately she reached out to grab the locket and opened it. Tears welt up in her eyes as she clutched the locket close to her chest and went to one knee sobbing. When she regained her composure she asked how I had found it and I pointed to young Jedi, "Ask him, he figured it out."

"It was in a Tacoma police report you made a year ago, you described the locket and the first two initials and last name of your grandmother with a date of birth of 03/13/69. I assumed that really means March 13, 1869," Jedi finished telling the story.

"She gave it to me the day she died asking that I pass it on in the family, it had been given to her by her mother when my grandmother was born," she told us. "The day it was stolen I was taking it to a jewelry store for cleaning when I recklessly left it in my car outside the Tacoma Mall. I was devastated when I found my car window smashed and the box gone," she said wiping tears from her eyes. "I can't believe you found this; a miracle," she said as she thanked us prior to her departure.

With little left to do we gathered up and left for the police department. When I got to my office there was a note attached to my phone from the captain.

"When you get back to the office grab your guys and meet me in my office, you're going on tour!" the note read.

I grabbed Pig, Rob, and decided to take along young Jedi. After what I had just witnessed him do for a little old lady, he would not be ignored. As we entered the captain's office he told us to find a seat and closed the door.

"What you guys did is nothing short of amazing. The chief was at a Police Chief and Sherriff meeting today and a Deputy Sherriff Sergeant from the Edgewood district announced that since Bulldog has been taken down they have not suffered one burglary in their community and I might add neither has Puyallup! A representative of WATPA has contacted our chief and wants you guys to put together an hour or so long power point presentation. They want you guys to spread the word and get other police departments to replicate what you have done. WATPA is paying the entire costs of the tour and is currently setting up dates and locations they have identified wanting the training, your skills, and your mind set. There will be one a month, so far they have made arrangements in Olympia, Everett, Spokane, Centralia, and two more they haven't yet told us of. You guys game?" the captain finished, asking with a big smile.

I looked at Jedi and asked, "Can you set up a power point?"

"In my sleep," he responded back.

"We'll do it," I said to the captain.

Over the next couple weeks a presentation was put together, mostly by Jedi with our support. When we rehearsed it we tweaked it and rehearsed it again and finally it was played out for the command staff. They loved it and in January of 2012 our first tour stop was Olympia.

As I watched and listened to Pig and Rob making the Bulldog presentation in Olympia, I thought back about those nights in the seventies and early eighties in Sumner, and the people I had met. Carl and his hat, Pig weaseling out of a ticket, Mable and her business, Frank the war hero, little dogs, men pretending, failures of fathers, a man with a bow and arrow, and another with a gun. Bulldog was a magnificent piece of police work that could only be completed by driven men and women dedicated to duty but it would pale to the pride I had felt when people of a small community would bestow on me the power of trust and faith in their protection. I learned to be humble, strong if needed, trusting, and compassionate. How lucky I am for being a policeman. At that time I thought retirement would be in a couple years away when I turn 60. Little did I know then that it was only just a few months away.

*Once the badge goes on, it
can never come off whether
they can see it, or not, it
fuses to the soul through
adversity, fear and adrenaline
and no one who
has ever worn it can ever
sleep through the 'call of the
wild' that wafts through
the bedroom windows in the
deep of the night.
(Author Unknown)*

Gangs & Teens

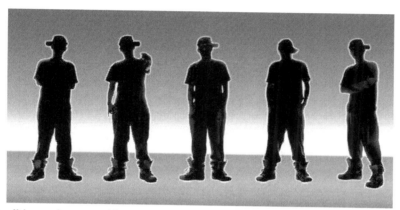

We all know how stupid teens and gangs can be. Yet there is no excuse for any bad behavior. There is a consequence for every wrong thing we do; and the earlier we learn this, the better. The "learning" part is never fun, yet hopefully it teaches us to correct our wrong. I believe I have been a catalyst of this learning experience for some of the teens and gangs I have dealt with in my cop career. As to whether they have learned from it or not, I don't know for the most part, except for one guy in the story you will read. I hope they all did. And even if they have not, at least I can say that I have done my part.

Tacoma was infested with gangsters, lots of gangsters, from the hilltop district to the Eastside and southern districts. Many of these gangsters thought nothing of shaking down some little kid for his or her fair ticket and away they'd go. These morons would then "gang up" with their gangster buddies and come to our quiet little town and of course meet other dumbass gangsters attending the fair on some little kid's ticket and let the turf war begin. Fights were common: gangsters fighting with high school kids, fighting locals, fighting other gangsters, and of course, my favorite, fighting the police. At times it was a free for all. The fair would let these idiots into the fair and then act surprised when all hell broke loose.

Chapter 22

Mace Rain

It was the summer of 1979 at O'dark thirty and I was in the office complaining to Carl about nothing out there to do.

"Kid" Carl said, "If you want to find something to do on a quiet night in this town, drag a bicycle out of the property room and take it for a spin, you'll hear it going on."

After thinking about it, I convinced myself that Carl might be right. It took some time, but the thought of me – pistol packing, badge wearing cop to throw a leg over an old crappy bike and take to patrolling the mean streets of little old Sumner, all the while wearing cowboy boots and a uniform – took a bit to set in. In time it would prove to be truly brilliant!

I found the right night. The drunks had gotten home and the town seemed to slip wearily away and now was all quiet. Or was it?

I had already scouted out the property room and located the best piece of shit bike they had stowed in there. It was junk, but the gears seemed to work and the important thing, its tires held air. I dragged it into the parking lot, hopped on, and away I went; cowboy boots and all.

After several minutes I realized this could be addictive. I loved it! I could hear people talking, fighting, the sound squealing tires, and racing engines. There was a lot going on, Carl was right.

I spent the entire summer riding a bike when the situations were right. I made note of the pitfalls and strengths and wondered what impact two cops on bikes riding the entire shift would have. In a properly prepared program and a bigger department this could make a difference in policing. It was something like the old cops of yesterday had done, walk a beat, but this time we would ride that beat, on bikes. I made notes and put them away, thinking that someday I might be able to use this information and develop a proper program.

Fast forward. It was now, a September night in 1994, warm and thousands of people out enjoying the Washington State Fair in Puyallup Washington. The fair was supposedly the 6th largest fair in the nation and tonight was proving it.

I was at the Gold gate to the fair, the main gate. My right leg was thrown over the top bar of my police issued Trek mountain bike. The bike was all black, complete with headlights and flashing tail lights that would turn on only when I needed lights. My uniform was black, mesh shirt, so the breeze would cool me down as I raced through the city streets at night hunting my next criminal. I wore a black helmet with a boom mic and earpiece mounted to the shell of the helmet and the entire system was push button operated from the handlebars of the bicycle, and or a button mounted to my black leather police belt. I wore black shorts with black socks and medium high 911 boots.

Puyallup bike cops were now leaders in "cops on bikes" programs and we were always being contacted by other departments for training and advice.

When I moved to the larger police department in Puyallup I brought with me the knowledge planted by Carl years ago, and the program was named "Wheelbeat". There were not two cops on bikes, but a unit of eight cops on bikes. Two of us had become national instructors for IPMBA, International Police on Mountain Bikes Association. It was worldwide and I was lucky enough to be part of it. Of course, Pig and Rob were along for the ride.

Cops like to stand around and talk, tell stories of their recent arrest, bitch about latest administration debacle, or make fun at something some dumbass cop had done. Tonight was no different. As this small group of cops gossiped, we monitored our radios for any activity and monitored foot and vehicle traffic on the nearby streets.

Tonight was packed; it was Tacoma night after all. The fair will give to cities' school districts entry tickets for the fair and the tickets are to be dispersed to the children of that school district on a given day. The fair would then proclaim that certain day as "Tacoma day" or "Valley day" and the kids of that school district would be let out of school half day early to attend the fair. Tacoma day was one of the more attended school days but it came with problems, big problems.

Tacoma was infested with gangsters, lots of gangsters, from the hilltop district to the Eastside and southern districts. Many of these gangsters thought nothing of shaking down some little kid for his or her fair ticket and away they'd go. These morons would then "gang up" with their gangster buddies and come to our quiet little town and of course meet other dumbass gangsters attending the fair on some little kid's ticket and let the turf war begin. Fights were common: gangsters fighting with high school kids, fighting locals, fighting other gangsters, and of course, my favorite, fighting the police. At times it was a free for all. The fair would let these idiots into the fair and then act surprised when all hell broke loose.

Fair cops were real cops, but hired by the fair to work a foot beat inside the fair grounds. It was their job to keep the place "fair like". Fair cops came from multiple jurisdictions and had permission through their home departments to work at the fair. They made good money. Anything that happened in the fair they handled. What occurred outside the fair was solely the Puyallup Police Department's responsibility.

Suddenly our radios barked out that 'fair cops' had corralled a large group of gangsters and was herding them out the yellow gate on the far side of the fairgrounds. "I could be there in less than a minute,, I responded. It would take considerably longer for a prowl car to arrive and even longer for cops walking a beat. I was off and screaming to the scene. Pig had indicated he was responding from the station located ten blocks away. I knew I'd be the first to arrive and as usual, greatly outnumbered.

I already knew what was about to happen. The gangsters had been fighting and flashing signs at each other, basically, gangster shit. Fair cops had gotten involved, but didn't want to write reports, just wanted them out of the fairgrounds, and they did so, roughly, so to speak. Some gangsters moved out of the gates talking their crap, others were physically tossed out and all were pissed off. Once outside they would turn their rage on normal everyday citizens. Gangsters would verbally insult women and children and the men of the family would protest, kind of what was expected of the man of the family, and he would flat out get his ass kicked in front of his screaming wife and terrorized children. It was like it had all been scripted. It was the responsibility of Puyallup PD to not allow this, and tonight was no different.

I smirked the first time I heard the ad on the radio about attending the Puyallup Fair. "Come dooo the Puyallup" was the catchy jingle line. It played over and over every year; it was a catchy line that, I felt, needed some help.

As I arrived I just couldn't help mumbling the words in gangster lingo, "I done came did the Puyallup, and the Puyallup did me." I smiled so slightly as I announce through my boomer mic, "244 Puyallup, arriving, yellow gate." I had a plan.

Pig or any other cops had not yet arrived so I flew by the gate glancing over at the chaos that was going on. About 30 gangsters, I estimated, yelling gangster slang, hand signs and threatening the cops still inside the gate. Families scurried from the area, trying not to attract any attention from the gangster group. I dared not stop, I'd be beaten to a bloody pulp and that wasn't going to happen. I knew of a spot next the gate that was concealed and out of sight and the dark would hide me and more importantly, what I was about to do. I wasn't about to wait till there was a victim that needed rescuing, I'd pick the fight!

After I passed by the gate I quickly veered off the road towards the fence that surrounded the fair grounds. My arrival had gone un-noticed by the gangsters. Up against the fence was a large ticket shed that was not used anymore. There was a space between the building and the fence that would conceal me but put me within a few feet of the angry mob, just behind a six foot wood fence that connected the ticket shed to the chain link fence of the surrounding fair.

Dismounting my bike, I laid it down so as not to be easily spotted by passers-by and I stepped into the dark space and pulled out my rather large can of mace.

I knelt down to a knee and looked through the cracks between the fence boards and thought of what I was about to do. This could work out and end the problem that was about to happen to some family, or I could be cornered by the crowd, that would be totally incensed by my actions, and the price would be heavy. Lastly, some dumbass do-gooder would figure out what I had done; or worse, witness it, and complain to the press or any other cop hater, and there are many, coupled with the complaints the gangsters would make, and the administration would hang me out to dry.

I had come up with a good plan, got into position without being noticed, no time to be shy, "game on assholes," I mumbled.

I let fly and judging by the angle of the stream of burning liquid that shot from the can, it would be raining down on the gangsters. I had let go a large burst of mace and now I stopped, shook the can and let go another burst till the can emptied.

I had to take a peek, and did so. I found a knot hole higher in the fence boards and it gave me a much better view of the calamity that was about to unfold before me. It looked like a small fog bank, like the ones you see melting down onto the bay, covering the area, and you could feel the thickening moisture as it slowly landed on you. On the bay I wouldn't have cared, but mace? Damn this was going to leave an impression, a lasting one I hoped. The ranting crowd began to suck in the fog as they screamed at the cops just inside the fence and the gates that protected the fair grounds.

The nonsensical ranting that roared moments earlier began to quiet as if they were all in chores, and their eyes widened as the moisture from the fog mixed with the wet in their eyes. Shit, I could even taste, smell, and feel some of the mace fog. Smelled like victory!

Now the spitting began, and they began wiping their faces with their do-rags and long baggy shirts and that only made it worse, they rubbed it in for me. The fog had coated their "colors" and now worked against their owner. This was beautiful. I took in the moment, but clearly had overstayed my unknown attendance. It's time to withdraw, while the getting is good.

Coughing, hacking, choking and spitting sounds told me I had indeed struck gangsta gold. I heard over my mic, "246 Puyallup, arriving yellow gate."

Pig had arrived but he stopped out front of the yellow gate and was watching the gangsters falling apart for no apparent reason. Then he figured it out. He hadn't seen me, but recognized the work.

Pig keyed up his radio, "46 to 44, where you at?"

I responded "over here in the dark, be there in a second."

Having already replaced my now empty mace can to my police belt I stepped into the light and retrieved my bike. I walked to Pig's location with the swagger of a victorious roman gladiator.

"Enjoying my art work buddy?" grinning as I spoke.

"Regular fucking Picasso; nice! When did you come up with that?" he asked.

"On the way here," I replied.

"I think you got a couple fair cops" he noted.

"Collateral damage" I replied, "or do I owe their pudgy asses donuts?"

"Best drop it, this will not go un-noticed" Pig warned.

"Creative police work rarely does." "Now let's herd these sons of bitches back to Tacoma," I barked, and with that we approached the caustic bunch.

We took a moment to pause and enjoy the scene before us. We tried to look like the cops inside the gate, innocent and ignorant as to what had hit these fuckers, and tried desperately not to start laughing. Although some of the cops inside were clearly pleased by my covert actions, some even grinned; we didn't have gates, fences, and barbed wire between us and "them".

They were hacking and coughing, one was throwing up. All were spitting up massive amount of snot and cussing up a storm. But they were basically helpless, rendered un-worthy of fighting cops. They truly had come to the Puyallup and the Puyallup had done them.

By now several more cops had arrived and soon it turned into a damn cattle drive. Pig and I strutted along behind the gangsters, pushing our bikes in one hand and twirling our flashy expandable batons in the other. We were packing an ass kicking and were looking for a place to deploy it. There would be no fighting, no arrests, nothing. These sons of bitches just simply wanted to get out this fucking red neck town. That works for us!

The mass of cops and gangsters completely blocked Ninth Street as we moved in a westward direction, towards Tacoma. As we passed by citizens, many nodded in approval. I wonder what they would have thought if they had seen what I did. Would they have approved? In public, probably not, trying to support the idea of being politically correct of the nowadays, but in private, I think they would have giggled with glee.

It took several blocks before the mass had disintegrated into the night. Cops were gone too, following what was left of the trouble makers, but their fire had been put out and their fair visit ruined. The remainder of our evening would be uneventful.

It was about 1100 pm and Pig and I rode silently around the fairgrounds, in alleys and parking lots looking for trouble but found no more that evening. We would stop and make fun of the views we had tonight, we could laugh now and laugh we did. Pig would do one of his classic re-enactments of some asshole he watched reacting to what mace will do to a person. He was hysterical and our laughing would reduce our stress of the evening. Following his act, we would ride off again, only to stop and comment on another view we had witnessed that evening.

We both agreed on one thing, silence would be golden for this event, at least for the time being, but someday, it would just be another story of small town cops. It would be told.

I couldn't help but think of Carl, his comment of hearing what was going on at night while riding a bicycle on patrol. How that idea he planted in my head so many years earlier had transformed into a window that gave me a vision to create Wheelbeat.

A cop on a bike had got to the yellow gate first, well ahead of any foot patrol cops or motor patrol cops. A predicted problem with criminals had been dismissed and life goes on.

Carl was dressed in his cowboy boots, hat tipped down to cover his eyes from view, rolled up sleeves of some ratty shirt with cigarette in hand smiling down on us. "Nice work kid."

In all fairness to the fair and its managers I would like to note that they have since eliminated "Tacoma night" and re-arranged how tickets are distributed throughout the school districts. They have also taken aggressive steps to eliminate gangster activity completely. "Colors" that are associated with gangsters and any gang signs have been completely banned from the fair and if any colors appear inside, they are either removed or the person is kicked out. Gang signing is also a guaranteed removal from the fair. Well done!

Chapter 23

Hey Larry, Over Here!

I believe I mentioned in an earlier story that there were times I couldn't believe I got paid to do police work. This happens to be one of those times!

It was October, 1995, the fair had come and gone and my little town was getting ready for winter. I was working my favorite shift, 6 in the evening till 6 in the morning, 12 hour shifts, 4 shifts on, then 4 off. After the fourth night of working, one was ready for the four days off.

My usual routine was attend briefing at 5:45, then hustle to the parking lot, check my patrol car one last time and leave. The department wanted no less than two tickets from each officer working, per shift. Don't confuse that as a quota, that would be illegal, but you better have at least your two tickets by the end of shift or there would be hell to pay.

I hurriedly moved to the street and found two unlucky citizens that would fulfill the department's "it's not a quota" quota, then I could begin some real policing, Wheelbeat.

I was usually on the bike by 10 at night, checking alleys, parking lots, and of course "Indian country". Indian country was a strip of woods that lined the Puyallup River banks on one side and civilization on the other; in between those two was "Indian country". The area was crisscrossed with trails and dirt road and was a very attractive area for narcotic and alcohol violation, or if one wanted to commit something more sinister, it was a good spot to go and not be seen.

Indian country had earned its nickname by the amount of crime that occurred there. So if you plan to go into Indian country, best have a partner or at least a viable backup plan cause chances are, shit would happen.

Smart cops usually didn't bother wandering into Indian country. The entire area was surrounded by sand that had been deposited there over the years and all one needed to do was ride the upper levee trail turned jogging path and check for tracks indicating if someone had entered into the alluring area. Nothing on this night was found.

I had recalled that recently there had been a rash auto prowls in some apartment and residential areas below the hospital. It was a large neighborhood where families were raised, jobs filled nearby, several grade and junior high schools, and freeway access.

And with success and comforts of living come nice cars, many of which contained magnetic valuables that people with money couldn't resist, and it also drew criminals to the area.

The weather was wet and now that fall had arrived the temperatures had dropped. During this time of year bike cops dressed a little warmer and were prepared for the rain that the northwest would bring. We had gortex everything –pants, jackets, and gloves. All in black with only the jacket bearing the word POLICE in large silver reflecting material. With this uniform we could remain out of sight most of the time and by simply moving into a lit area we would only then be clearly visible. It was perfect for our needs.

I had finally worked my way to the area across town from the Indian country. It was quiet and I slowly rode through the neighborhoods and apartment building staying undetected, always watching ahead for movement. At times I would find a dark place that afforded me a view of an area, usually a long strip of road where I could easily see movement telling me something was going on.

I had found a spot in the middle of long hedge on the North side of a set of apartments named "Rattle Back", right at the base of South Hill. It was a notably good piece of real estate for me to hunker down in, giving me views of four parking lots and two long roadways. I stood, watched, and listened.

After about 20 minutes, I heard an apartment door open just above me, where I was standing. Two young men stepped onto the landing then ran down the stairs into the parking lot. Both got into a white piece of shit 4-door Honda Civic.

I'm not sure what the attraction is to Hondas but kids seemed to love them and so did criminals. They were easy to steal. I could do it simply with a shaved key. In the coming years it would prove to be a useful skill that I had to use on occasion.

As the young men got to the car, I recognized the passenger as a kid that had been to my home on several occasions to goof off with my son. As the two progressed into Junior High they slowly parted ways. At the time he was a good kid and never gave me any problems. His name was Larry.

Larry pretty much looked the same as he had when he was but a boy, just bigger and now perhaps 19 or 20 years of age. I did not know the other kid. I watched as they drove off eastbound on the nearby street. They had not noticed me.

I continued watching and listening.

Another 30 minutes passed and I heard radio traffic from a 911 center put out to motor patrols that a homeowner had just caught two young men breaking into his truck parked on the street in front of his house. The victim reported that the young men had run from his vehicle on foot, Westbound, but felt that they had left their car behind in their haste for escape. The victim stated the car was a white 4-door Honda Civic. Soon thereafter I received radio reports of the descriptions of the suspects and I was now convinced it was Larry and his buddy.

As I began riding towards the area to assist in searching, which was close, less than a mile, it hit me. "They were running and left their car behind" could only mean one thing: they're on the way to me! Why leave now? This is going to get interesting.

I notified radio that I was sure who they were and where they were going and asked that patrol cars stay back till I needed help. This brought a flurry of questions, of which I had no time to answer as I had already detected movement about three blocks away and heading towards me.

It was the young man that I did not know, the one that had been with Larry. He was alone and running for all he was worth, glancing over his shoulder, looking back. I was still in the hedge row, surrounded by tall thin cedars that were bushy and provided perfect concealment in the dark and best yet, lined the sidewalk this young man was running on.

As he got closer to me I quietly removed a set of handcuffs from my belt and was prepared to use them when he slowed and looked one last time over his shoulder. Then he stopped directly in front of me, back turned and completely unaware of neither my presence nor my intentions.

It was too simple, within seconds I had him, arms and hands behind his back and he had by now glanced over his shoulder and saw a policeman. It was the usual look of astonishment that I had witnessed many times before. Having the handcuffs in place I pulled the young man back into the darkness of the bushes that had concealed me so well. I introduced myself and asked what his name was. He said "Jeff".

"Well Jeff, you and your buddy broke into a car in my area and I'm afraid to tell you, you're under arrest." I got no response.

I continued to watch for Larry to arrive and didn't have to wait long. However, Larry was on the same street as I, but he was across the street and had yet to cross to my side. If he didn't cross soon, he would be past my location and therefore difficult to snag since I already had one guy in hand. I had a plan, and things were going to get fun.

I whispered into Jeff's ear and told him "I'm going to push you out of the bushes into the light and I want you to yell to your buddy saying COME HERE, ok?" I said.

Jeff simply looked over his shoulder at me and said "fuck you". Predictable and yes, understandable but it had been worth a try, so now plan "B".

Larry by now was almost directly across the street from us. Now or never I thought. I pushed Jeff out into the light. I had grip on the back of his jacket between his shoulders with my left hand, had a firm grip of the handcuff chain with the other. Only Jeff could be seen by Larry, all but my hands remained in the dark and Larry would not be able to see me.

I yelled "hey Larry, over here."

Larry stopped and looked directly at me and Jeff but only saw Jeff. Larry, upon spotting his buddy, responded with a big toothy grin, looked up and down the street and ran to me. As he got close I pulled Jeff back into the cover of dark and within seconds Larry was across the road looking over the street for any sign of the cops.

He saw nothing, till my right hand burst from the bushes and I grabbed him by the front of his jacket. As I pulled Larry, I stepped into him and his forehead hit the front area of my bike helmet.

There we three stood, on the sidewalk, 1:30 in the morning: Jeff in handcuffs and the connecting chain in my left hand; Larry and me, nose to nose, and me with a solid grip to his jacket.

"What the fuck, Larry? Breaking into cars now?"

"Sorry Mr. Gill … huh Officer Gill" Larry blurted out stuttering as he spoke, clearly rattled by the surprise of my sudden appearance.

"I'm very disappointed in you!" I muttered. "Turn around Larry; you get bracelets too, no favoritism here."

With that, it was over, Larry kept saying he was sorry and kept his head hung low.

While waiting for a patrol car to show up and transport the two, Jeff started giggling to himself.

"What's so funny Jeff?" I asked.

Then Jeff busted up and yelled "Hey Larry, over here!"

It brought a grin to my face but I clearly understood now it would be awhile till Larry lived this one down.

I was outside and basically doing nothing when my son stopped by. He was rummaging around my garage looking for something when we started talking. Then he asked if the Larry story was true. I wasn't sure what story he had heard, then he cleared it up. Seems as though he had been attending a large party several weeks earlier and in the middle of the bustling noise of the party someone yelled "Hey Larry, over here" and the crowd busted up laughing. Larry had just arrived at the party. My son said Larry turned red but clearly it wasn't the first time he had heard it.

"Yes, it's true," I said. "And I got paid to do it."

Authors note: Last time I heard Larry is a good guy and a productive member of our community. He simply made a mistake and lord knows I've made mine.

Rotten Fruits

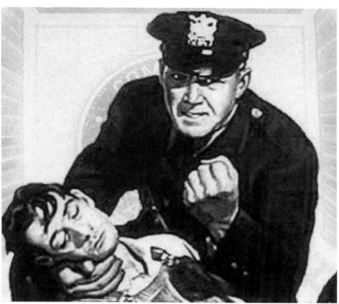

It would be nice to have no rotten fruits in the basket. However, you and I know that sometimes bad fruits get in the mix of the good fruits. They all look the same until you discover the rotten ones. Sad to say, the Police Force is not exempted from these bad fruits. It is not good though to assume that just because there are bad fruits, everything is bad. Let me now expose to you some of the rotten fruits I have directly encountered in my career.

I was standing next to my open door of the driver's seat and had continued my wipe down process. Manning walked over to my patrol car and looked into the back window of my car to see whom I had in custody. Manning was not alone. He had with him a young guy, one I knew, one I had shared many a trips with to the police academy, Jim. We shared rides to Burien every morning. One week mine, the next week his', rotated the weeks till we finished the academy and helped each other study when there was a need.

Chapter 24

Bully with a Badge

It's about surrender, discipline and jurisdiction, mixed with the confident responsibility of the conqueror for the protection of the conquered (Author Unknown).

It was the summer of 1980 and I had completed the Washington State Police Academy several months earlier. I spent many hours seated in an abandoned grade school filled with desks meant for children that was now turned into a police academy. Actually the academy lasted only about seven weeks and we were turned lose, back to communities be it police departments or county sheriff. Since I had three years as a military policeman and now about a year and a half with civilian authority, I no longer considered myself a rookie. Seasoned cop, not yet; I had plenty to learn, but the difference of right and wrong, bullshit and truth was something you are raised with.

I was working graveyards alone when I received a call of a man wearing only Levi's jeans and was pounding the front windows of the Rainer Bank off east Main in the eastern area of town. I responded quickly, and as I approached I found what the caller had described. He looked to be about my age and build. No shoes, no shirt, and pounding on the large plate glass with his fists. He hit the glass so hard that it "rippled" with his impacts all the while screaming at the top of his lungs. I got out of my car and approached cautiously, more than willing to let the man wear himself out on the glass, better than fighting with me. I could make out in his screams that he was upset at his girlfriend, it sounded as though their relationship had come to an end and now his heart was broken. I was worried the glass would soon give way also. I quietly slipped my mace can out of its holder and concealed it in my left hand and approached the man.

"Hey, hey, calm down, calm down, talk to me, talk to me," was about all I could get in between the pounding and screaming. His screams began to quiet and the pounding of his fists slowed and his tears flowed.

He turned to look at me and said "fuck you, go ahead fucking arrest me you asshole."

"I have no intentions on arresting you, let's just talk," I responded.

By now I had slipped the mace can back into the right pocket of my jacket hoping I wouldn't need it. The man turned and attacked the window again with about the same velocity as he had displayed earlier. Enough is enough; I grabbed him and pulled him away from the windows and pushed up against my patrol car effectively pinning him against it.

"Just calm the fuck down and talk to me," I said as I stood there basically hugging him against the car.

His body didn't relax and exploded pushing away from patrol car. I simply stepped aside and used his force against him and down we went. He was now faced down on the asphalt with me behind him. I struggled for my handcuffs all the while maintaining my current dominate position on top of him. I slipped one of the shackles on his left wrist then twisted it against the inside of his left wrist bone. This is extremely painful and soon the second hand cuff was in place. I stood him up and leaned him up against the patrol car, again. He leaned there with his head hung low and sobbed. I was busy with a towel wiping sweat from my arms, his sweat, and then wiped his face. I continued to stand there as he slowly regained his composure. I contacted my dispatch that had been trying to check on my "status". I told her I was okay but she had already contacted a nearby city and asked for a patrol car to check on me as I had not answered my radio.

"You can cancel them," I said over my radio.

"Received" was all she said.

"Talk to me, what is this all about?" I asked.

"My girlfriend left me for another guy," he said.

Tough spot for a guy or gal I thought to myself. "You must have loved her, you were going nuts," I said.

"Never been in trouble with the law when I was with her; never was in handcuffs for the last two years with her; she is gone for two hours and look at me, in handcuffs," he said.

"Not her fault, you own this one," I replied.

I glanced up and noticed a patrol car from a neighboring jurisdiction enter the parking lot. I knew who was driving it and didn't much care for his type of police work. He was old school, real old school and loved to kick people's ass.

"Great, those guys are here," he said. I used to live in their town and they'd kick the crap out of me" he spoke again.

"Get in my car," I said as I opened up my back door.

The guy slid into the seat and I shut the door.

"Manning, Officer Manning what brings you to our little town?" I asked him.

"Heard there was a problem, you might need help," he answered.

"Nope, under control, guy upset about losing his girlfriend is all," I responded.

I was standing next to my open door of the driver's seat and had continued my wipe down process. Manning walked over to my patrol car and looked into the back window of my car to see whom I had in custody. Manning was not alone. He had with him a young guy, one I knew, one I had shared many a trips with to the police academy, Jim. We shared rides to Burien every morning. One week mine, the next week his', rotated the weeks till we finished the academy and helped each other study when there was a need.

"That's Thompson, he's a fucking prick," Manning said with a bit of glee in his voice. "I've kicked his ass more than once," he bragged.

Of course this lit Thompson's fuse and he responded back at Manning calling him about every name in the book.

"Why not," I thought to myself, "can't touch me, I'm already inside a police car."

"What did he do?" asked Manning. "We heard the call over the scanner but what happened when you got here?" he asked of me.

"Not much, he was pounding on the windows, wouldn't stop so I had to take him," I responded, throwing my towel across to the passenger seat.

"Did he fight you?" Manning asked.

"Little wrestling, nothing much," I responded not showing like I much cared.

"We have to get him out and kick his ass properly," Manning stated.

The comment simply threw Thompson into a rage and more name calling was directed at Manning.

"Naw," I responded, and then I said "he's upset at his gal for leaving him for another guy and now you're taunting him."

I noticed Jim smile at my comment. Then Manning did something I'll never forget; he reached down and unlatched the rear door where Thompson was seated. As Manning began to open the door I banged it shut using my left hip and quickly turned to Manning face to face.

"Not happening," I said.

I later questioned myself if I would have done this a year earlier or even six months prior. Would I have had the courage to stand up to a big valley bull as cops referred to themselves back then? I like to think that I would have, but that time had passed and I was sure of what I was doing now.

There we stood in the night, face to face; I could feel his pudgy mid-drift against my jacket, neither blinking in a show down of old school verses new school. Jim was watching too; he knew I was right. He was the first to speak to try to break a stalemate of two men with guns and badges locked in the silent battle of two valley bulls.

"Come on Manning, Gill's got it handled," Jim said.

I flat refused to be the first to blink.

"My town, my arrest, my responsibility and by the way fuck you Manning," was what I hoped he saw in my eyes.

Manning smirked and broke the stare and as he turned said, "you know if you touch a cop, you get your ass kicked."

"I'm perfectly aware of the rule, but not like this," I responded.

Manning walked back to his car telling Jim "let's go". Just prior to Jim turning around he used his right hand and crossed his chest and tapped his badge, then nodded to me. I took a deep breath and let it out trying to recompose myself. "I wonder if Manning will ever respond to back me up after this," I silently asked myself. Oh well, point made.

I climbed back into the patrol car with Thompson seated behind me. I noticed Thompson in the back seat fidgeting, trying to move to the middle of the rear seat. When he got there he stuck his head through the opening in the screen and simply said "thanks" then slid back in behind me. We got to the back of the station and I coded us through the back doors. Thompson was not a problem anymore for me. The handcuffs were removed; he was provided an orange jumpsuit and placed in a cell with pillows, blankets, and two bunk pads.

I did a half page report for the judge to read the next morning then attached a hand written note for the chief to read.

Chief, Thompson had a bad night that could have been a lot worse. You might want to speak to the judge. I'm okay if he dismisses the disorderly charge. I don't think he will be a problem for us again. Gill

I placed the report and a copy of the hand written note into the chief's mailbox and went back to work.

A Short Essay

I decided to include this portion as a follow-up to the previous story you just read. How I wish all cops are good cops. Unfortunately they are not. Some are just so proud of their badges, not to mention their education. This is the reason why I want to share this one with you. It is a document that I wrote after a Captain that oversees sergeant meetings asked that all department sergeants write a short "essay" on why they wanted to be a sergeant.

I was absolutely pissed off by his request. He was about the same age as my daughter and had pole vaulted into ranks because of his education and intelligence, but had spent no time whatsoever as a detective or any special unit to include SWAT. This I felt was nothing more than a home work assignment and it took me off the streets during the "Bulldog" operation where I really belong. This was required writing and therefore an opportunity for me.

The entire document took me about 10 minutes to complete and then I set it aside for the next month's meeting. Somewhere along the way someone must have spotted it because I was told the captain had learned of it and was going to cancel the "homework assignment" not wanting to be embarrassed. At the next meeting the captain did cancel the project saying simply "we are too busy". By the time he got back to his office it laid on his desk before him!

So, You Want To Be A Sergeant?

Yes I do and will be one when I'm ready.

I will earn it on my own terms, no where will you find "butt kisser" on my resume.

Why do I want to be a sergeant? Not sure really. After all, the hours suck, 24-7; you will work harder and smarter than ever before and if you have ever been frightened, hang on, because this is going to take some serious intestinal fortitude.

I know I will have to be smart and surround myself with the best people I can get my hands on. I will look for people with three qualities: enthusiasm, common sense, and courage. A college degree will not be on that list.

I will then have to be humble myself, to be their servant. I must provide them with training, give them direction from my experience and guidance when they struggle, and praise them in their victories.

I must be their protective liaison from administration; their champion from micro managers and jealousy.

Lastly, when the time comes, I will need to have the strength and wisdom to get the hell out of their way.

Yes, I want to be a sergeant, I need to be.

Sgt. D. L. Gill
Puyallup Police Department
Special Investigation Unit

Chapter 25

Cop on Cop

I'm not sure where Justin came from: a volunteer fireman somewhere; a pretend cop from somewhere else; but now he was here and had made it through the police academy. We got along fine at the start, as most new relationships do, but within a year or two our relationship slowly unraveled. I had noticed "things". Working graveyards he would "disappear", not show up at calls and sounded like he had been awakened over the radio when called by dispatch. Sleeping cops pissed me off and terrorizing their ass was top of my list. But I couldn't find this son of a bitch. I knew he was not that talented to hide from me so he had help, a garage door opener, but where could he be?

Justin and I were working graveyards and I had just gotten out of bed when the phone rang.

"Hey this is Justin, been working on my car and it's still not fixed, can I get a ride work with you?"

"Yeah, I'll be there at 2230 hrs, give you a ride," and with that being said I hung up.

I spent the remainder of the evening goofing off with the kids, getting them to bed, and conversation with the wife. I left the house at about 2230 hrs and drove to Justin's townhouse located in the same neighborhood as mine. When I arrived he was not outside waiting; so I waited, and waited some more. Finally I knocked on the front door and got no response. Dumbass fell asleep, worked all day on his car and was nap cramming before work. I knew I'd be working alone that night even though Justin would be in a patrol car, somewhere.

Having gotten no answer to my repeated knocks I tried the door knob; unlocked. Now I know cops, how they think and how they act. Most all live in single family dwellings, six foot fences around the house, big dog that will eat an intruder and a gun in most all rooms; well hidden, of course. But leaving your front door unlocked while sleeping is total bullshit.

"Hey Justin," I yelled. No response, so I entered and again yelled "hey Justin," and again, no response. I wandered through the place to his bedroom. I knocked on the door and said again, "Hey Justin, you awake?" no answer. "Shit" was all I could muster. I tried the door knob and of course, unlocked, so I turned and cracked open the door. "Hey Justin, you're in here?" I asked. I slowly opened the door shedding light on Justin with his back to me lying on the bed. Then in flash Justin spun around and brought a 357 handgun up pointing at me.

"Sorry, I was sound asleep, keep this gun under my pillow, you startled me, give me 5 minutes I'll be ready," he said.

"Yeah right," I mumbled as I walked out not buying a single line of this bullshit display; it was planned out, but why?

Actually it was the first card pulled off his now dwindling house of cards career; he should have never let me in his home. I stepped into the kitchen area to await the idiot getting ready for work. That's when I spotted it: a buck knife; not just any buck knife, but my buck knife. It had come up missing in the previous months and I had given up all hope of ever finding it again. I examined the knife closely; no doubt about it, it was mine and Justin had it. I had put out a note to the department that the knife was missing and if you were to see it, put it in my locker, and then I thanked them in advance. Fucking Justin had stolen it from my locker.

This knife was given to me by my father just prior to me joining the Army and I had worn it throughout garrison duty as a military policeman stationed in Alaska. The knife had gone everywhere with me and I was upset at losing it and now enraged that it had been stolen by a cop. Well that title will disappear, cop, my rage would be concealed and I would work to seal Justin's fate. I slipped the knife into my pocket.

Justin came out of the back of his house and looked to be ready for work. We left and not a word was spoken during the 10 minute drive to the police department. I had already decided to watch, learn, and figure Justin out; and if he would steal another cop's property then he would certainly steal from the public.

I called Pig and downloaded a catharsis of anger on him; told him of the night and what had happened in the gun and knife incident at Justin's home.

"You're taking notes, right?" he asked.

"Duh" was my simple smartass reply.

"I'm on board; I don't work with him much but will let you know if I hear or see anything," Pig said and with that the conversation ended.

Couple weeks went by and nothing new developed; but then Justin did something out of the norm, he stopped at KC's Caboose for a bar check. Odd, something he rarely did but I'm sure he was looking for some personal gain. I parked just around the corner from where he had parked out of sight. I quickly moved to his parked car and in seconds I was inside his car with a spare key I had had made for this very purpose. I looked at the visors and sure enough there was a small metal clip, like the one you find attached to a garage door opener. I flipped the sun visor down and there it was: a garage door opener; he had a friend nearby, someplace safe where could sleep his shift away.

I didn't touch the opener and left it where he had put it. I pulled out my can of mace and sprayed it into the intake to the defrost system to the car. This would be a quick strike for the stealing of my knife. Justin was useless and I didn't want him working; so dismantling him now, for at least one shift, would mean nothing to me. It will just make me feel a little better for stealing my knife. I quickly got out of the car, re-locked it, and returned to my patrol car.

"Incoming asshole," I mumbled to myself as I drove off.

It was about 15 minutes later when Justin called me on the radio. "Hey can you meet me at the intersection of Wood and Main?" he asked.

"Sure, en-route," I replied. I was actually surprised he had made it that far.

As I arrived there sat his car: driver's door wide open, blocking the left turn lane in the middle of town, overhead lights flashing, and Justin outside his car. He was a mess. I was doing my best to keep my gleefulness in check.

When I got to Justin he showed all the signs of a good macing: snot dangle freely from his nose, tears stream like creeks down his cheeks, and all he could muster up was "what the fuck is going on?"

"I got in my car and this is as far as I got before I had a snot explosion," he whined on.

I looked inside his car, like I give a shit, looking as bewildered as he.

"What the hell happened?" I asked.

"Don't know," he replied "but can't work tonight," he claimed.

"Well I'm not driving your car back, your job," I said. "Smells like mace," I mentioned to him.

"No kidding, but how?" he asked me.

"You were just at the Caboose, bet someone has a can of mace and fogged your vents, seen it before," I lied.

"Fucked me up," Justin continued looking as though he were crying.

Cars past by looking at us, especially Justin; not often you see a cop standing in the middle of main street crying. I offered no pity, had none but wow was I dying from laughter inside. After about another 15 minutes Justin rolled all the windows down on the car and with his snot-covered face hanging out the window. He slowly drove the car to the police department. Justin changed to his plain clothes and drove home. The dispatcher wanted to know what happened.

"Don't know," I said with a smile.

"Something tells me you do," she remarked.

I just smiled and left.

Get used to it asshole, that was just my first strike, and I'm just getting warmed up, I thought to myself.

The next day I called Pig, filled him in on last night's mission. "Yeah, he has a garage door opener in the car, took it with him when he left last."

Pig was still laughing about me macing the intake vents of the car. "Yesterday I heard the Chief complaining to his secretary about how many stamps the department was using," Pig stated. Chief said "we are always out."

"That's got to be Justin," I said.

"You know he collects police department patches from all over the USA," Pig stated.

"Postage," was my only reply.

"Yep," Pig said.

More weeks passed by and Justin continued with his lazy ass stealing ways. On one of my days off I stopped in at Dale's Pharmacy in town, which I do regularly. Dale was an old family friend and our pharmacist forever. I picked up a couple of items and Dale dragged me aside.

"You know, every time I come to work on certain days my newspaper is missing," Dale told me. "It's always the same five days, Wednesday thru Sunday mornings, paper is gone," Dale complained. "I love reading my morning paper and it's never there," he complained further.

"How long has this been going on?" I asked.

"Couple months," he replied. I was doing the math in my head.

I worked with Justin Tuesday thru Saturday, getting off Sunday morning for our weekend. It's been about a couple of months working that shift; asshole was stealing from Dale.

Tuesday night rolled around and I went to work as usual, with Justin. Nothing unusual happened till bout 0600 hrs. I had parked my patrol car; or should I say hid it near Dale's Pharmacy. I found a spot that gave me a clear view of the front door and waited. I didn't have to wait long and a Tacoma News Tribune truck pulled up out front and the driver got out. He tossed a tightly wrapped bundle of newspapers onto the front door area of Dale's then carefully laid one untied newspaper on top of the pile. The driver jumped back into his van and away he went.

Seconds passed by and I heard the sound of an engine start and there was Justin. He parks the patrol car exactly like the newspaper man, gets out of his car, walks to the stack of newspapers, and collects the lose one on top.

"Fucker," I said to myself.

I remember when I first started in Sumner, Carl told me that there will be times you're in a restaurant having coffee or a meal and when it comes time to pay the waitress will say "This is on the house, or cop's money is no good here, trying to get you to their favor." "Never allow it; never," Carl said. "You politely say thank you but you can't do that and if they persist, lay the amount of the check plus tip on the table, tip your hat and leave, ok?" he finished.

Frankly, stealing newspapers, stamps, and a knife are a lot worse. Public trust is in the balance here; best nip in the bud now then read about in the newspapers later.

The shift ended at 0700 hrs with Pig relieving us. Nothing was said; I just nodded and smiled at him as I left, but he knew what I just told him. Five hours later my alarm went off. I got dressed and called the department.

Pauline answered, "Hello, police department."

"Gill here, Chief in? Need to talk to him."

"Hold on, I'll patch you, through."

"Chief of Police, how may I help you?" the chief spoke.

"Hi Chief, Gill here, need to talk to you; important. This afternoon, will you be around?" I asked.

"I'm already waiting on you," he replied.

"15 out, be there soon," I responded and the conversation ended.

Arriving, I made short work of introductions with the office staff and found myself at the Chief's office knocking on the already open door.

"Come in, have a seat," he said.

I entered and as I did I laid my knife on his desk then sat down. He gave me a puzzled look. I recalled he had on his eight point hat, full uniform with awards, and badges of his past life, tie, all jeweled up in gold. He earned it.

"Your knife, you lost it, you found it, where?"

"That's why I'm here to talk to you, low on postage stamps?" I said in asking manner.

"Yes he said, this is not going to have a good finish I take it," ending his statement.

"No it won't, has Dale called you bitching about the theft of his newspaper every morning, Wednesday through Sunday?" I asked.

"Like clockwork, every morning about 0800 he calls; quit screwing around, what you got?" said the Chief wanting answers.

I relayed the story starting with the gun bullshit that Justin had pulled and the finding of my knife, stamps, and then what I had watched him do at Dale's business. Chief was pissed off, although he would not verbally tell me; I could see it in his eyes and mannerisms.

"Who knows of this?" he asked.

"Just Pig," I replied.

"I should have assumed that," he said knowing Pig and I are close. "Let's keep it that way till I do an internal investigation on it and I'll let you know," he stated.

Conversation was over; it was time to go home for a short nap before everyone arrived home and the house would no longer be sleep-able.

Couple weeks had gone by when I caught a glint of something in the dark I had not noticed before. It was 0430 hrs and there was a car hidden in the dark near the back of Nelson's Candy off main, but across the street and away from Dale's business. I found a place to park near the police department and walked back to the location on foot. I found the car; it was running and two men were seated inside on the front seat. I recognized the car; it was the Chief's and probably a lieutenant with him. None of my business anymore, and I turned and walked away.

Another week flew by and I was getting ready to go to work when the phone rang.

"Hello?" I answered.

"Hello, it's Justin. I need a ride to work tonight; came outside and my tire was flat, don't feel like fixing it right now."

Rock and hard spot, I thought to myself. "Ok, be there in a couple," and hung up.

As we pulled into the rear parking lot of the police department, I about died; Chief's car and a lieutenant's car. Old Justin was going to get hammered tonight and I just drove him to the slaughter. *Wonderful* I thought to myself, but I didn't start this fight, Justin owns it.

We walked through the back door and into the front office, Justin anxious to know what was going on; me, knowing full well a shit storm was about to hit. Might as well get ready for work; I'll be working alone again, this time for real.

Justin was fired from the department. He was rehired by a neighboring county sheriff that stated anybody that doesn't get along with that Sumner chief can work for me. Four years later Justin beat the crap out of a motorist so badly it cost his county 2 million to get the lawsuit settled. Three years later Justin was promoted to sergeant, and at last check is already retired.

Let's Laugh Again

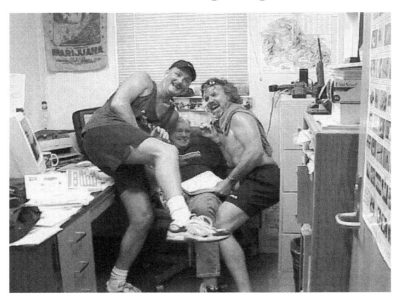

Laughter is the best medicine. It is a good break from something serious, irritating, sad, or whatever other emotions are stirring up in you. So I want to make you laugh again, or at least make you feel lighter. How about just to make you say, "Good for you!" or "Yuck!"?

Frank invited me into his home. We sat at his kitchen table, sipped coffee, and I told Frank what had happened and what we had done. While telling him the story I noticed a Purple Heart medal hanging in a display case in the front room. Frank was laughing his ass off when I told of the dog shit and the note. He slammed his big hand onto the kitchen table and it spilled a bit of our coffee from the impact. We continued to talk for a bit but I did not mention anything of the war nor the medal that hung in the room. Frank had hidden those thoughts and right now was enjoying his newest story told to him.

Chapter 26

Dances with Dogs

Karma means I can rest easy at night knowing all the people I treated badly had it coming (ROTTENeCARDS).

Dispatch had called me and sent me to an address just behind Sumner High School. There is a resident living in a home that had just interrupted a theft in progress. The time was about 0145 hrs. The victim stated that someone had broken into his car and stole his new cassette stereo deck. Eight track stereo players had been all but replaced by the new fancy better sounding cassette decks of the time.

As I arrived at the home, I recognized it. The gentleman that lived there was a World War II veteran and had done battle in the European theater. Although Frank never talked about his experiences of the war, all that lived in Sumner knew he had been there in battle, and now made Sumner his home. People like Frank are precious, no matter where they lived.

Frank met me at the front door wearing a robe and slippers, and invited me in. He stated that he had been awakened by noise in his driveway and when he peeked out his bedroom window noticed two young men walking from his car to a small Toyota car parked near his home. Frank also stated that he didn't bother to wear robe or slippers and moved quickly from his bedroom to his front door dressed only in his mighty 'whities'. He noticed that the window to his passenger door had been shattered and the stereo was gone. Frank heard the suspect's car start and he ran to the edge of the road as the vehicle sped off, driving directly in front of him. He told me that the first three letters of the license plate was AHC, and it was a Washington plate. Likewise, he stated that the car was green and the last thing he noticed was the sound of barking dogs, "those small yappy type dogs," Frank said.

Frank was upset, not only about the theft of the stereo but the breaking of his window.

"The car wasn't even locked," he said.

I gathered the necessary information and assured him that I would spend the remainder of my shift looking for it and would contact him before I go home if I do find the car and thieves that occupied it.

I called Pig on the radio and gave him the description of the vehicle to include the first three letters of the plate, AHC.

I was working the graveyard shift, 2300 hrs till 0700 hrs the next morning. Pig had landed a chance at working the much desired 2000 hrs till 0400 hrs. After 0400 hrs I'd be alone with only a dispatcher, but I was used to the arrangement and didn't mind.

At about 0245 hrs Pig contacted me and stated that he had found the vehicle parked near where an old burnt out bowling alley had once stood. He said that the occupants were probably at 805 Parker Road, an armpit of apartments and problems. Pig and I met up a couple blocks away from 805 Parker Road and made our way to the apartment complex. We at first thought that maybe the prowlers were in the apartment complex prowling cars, but after a thorough inspection of the parking lot revealed nothing. So were they there visiting? We made our way to their car to have a closer look.

The car was the one Frank described to me earlier, complete with two yappy little dogs. On the passenger floor boards lay wire cutters, a large flat tip screw driver, and a window punch – tools of the car prowler trade. We ran the full plate for information on the owner and learned it was out of Auburn, Washington. Dispatch began cross checking the registered owner for wants and warrants as well as drivers status. This was a time consuming effort back then so Pig and I disappeared into the shadows and waited to see if the two men would return to their car and us.

As we waited I told Pig of the story about Frank and his battles in Europe during the Great War. Pig mentioned he too had heard of Frank, a local community hero. Pig and I had both been in the military prior to our collision in police work.

"Could you imagine one day you're finishing boot camp and the next day you're shipping off to war in Europe and you're only 18 years old?" I asked Pig.

"Could you imagine the same 18 year old kid riding in a landing craft heading for hell and good chance at death on D day?" Pig quizzed me.

"Did Frank land on the beaches?" I asked.

"I don't know," Pig said, "but can you imagine the fear and courage those men had?" he continued.

"Damn, those are special people," I said softly still looking at the suspect's car. "Look, I'll stand guard here, why don't you check the town and when you return I'll check town and by then you'll be getting off. I'll figure out by then what I'm going to do about this car."

Pig agreed and made his way to his car and made the rounds of our little town. I thought back about the conversation Pig and I had just talked about. I tried to imagine what that ride in a landing craft on D-Day would be like. I realized I couldn't; no one that wasn't there could. It is impossible to imagine the horror that waited on those beaches for those brave men. I was still staring at the car and walked slowly towards it. The night was still and quiet; I enjoyed moments like these, quiet and intimate like. I arrived at the driver's door and noticed that something had changed. There was something different inside the car.

Between the two front seats one of the dogs had left a fresh pile doggy poop, coiled neatly like a freshly served soft ice crème cone. I grinned at the sight. I know there is a God and he just used the dogs to serve up justice for Frank.

I smiled as I slid my flashlight into a sap pocket of my trousers. I slowly began walking in circles around the car. I used my right knuckle of my right hand to tap on the side of the car so the dogs inside could follow my movements circling the car. I kept count but lost after seven trips around the car. The dogs were having a fit, bouncing all over the car and at me circling it, slowly. I continued my movements and the dogs continued theirs. As I came to a stop at the driver door window, I slowly eased my flashlight from my sap pocket and brought it to bear on the driver's window. In a flash I saw what I predicted would occur: dog poop spread throughout the interior of the car. It was even on the driver's window. *What an asshole* I thought of myself. But I was no coward and would not slink away in the night. I noticed that Pig had been watching from a distance probably wondering what the heck I was up to.

I took out my notebook and began a note.

This car was used in a car prowl earlier this morning. The victim gave us your description and your car description. I made a few laps around your car checking it for the missing stereo and only noticed the burglar tools you used on the floor. I believe the dogs were busy protecting your car and made a little mess.

D. Gill SPD 112

I put away the pad and pen then carefully slipped the note under the windshield wiper in front of the driver's seat. I was daring them to complain which would mean they would be identified.

I walked to Pig and as I got there he was intently looking at me; I glanced down then back to him then down again. I was purposely looking like a guilty kid trying to get something over on my parents.

"What did you do?" Pig asked.

"Being bad," was all I said.

"What the hell did you do?" Pig continued to pry.

"Just go look, and read the note," I told him.

Pig didn't hesitate; he turned and briskly walked to the car and looked inside the car with his flashlight. The dogs attacked. Then he grabbed the note and read it. Pig folded the note and carefully replaced it and walked back to where I was standing. As he arrived he had a big evil smirk to his face and was controlling his laughter.

"Do you think they'll complain?" he asked.

"Doubt it, they are cowards," was my response. "I hope they never come back to our town," I then said.

Pig and I moved to our cars and Pig was soon on his way home. At around 0615 hrs I drove by Frank's home and noticed he was sitting in the kitchen with coffee and his morning TNT, Tacoma News Tribune. I parked out front and walked to his front door and knocked. Frank answered the door. No hi, no glad to see you, just "did you get them sons of bitches?" he asked.

"No, but found the car with the yappy little dogs," I replied.

Frank invited me into his home. We sat at his kitchen table, sipped coffee, and I told Frank what had happened and what we had done. While telling him the story I noticed a Purple Heart medal hanging in a display case in the front room. Frank was laughing his ass off when I told of the dog shit and the note. He slammed his big hand onto the kitchen table and it spilled a bit of our coffee from the impact. We continued to talk for a bit but I did not mention anything of the war nor the medal that hung in the room. Frank had hidden those thoughts and right now was enjoying his newest story told to him.

As I left I got close enough to the display case to note the date on the medal, "June 6, 1944."

Chapter 27

Crazy People

In all the years of work that Pig and I had, we came across many flat, crazy people. All sorts! Some wanted and tried to kill you or someone else; some had simple quirks or activities that were a delight to watch; and then there were those that were just simply nuts. These are a few encounters we had with these crazy people, broken down into short stories.

Number one
It was a sunny afternoon on a Saturday in the early spring and I was working day shift assigned to the South Hill district. This area would need the attention of at least two officers on patrol and at times three would be assigned to it. This district was unique at that time, as it had a crime prevention office located inside the mall. It was a handy place to eat lunch, take a break, or write reports and not be bothered by anyone other than the radio. Today I was using a bicycle making it easier to move through traffic and quicker to respond to calls. I was working my way back to the mall and the office to finish up on a couple of reports I was working on when dispatch reported they had received a call of a suspicious male behind the mall, near the cinemas. The report was that he was acting odd amongst the cars and the caller believed he may be up to no good. I responded to dispatch that I was "in the area, doing a sneak and peek". By using the words "sneak and peek" motor cops knew I was watching and to stay out of the area until I determined if the suspect was involved in criminal activity.

It didn't take long to find him. He was amongst the cars, dressed as described – jeans, long sleeved shirt, bib apron with the name of a pizza business on it, and a baseball hat also displaying the pizza business name. He had thick hard rimmed glasses and looked to be about 30 years old. What really stuck out about this guy is something the dispatchers had not been told about or choose not to relay to me: he was carrying a sack. It was a simple paper sack like that of a lunch sack one would carry a lunch in. And the way he carried it was just very odd. It looked as though there was something in it but nothing very heavy, as it did not sag. The top of the sack was neatly rolled down forming a seam that people commonly do with such sacks. It was how he held the bag that screamed goofy. He held it tight fisted with both hands clutching it, up close to his chest but pulled in close to his body and he never, not once put it down to his side like a normal person would do. Also, all he did was walk the same area; in between the cars, alongside the cars, by the bumpers of the cars, but did not leave the little area of that parking lot. He reminded me of watching pac man wander the screen in front of you with no finish line or start area, just keep blazing a trail but staying in the confines of one area.

Enough is enough! It's time to find out what he is up to. As he rounds yet another corner he comes face to face with a blockade with a badge.

"Got a report you were acting suspicious out here and after watching you for the last five minutes I must agree with the person that called the police. What you doing?" I asked.

"Nothing," he said finally looking at me.

"Beside nothing, what else you got going on?" I asked.

I noticed when he looked at me he had full loads of double barreled snot coming from his nose that had increased the mass size of his Hitler styled mustache. Yikes! Again he said "nothing" but he was twitching glancing about.

"What's in the bag?" I asked and again he replied "nothing". "If nothing, let's just throw it away then," I told him and he said "can't".

"Why can't we throw it away?" I asked.

"I don't know, just can't," he said.

"Do you have identification?" I asked of him.

"Yes," he answered, still just standing there twitching and glancing about.

"Show me some identification," I ordered.

This causes extreme twitching and glancing about and now a snot bubble begins to form then pops. I looked at the name of the pizza shop he apparently works at.

I made a mental note to myself, "never ever … ever eat at that place, never!"

"Need to see your identification, tired of messing around with you," I told him.

His twitching is fanatical now and another bubble begins to form. He neatly places the bag on the hood of the car we are standing next to and reaches for his wallet. The snot bubble pops. He pulls out his Washington State identification card, not a license to drive, just identification card. He looks at the bag, checking it visually. Another snot bubble forms. I gave his name and date of birth to dispatch to check for wants and warrant or anything else they can figure out. I reached over and suddenly grabbed the bag. It is light but there is something in it.

"What's in the bag?" I asked again.

"Don't know," he replied.

Huh, same question, different answer. The biggest bubble yet pops.

"Maybe we should find out together then?" I said in an asking tone. No reply, nothing, he stares at the bag.

"What you say we explore this together?" I again asked. Nothing, not a word, no twitching either, just stares at the bag. I handed him his identification.

"I'm going to look in this bag, okay?" I asked him one last time.

As he put his identification back in his wallet he shrugged his shoulders and nodded his head, and I began to slowly unfold the top of the bag. By now

I've already made assumptions of the contents of the bag. My number one choice is marijuana to sell; the number two is money to buy marijuana. Those are my two top picks. More of the bag began to unfold, and as I opened it and saw the contents I jumped about a foot back and dropped the bag.

"What the fuck you got those for?" I yelled at the guy. It was a paper bag full of **used** condoms.

"I don't know," he answered back to shuffling, twitching and looking about.

I pulled out rubber gloves I keep in a pouch on my belt, slipped into them, and opened the bag making sure the condoms weren't being used to hide something. They weren't, just a collection of used condoms.

Dispatch contacts me, "dispatch to 244".

"244," I answered back.

"Your subject is a 414 with multiple stops and mental contacts," dispatch said to me.

I wanted to say "no shit" but elected to say "received".

414 is police jargon for a crazy person. I grabbed the bag and its contents and walked to the dumpster, flipped open the lid, and tossed the bag into the dumpster. I walked back to the guy and told him "I'm watching the dumpster all day and all night, don't come back to it now get outta here." Another snot bubble pops as he turns and wanders off. Unless they are a threat to themselves or others, they have the right to wander among us. So be it.

When I got home that night I told my wife about the guy and bag of used condoms. To this day, after over 20 years have passed, every time she sees one of those pizza restaurants she says "never eating there".

Number two

It was a colder winter night and I was working graveyards in Sumner. I had been hired only weeks earlier and was out and about as patrol. Working with me was Sergeant Luke on the 2000 to 0400 shift. I had just driven by the police department and noticed Luke was at the department lobby probably bullshitting with Howard. Howard was dirt old at the time and was about ready to retire, again, and move to Las Vegas for his end game. The two men enjoyed each other's company and thus they spent it talking. I wandered about for another 10 minutes when Luke called me on the radio and told me to meet him at an address on Cherry Street. Then he asked if I had my eight-point round hat that I had been issued to by the chief. "Why?" I wondered. "Why did he care if I had my hat?" Luke hated the damn hats as he called them and I had yet to see him wear one. "Yes I got it, be there in 3" I responded. As I arrived Luke was standing in front of the house, no coat, and wearing that "damn hat".

Luke was a big man, not a sloppy fat man but well groomed and well-dressed heavy man that wore his trousers up around his waist unlike other portly men that let their bellies sag over the top of their belts. Luke was a sergeant and had always been a sergeant. When I was 16 he stopped me for traffic violation. He was a sergeant then and he wrote me my first traffic ticket. Everyone in high school feared "fat Luke" as we, including me, named him. He was a ticket writing machine with a fearsome reputation. I didn't know then what I know now; he was earning his taxpayer's pay.

Now we worked together and I, like him, wore a silly eight point hat. As I approached Luke I slipped on the rather cumbersome hat and asked "what's going on?"

"You need to grow into the hat boy," he said to me then turned and said "follow me, keep quiet, and learn something, you'll be back here someday."

The home was old. Even in 1979 I could tell it was a turn of the century house. Luke opened the front screen door that was "ratty", to best describe it, and knocked. The door opened to a little old lady that wore a shawl and had gray hair, lots of it, and she let it hang straight down and she was wrapped in heavy dark purple robe. Nothing unusual except for one thing -- her head, tops of shoulders, and hands were covered in aluminum tin foil!

"Oh thank you Mr. Luke for coming over at this hour," she said.

"Hi Rosemary, what's going on, demons again?" Luke said.

Suddenly I understood the "you'll be back here" comment Luke had made to me moments earlier.

"Yes it is Hank, they got him again. He's fighting but getting tired and needs your help," she spoke with great concern and pointed to Hank.

Okay, I admit things had gotten weird as we greeted Rosemary wearing foil but now it was a fucking freak show. There lay Hank, on a sheet of three quarter inch plywood held off the floor by two saw horses. There was no foil "on" Hank but it covered the plywood under Hank, and Hank was covered with a white bed sheet. The room was dimly lit and those little hairs on the back of my neck were full on erect!

Rosemary's attention turned to me and I could feel my feet sweating. Last time I felt that was the night I got married.

"You're new?" she asked.

"Huh, yes ma'am," I stuttered out.

"What's your name?" she asked.

"Gill," I answered.

"Mr. Gill, thank you for coming to help us out," she said.

Her eyes were bright and had that "I'm fucking crazy as a pet coon" look to them and her hand was cold when I shook it. I glanced at Luke. He was peering back at me to see if I shit myself yet. I remembered Luke always had a toothpick in his mouth. Using his tongue I could watch him spin that pick, twirl it and not once take it out of his mouth in conversation. Bet his ladies loved him! He motioned me further into the cavern of crazy and I followed his lead. I watched as he walked up to the horizontal Hank lying before him. Luke quickly pulled back enough of the sheet to expose Hank's head and neck then did a quick artery check to make sure the old fart was still alive. Luke smiled and winked at me as he re-covered Hank's head.

"How long they had him Rosemary?" Luke asked of her.

"About two hours I suppose," she answered.

"Call me earlier next time; it's harder to rid them damn devils if they stay in there that long," Luke said.

"Sorry Mr. Luke, I thought he was sleeping," she said.

My head went spinning, *"he's laying completely covered with a sheet, on a piece of foil covered plywood, supported by two sawhorses, in the middle of a mostly normal looking front room, and you thought he was fucking sleeping?"* was all I could think. *'Oh, that's right, you both are fucking crazy"* was my closing thought on her latest statement.

Then I wondered if maybe I was the only sane one in the room when Luke began a little chant as he circled Hank.

"Leave this man, you devil dogs, he belongs to the Lord" ... "Leave this man you devil dogs, he belongs to the Lord."

Luke repeated the chant several more times all the while walking a slow circle around Hank. Luke suddenly stopped and pulled a slight bit of the sheet down off Hank exposing his forehead, and he looked to Rosemary as she was already armed with the roll of aluminum foil and moving in to help. What had been earlier covered up by the "now removed sheet" was covered by foil, Hank's forehead. Luke began the chant again and the slow walk around Hank. The process repeated itself several times over until Hank was covered in foil to his abdomen and bed sheet from there on down. All I could think of was *"please have your crazy ass private parts covered up, wear some fucking trouser you nut job."* Luke chanted yet another round and did the walk around one more time and yanked the sheet off exposing the lower half of Hank, and thank God his pajama bottoms were on. Rosemary was busy covering Hank's lower half. Luke glanced at me, twirling the toothpick and winked.

"Ready Rosemary?" he asked of her.

"Yes Mr. Luke," she responded.

Luke moved to the head area of the plywood and Hank. He leaned forward and placed his big hands on the plywood covered with foil now almost hovered above Hank. Rosemary had moved off to Hank's left and her little hands tightly gripped in a praying manner, her eyes closed tightly and her lips moved saying God only knows what prayer. Luke then said, "Rise Hank, you're free." And with that Hank shot up to a seated position on the plywood.

"Thank the Lord," Hank said, "Thank the Lord."

Moments later after many thank you and just as many God bless you directed at Luke by the crazy old folks, we left. Once outside all I wanted was answers. Before I got started Luke looked at me and said "get that silly fucking hat off and meet me at the station."

"Okay," I responded.

I arrived at the station and parked out back. Moments later Luke arrived and we coded through the back door of the police department.

"Want a cup?" he asked me.

"Why not, wish I had a shot of whisky to add to it," I replied.

Luke smiled as he poured the cup. "Go ahead, ask away" Luke said.

"The eight point hat," I asked.

"Better than wearing foil," he responded.

"The foil, what's that about?" I asked.

"Keeps demons out of you," Luke answers.

"Bed sheet covering Hank" was my next enquiry.

"Demons can leave Hank's body through the sheet but not foil," Luke responded.

"Which one of you guys figured all this out?" was my next question.

"Hank and Rosemary arrived here from the Midwest about 15 years ago, brought crazy with them. About every six months or so someone has to go do an exorcism and it took us trial and error to get it perfected," Luke answered.

"Does Carl do this?" I asked.

"Yes, he is one of the best and loves it when a new guy is with him," Luke answers.

"Great, so in six months I'll have to do it," I said.

"Look, we are pretty sure they have these little episodes after foil goes on sale at the Thriftway near their home. It was probably on sale last week," Luke mentioned.

I quickly searched for an old newspaper but found none. "Any other crazy people around town I need know about?" I asked Luke.

"Lots of them son, but that's half the fun, let you find them and figure it out," he responded.

Three and half years passed by quickly and now I was working with a new guy. He had an odd last name for a cop so we just called him Pig. I was working 2000 to 0400 and he was working the graveyard shift when I got a call.

"Sumner 112," my Sumner badge number, Rosemary on Cherry Street just called, "Hank's in trouble."

"En-route Sumner," I respond.

On the way I called Pig on the radio and asked him if he has that silly eight point hat the chief had issued him. I arrived before Pig and was standing in front of Rosemary's and Hank's home wearing that silly hat when Pig arrived. Pig got out of his car and walked to me.

"What's going on?" he asked.

"You look funny in that hat, just follow me and learn; you'll be back in the future," I responded.

I turned and opened the ratty storm door and knocked. You all already know what happens next.

About two years later Rosemary passed away and three weeks after that Hank died. The only people that attended their funerals was a pastor, couple church folks, neighbors on Cherry Avenue and three Sumner cops. When a small town loses sweet crazy people, the little town loses a bit of its character.

Number three

"He wants to meet you down the street from his house," the dispatcher said, "doesn't want the neighbors to know he called the police," she continued.

"112 Sumner, tell him I'll be behind the warehouse at the end of the street, have him meet me there" I told dispatch.

"Received," she responded.

The neighbor had called and said he had weird neighbors and saw "things" that concerned him and wanted the police to check them out. This is not an unusual call, had many of these type calls and usually they turned out to be nothing, but this one would be flat ass nuts.

I had only waited a couple minutes when a small red truck rounded the corner and drove to my location. I got out and met the man. His name was Jackson and he looked familiar. In a small town strangers were rare; thus I had seen Jackson out and about in my little town.

"Thanks for meeting me officer," were his first words.

"No problem, what's eating at you?" I asked.

"Two, three months ago we got new neighbors to the east of us that are doing some strange things," he started.

Jackson told me that he and his wife had noticed the man and woman renting the house didn't own a car and walked everywhere they went. He continued and stated: "furthermore, they walk around in capes at times and I noticed the man wears make up, the kind that lightens his skin and lipstick. Both have their hair dyed black and I'm sure I once seen a coffin in the front room."

"How old are they?" I asked.

"Around thirty I think," he responded.

"Okay I'll do some digging and maybe find out what they are all about, call you when I learn something," I said. With that we shook hands and left.

I drove to the police department and began searching our file. It was pre-computer ages so everything had to be done by hand and phone and 3 x 5 cards in stacks of metal file cabinets. Nothing was found. Pig had arrived at work and I shared the story Jackson had told me.

"Wow, kind of spooky," was his comment.

"They're new in the neighborhood, why don't we go introduce ourselves?" I said. "What's the worse they can do to us, tell us to leave?" I continued.

"Bite us," Pig said with a smile.

"Heck I'm going to stop by and say hi, want to go?" I asked.

"If for no other reason, just to see you do it will be worth the price of admission," Pig said.

I climbed into my cruiser trying to figure out what my opening line would be. "Hi, I'm here because the neighbors think you're crazy and wanted me to check" I figured would mean I'd be tossed off the porch. *"This is a small town, act like it"*, I thought to myself as I parked out front of the home. The curtains were closed, and the curtains were black as was the front door. I climbed out of my car as Pig arrived and he was already smiling as he watched me move to the front of my car and the sidewalk out front of the house. It had been a warm summer day and the sun was still out but near setting, figured I was safe. I had no idea what would answer the door or if I would even be acknowledged. I reached out and gave the door three knocks. Moments passed then the door unlocked and slightly opened.

"Hi," I said in a friendly tone.

"Why you here?" the person asked. I could see the white like painted face and dark lipstick that the man was wearing along with a cape and full collar and dressed in "vampire attire".

"Well, I knew you all had just moved into the neighborhood and I would like to introduce myself to folks that live in the area I work," I said in a very friendly tone.

The door opened wider and now I had a view of the interior of the home and a lady that stood closely behind the man. She too wore a little vampire outfit with high heels of course. Then I saw the tell-tale sign of crazy ass people, their eyes, *"bat shit crazy eyes"* I thought to myself. I also noticed the ends of two coffins in the front room.

"That's cool, what you do with those?" pointing to the boxes in the room.

The words I spoke were like a wrecking ball knocking down any walls they might have had; suddenly there was a cop on their doorstep interested in them.

"We sleep in them, look," he said motioning me into the house.

As I stepped in, Pig had caught up and was now on the door step.

"Can my buddy come in?" I asked.

"Check these out Pig," I said.

"Yeah, come on in, we got these things hooked up to stereo complete with speakers inside," he said.

He and his girlfriend began showing and telling us what the boxes did for them. They were real coffins -- bright, shiny, and comfortable stuffing found within a coffin. I noticed three handles down each side of the coffins. These things were the real deal! They slept in them and could control the sound of the music that came into the coffins. I noticed there were no latches on the boxes; they had been purposely removed.

Understandable, if you got into a fight with your girlfriend then slipped into your coffin for a nap she'd probably feel justified to latch the lid down and crank up the stereo and think that was a perfectly normal process of retaliation because after all he's a man, therefore a verified asshole.

I looked about the room as the two entertained Pig with crazy shit. No pictures, nothing. I saw a small table and two chairs in the kitchen and again no pictures and more black curtains everywhere. I still didn't know their names so I had work to do.

"I forgot to introduce myself, Officer Gill, you can call me Mr. Gill if you prefer," I said to the couple.

"I'm Terry Stackman and this is my wife Samantha," Terry said.

We chatted for a bit longer then I pulled out a piece of folded paper that had emergency contacts – phone number to the city, fire department, and police.

"Keep this around in case you need to contact us or need any help," handing it to Terry.

"Thanks," he responded.

We shook hands and bid farewell. The sun was getting very low in the skyline and leaving the two vampires before darkness took over seemed to be the prudent move.

Once outside Pig and I left and met just down the street behind the warehouse.

"They are flat fucking crazy," he said.

"Yep and probably wards of the state for their income," I responded.

"I'll do a background, you figure out where they come from," I asked Pig.

"She said Tacoma when I asked," Pig stated.

I returned to the police department and found nothing of their names in the file we kept. I made a few phone calls to contacts I had at the Tacoma Police Department and learned that the vampires had several contacts with the police department and were listed and verified as 414. There was no criminal history and they were just peaceable crazy people that dressed and acted like vampires.

I called Jackson and informed him of my findings. "I have found absolutely no record of the folks engaging in any criminal activity" I told him.

"So they are in fact crazy people, but harmless," Jackson said.

"I'd keep a wary eye on them but get to know them and the entertainment factor is going to cost you nothing," I told him.

Jackson laughed at the comment then thanked me for checking on his crazy neighbors.

Three years later when I left Sumner police department for Puyallup, my harmless little vampires were still happily living in their boxes, bothering no one.

Number four

I had never officially met Hazel but had heard stories of her and knew her on sight as she had been pointed out to me by Carl, Luke, and other members of the police department. When I asked about her they usually said nothing other than "you'll figure it out one day" and of course I did.

I was parked in a parking lot of a gas station monitoring traffic flow when I spotted the heavy set older lady seated in her familiar wheel chair rolling the wheels with her hands and her right foot that help pull her along the paved sidewalk. As I watched her I could see she was chewing and would occasionally spit off to the side of the sidewalk. There was a dark dribble streak down the left corner of her mouth from the chew. When she got to the intersection she didn't hesitate much and wheeled herself into the cross walk with disregard for passing traffic. This always called for excited motorists to find a way to stop and not get rear ended or hit a woman in a wheel chair in a cross walk. That would cause a pain in the ass moment for the driver in a courtroom sitting with a wicked civil attorney that Hazel had hired. Someone in a car honked but Hazel paid them no attention and just continued her rhythmic pattern of movement down the sidewalk in her wheel chair. After crossing the street she angled off to her left and left the side walk onto Harrison Street. Harrison Street has no sidewalk thus forcing Hazel to travel west bound in the east bound lane on the edge of the black top narrow old road. There was an automotive dealer ship that occupied that corner of the intersection and the cars that parked along Harrison Street did not parallel park; they pulled or backed into the edge of the building that was there.

About then was when I noticed the backup lights to one of the parked cars come on and begin to back out of it, space, and back onto Harrison. The driver carefully began backing up but before his rear wheel got to the pavement he spotted Hazel and stopped the movement of his car. He simply sat there waiting for Hazel to pass by. Hazel had a different, creative plan but she had missed one important factor: me watching from the parking lot of the gas station. As Hazel got closer to the car she began to veer off from the lane of travel and towards the rear quarter panel of the man's car that had stopped to allow her to pass by. I watched as she intently wheeled herself into the side of the car and come to clunking stop. I was riveted by the display. Hazel then began rocking side to side and finally got the chair to tip over in the proper position and for all intent and purposes looked as though she had been knocked over by the car. She lay there motionless as the horrified driver climbed out of his parked car.

I slipped my patrol car into gear and made a short drive to Hazel, her chair, the car, and the driver. As I arrived I got out and introduced myself to the driver first then bent over, and with my hands on my knees looked at Hazel

"Yep, bat shit crazy eyes" I noticed.

"And lady, what are you doing?" I asked of Hazel.

"He backed up and knocked me over officer, I'm hurt, need an ambulance," she painstakingly muttered out.

The driver then interrupted and said "that's not true officer," and I stopped him.

"Hazel, knock it off, I was parked across the street and saw what you did; this gentleman was stopped and you veered off the road into him then forced your wheel chair to topple over," I said with a no bullshit tone to my voice.

"I have good intentions to arrest you for false reporting," completing my statement.

Hazel glanced at me and looked at me with those crazy ass eyes then closed them and began wiggling herself out of the chair and now she was sitting on her butt on the edge of Harrison Street. I picked up her wheel chair and righted it and placed it next to her on the street. I was now standing in front of her and she simply reached up to me with one of her dirty hands and I grasped it and pulled her to her feet. She then slowly turned around and backed up to her wheel chair and then sat down in it. She then, without saying a word, began her usual rhythmic movements that would power her wheel chair down the street and to her home. I watched her slowly move off into the distance. The driver was a bit stunned.

I turned to speak to him and I got his name and address as I would write an incident report that would be damning to Hazel if she ever tried that maneuver again.

"She nuts or something like that?" the driver asked.

"Did you not see her eyes?" I asked him.

"Yes, I noticed," he replied.

"Then you know the answer to that question," I said. After a few more comments we parted company.

Months passed by then one evening I arrived at work at 2000 hrs. When I got to the police department, Pig was in the office waiting for me.

"Hazel called about an hour ago and wants an officer to stop by. She says she is having a prowler problem and wants to talk to the police about the matter," Pig explained.

The chief had put out a department memo that ordered no officer go to Hazel's house alone; "take a witness" was pretty much what the memo stated.

"Okay, let's go find out what she wants" I told him and out the door we went.

I had never been inside Hazel's house; only heard the horror stories from those brave few that entered her house of crazy. As we arrived, the place was a mess outside and there was a wood-constructed wheel chair ramp leading to her front door. The porch light was on and the angle of the light was extremely crooked. *"House of horror"* I smiled to myself. Pig met me on the street out front.

"She has six wiener dogs," I warned my shiny friend.

Personally I love wiener dogs. They are stubborn and when you try to train them they are actually training you. I know because I have one, and I love her to death. Besides, anything that will run head first into a dark hole hunting for a bad ass badger has my complete respect. I'm glad they don't weigh 200 pounds or they would eat people.

We arrived on Hazel's porch and knocked on the door.

"Who's there?" she yelled from inside.

"The police," I yelled back.

"Come in," she yelled back.

The wiener dogs are going ballistic. "You first" said Pig and in I went.

Wiener dogs were all over me giving me the sniff test. Then Pig entered and they attacked him. Pig got not just a sniff test but a full blown wiener dogs' brawl. Pig was not amused by the dogs or the rancid odor of the interior of Hazel's shack. Hazel yelling at the wiener dogs to shut up had no effect. Pig was having a fit. The dogs were jumping onto his spotless uniform with shit clad claws and one has gotten a hold of the back of his trousers and is fiercely shaking its head thinking that it has his prey close to death. I thought of helping but this was just too damn precious to intervene.

"Let's go to the kitchen," I yelled at Hazel and she began moving in that direction.

I couldn't help but notice that on the right tire of her wheel chair there was what looked to be a Tootsie Roll candy stick squished cross wise on the rubber tire that stuck out on each side. It wasn't a Tootsie Roll, it was wiener dog poop. As she rolled along I kept waiting for her hand to grab it but no such luck yet. We arrived in the kitchen and Hazel turned to talk to me.

"Shut up!" she screamed at the dogs then said "god damn dogs" and began to tell me some bullshit story about a prowler. I tried to listen to her but looking at her crazy ass eyes was just little more than I could do; but watching Pig fight off wiener dogs was riveting. I couldn't see Pig but would see a boot swing up launching one of the little guys into the air that had been hanging off the back of his trousers. The pooch flew past the opening of the door, landed, then simply raced back into the fray re-engaging Pig and the other five attack wieners. Hazel continued to shout how she thought some guy was looking into her windows at night. That would be a tough task considering the house was nearly engulfed with blackberry vines but I continued to listen and watch the Pig fight wieners.

Hazel wheeled around her wheel chair and this time got a firm grip on the turd that was impacted on the wheel of the chair. She didn't even notice! I saw Pig dart in front of the door and jumped up onto the couch. Wieners got short legs so he figured he can rise above them but those little shits can jump and soon four of them were on the couch going nuts with the Pig. Hazel was still yelling her story to me over the barking wieners and I was still acting like I gave a shit, but now was completely committed to watching Pig do battle.

I noticed dog shit all over the place and the smell was even worse in the kitchen and I could see urine stains on the linoleum floor. Then I noticed Pig lose his balance and fall slightly backwards banging up against the wall the couch was up against. This forced the couch away from the wall about a foot and as Pig turned to retreat off the couch abandoning his "height is safety plan" he suddenly stopped and peered over the back of the couch. I could tell he spotted something behind the couch. The dogs were relentless and so was Hazel screaming at me about the prowler only to be interrupted by the occasional shouts at the wieners. *"House of horrors"* I thought; now I know why the others called it a house of horror. Pig kept pushing the wieners off the couch then would look behind the couch again. I was curious as to what he had found. Pig glanced at me with that fiendish grin of his that tells me it was something good. I stepped out of the kitchen followed by the still yelling crazy Hazel that has collected another wiener dog turd, this time on her left wheel. I didn't care to watch the yet another turd squish through the hands of crazy Hazel. I turned away just as Pig reached down behind the couch with a rubber glove on and pulled up a magazine. I stepped in front of Hazel with my back facing her and Pig turned the magazine front towards me and there I saw the name of the magazine "Playgirl"! Pig quickly flipped the magazine over the back of the couch and swept it clear of wieners then stepped down and shoved the couch up against the wall.

Hazel finished yelling her problem prowler story to me and I yelled back, "we will put you on patrol check so don't be alarmed if you see one of our powerful car mounted spot lights shine through your windows."

Pig and I retreated to the front door. The wieners were nonstop barking and aggressive with Pig but not aggressive with me. They must have sensed that I liked wieners. As I stepped out onto the porch I yelled bye to crazy Hazel and she yelled bye back. As soon as the door shut, the wieners stopped barking.

"That was a "what the fuck" moment" Pig said. "There must have been ten copies of Playgirl magazines behind the couch" Pig told me.

"Crazy Hazel still has some game I guess," telling Pig.

"What she want? Couldn't hear a damn thing over those dogs barking at me," Pig asked.

"Something about a prowler, but I think she wanted some attention," I answered.

"I'm going to the station, going to shower and change out my uniform, I smell like the inside of her house. Got it covered?" he said and then asked of me.

"Yep, got it covered," I answered.

With that, Pig drove off into the night and I stood out front of Hazel's house looking at the brush and blackberries vines that engulfed the place. I found a cigar in my car and lit it. I wanted to rid myself of the smell of the inside of the house and I could do it with the cigar. *"Crazy Hazel and her house of horrors"* I thought to myself as I drove off with a chuckle.

I'm not sure when Hazel died but it was after I had left for Puyallup that I heard she had a heart attack while wheeling down the sidewalk somewhere in Sumner. They found her slumped in her wheel chair and she looked as though she had simply fallen asleep. I hope the wieners found a good home; they deserved it.

The next morning when I awoke, I got dressed and looked for my new boots. I found them next to a large chair at the fire pit, not where I had left them. As I began putting them on I discovered that someone had used them to collect peanuts shell discards from the night before. Even as a young boy I was not amused and I demanded to know who was responsible for the deed. Finally my mom told me that Warren had used both my boots for "garbage". I was pissed off and vowed revenge someday, and I actually never forgot it.

Chapter 28

Payback

There never seemed to be a moment at the Police Department when, no matter what was going on, there was an underbelly of humor of "capers" being planned or played out. This is one of the better ones.

Warren arrived for work as he usually did – pudgy belly, bald head, and of course talking. In fact when Warren talked, the only way to get out of the conversation was to simply walk away from his porcelain dust and he would, believe it or not, continue with the conversation, sometimes completely alone. He was an elder of the department having been around for, well over thirty years, and never had any intention of becoming a sergeant. He loved to park along a street and run radar. This was Warren's passion and he did his job well.

I first met Warren when I was a young boy at Flaming Geyser Park in King County along the soon to be famous Green River.

In the years to come the name Green River would mean two things: one the river; and two, sadly, Gary Ridgeway, the Green River serial killer. Ridgeway was probably one of the most prolific serial killers known in modern times.

My parents spent several summers camping along the green river with family and friends. One family had an older son named Warren, a young cop back then. At times he would show up and spend the weekend among family and friends camping on the green river.

This particular weekend I had been given new boots by my dad as I loved to fish and do whatever boys do next to a beautiful river. That night we would gather around an oversized bonfire for marshmallow roasting and storytelling. Around 2200 hrs our mother would send us to bed. That night was no different.

The next morning when I awoke, I got dressed and looked for my new boots. I found them next to a large chair at the fire pit, not where I had left them. As I began putting them on I discovered that someone had used them to collect peanuts shell discards from the night before. Even as a young boy I was not amused and I demanded to know who was responsible for the deed. Finally my mom told me that Warren had used both my boots for "garbage". I was pissed off and vowed revenge someday, and I actually never forgot it.

This morning it was a Sunday, 0600 hrs. It was years later after the Green river camping trips had long ended. As the briefing ended, Warren began telling the squad that he had spent part of his weekend mowing the lawn at the Mason Temple Fellowship, a club Warren proudly belonged to. He complained a bit about how warm it was getting, and pushing the lawn mower around was hard work.

I asked Warren if he remembered how he had put peanut shells in my boots on the Green River so many years earlier. "Yes" he answered, and then delightfully told the squad of his stunt that would surely piss off the new and young owner of the boots at the time.

Little did Warren know that he just loaded "my gun", so to speak. This summer would be hell for him; I'd make sure of it.

After several weeks the squad rotated to grave yard shift, 1800 hrs to 0600 hrs, 12 hours working graveyards, and usually there was little to do after 0300 hrs. I did not wait. I parked behind the Mason Temple about 0330 hrs; out of sight from the main road, and opened the trunk of my Crown Victoria. I glanced cautiously around and I was sure I was unnoticed. I pulled out a hand held lawn fertilizer and a large bag of fertilizer. I filled the contraption with fertilizer and began making my rounds. I remembered, smiling to myself of the promise I had made so many years before, revenge!

Warren was right about one thing, the lawn was big and it took me almost twenty minutes the first time I fertilized it. I had to make many trips to the bag of fertilizer in the trunk of my car to refill the machine. I would have been easily spotted but no one ever noticed. From then on through the summer I would always fertilize the Mason Temple lawn on the first night of our night shift.

August had rolled into September and the Western Washington Fair was at our doorstep. Although Warren had transferred back to a dayshift squad I had remained with the graveyard crew, and continued to fertilize the Mason's lawn.

It had been a couple of months since I had sat through a briefing with Warren and today I was working overtime at the fair. Warren was also one of the overtime officers and took his place across from me at the briefing table. The sergeant had yet to speak, so bullshit was being spoken fluently among the officers. I decided that now would be the moment to spring my trap.

"So Warren, are you still mowing the Temple lawn?" I asked.

"Yeah, I must say that I have never seen that lawn grow like it has this year. I can mow it one day and then two days later it is ready for a mowing. I think this maybe will be the last year I will be doing this; too old for that kind of labor," he whined.

I grinned, he was mine for the cleaning and payback would be slowly dealt out.

"So Warren, you been keeping it fertilized?" I asked, grinning of course.

"No way, the last thing that lawn needs is fertilizing, I never seen anything grow like it in my life," he questioningly stated.

"Is it still green?" I asked.

"That's the other odd thing; it is rich green, never seems to give up growing or looking good!" he continued to whine.

I had turned on a water hose and let it water the lawn the best I could the entire time that I had been fertilizing it.

"Damn mystery, isn't it Warren?" I mused.

Warren looked at me, he knew something was up. For once he was quiet, looking at me. Good time to put him out of his misery.

"Well, you old fart. Do you remember those new boots of mine you gleefully filled with peanut shells and garbage many years ago along the Green River?"

Warren looked at me sternly, "Yeah, what you been up to?"

I grinned like a Cheshire cat and spoke as though all my words had a pointy end. I leaned forward, squads' attention fully on my next words and said, "all summer on the first day of my four night work shift I had parked my car behind the Temple and used a hand held fertilizer to fertilize and water that damn lawn, I wanted you to work your ass off."

The remainder of the squad of cops sitting around the table erupted in laughter. Warren sat, a blank expression, and then he slowly smiled and laughed, shaking his head as he did.

"Well done Mr. Gill, well done," Warren said.

I took Warren to dinner that evening. After all, I had and still do have immense respect for him.

Arriving, the guy on the ground was stunned and a mess. I quickly radioed for fire and aid to be dispatched to my location. Dispatched asked what this was in reference to so I simply say "blunt force trauma to the head from a bowling ball." Radio was silent then dispatch asked me to repeat and I did, "blunt force trauma to the head from a bowling ball." "Received," was their response.

Chapter 29

First Episode of Jackass

I had noticed an upturn in activity in the rear parking lot of Puyallup's one and only bowling alley. Car prowls and fighting mostly; but things were slow tonight and so I found a place where I could watch the parking lot but not be seen.

I'd been there about 25 minutes and saw very little activity when two young men in their early to mid twenties, come out of the back of the bowling alley. When they got some distance from the doors and off in the back corner of the parking lot one of them removed from under his coat a bowling ball. Really, a bowling ball he had stolen from inside the bowling alley?

Both men looked closer at the ball then the one without the ball backed up. The one with the ball elevated it far above his head then with a violent force threw the ball onto the asphalt. He quickly inspected it as did his friend. I could see them pointing to the ball, looking for damage. The man with the ball again raised it high above his head and again slammed it into the asphalt. The ball was once again inspected. The other man, slightly bigger than his friend, decided to give it a try and took the ball; he too raised it high above his head and slammed it into the asphalt and the ball was re-inspected. They appeared disappointed.

The smaller guy took the ball and ran across the lot and slammed it into the asphalt, guessing his speed would help break it but same results; no damage. They stood there; the big guy had a foot on the ball as they talked. Clearly they were trying to break it but frustration had set in and now they pondered their thoughts as to what to do next. I suppose I could ask if they had stolen the ball but it was killing me as to what they were going to do next; so I watched. They both lit cigarettes and as they smoked and talked the tall man tilted his head back to blow out smoke, and it was suddenly like a light of the best idea entered his brain. The entire area out back and to the West side of the bowling alley is a business that creates cement pipes, manholes, and all sorts of cement fittings used in construction of roads and sewers.

This guy had noticed a cement pipe, standing on end that was about eight feet across and 16 feet high. The pipe was perched next to the parking lot and no cars around it.

Maybe they were thinking the asphalt flexed too much on impact and cement don't flex. I'm frankly at a loss as to what this guy was thinking.

The tall guy picked up the bowling ball, raised it high above his head, and sped off. He was running flat out and when he got within six feet of the cement pipe he threw the ball at the pipe. Direct hit, dead center, and it bounced directly back and smashed into his face. The last thing to hit the asphalt was the guy's feet; the first thing was the back of his head. His buddy ran up to him and just stood there looking. The guy on the ground didn't move. I jumped onto my bicycle and pedaled over to investigate.

Arriving, the guy on the ground was stunned and a mess. I quickly radioed for fire and aid to be dispatched to my location. Dispatched asked what this was in reference to so I simply say "blunt force trauma to the head from a bowling ball." Radio was silent then dispatch asked me to repeat and I did, "blunt force trauma to the head from a bowling ball." "Received," was their response.

I knelt down next to the guy and could see he was breathing; but he was missing most of his teeth clearly a broken jaw and his nose was, simply put, flat. I noticed blood oozing from the impact of the back of his head on the asphalt. Some of his teeth were sticking out of his shredded lips and many lay in pieces on the asphalt. I glanced at the ball, not broken.

"What were you guys trying to do?" I asked.

"Ed was mad at his ball and decided to break it."

"Did he have a bad game or something?" I asked.

"Yeah, guess you could say that."

"Do you think the level of intoxication is why his game was bad and his face is basically now gone?" I pressed on. He didn't answer.

I checked on Ed's breathing and he was fine and he was beginning to show signs of coming around. Ed did mention something about stupid but he was tough to understand. Fire department arrived and began providing aid. Soon an ambulance arrived and Ed was taken to Good Samaritan Hospital for care.

A fireman wandered over to me and asked how the guy got hurt. I told him what I had seen and I thought he was going to pee himself laughing.

"You're kidding," he said, getting his composure back.

"Nope, it was quite the show," I responded. The fireman wandered back to his rig still laughing.

I entered the bowling alley and found the manager, Tony. I asked him if the two guys we were out in the rear parking lot are known to him. Tony said their names were Don and Ed. Tony described them as dumbasses. I agreed.

"That ball they had in the back lot, is it Ed's?" I asked.

"Yes, he gets them from garage sales thinking his game will get better then gets pissed off when his game doesn't improve."

We made some more small talk and I left.

As I threw a leg over my bicycle seat and strapped down my helmet I spotted the bowling ball one more time. It sat lonely in the far corner of the lot, barely a scratch on it.

Cops in Schools

Cop life is not all cop-related work. Sometimes we get to do things that are really fun. Two of my funnest times happened in schools: one was when I was invited to give a talk; the other one was a training scenario. As you read the next chapters, you will see why it was most fun.

I heard a collective moan from the crowd. I continued on talking of positive mental attitude; seeing success and never thinking of failure. Pretty standard thought process plus, currently, teasing them for the answers they were seeking. I moved the story to Hawaii and what it was like to acclimatize yourself, all the while recognizing the world champions training next to you. The students almost glared at me but remained polite, but I knew I was pushing their limits.

Chapter 30

Shoot
Don't Shoot

It was October 6th, 1984. I stood in knee deep water in "dig me beach" on the Kona Coast in Kona Hawaii. I was shoulder to shoulder with some of the best athletes in the world and it was Ironman Day. The world's best and fastest athletes would be discovered, personnel battles fought, personal goals accomplished and hearts broken; thus is the world of athletic competition.

I had 27 sponsors for the race, all police departments from the Pacific Northwest. When they learned that a cop was going to compete for and in a world championship they wanted to be part of it. They had sent money to fund the effort and for that I'd wear a light jacket proudly displaying their department patch.

It had been a long journey to get the honor to stand on this beach and wage battle with the world's best. The journey had not been traveled alone however; such training involves family and co-workers support and I would always be grateful for that.

During the training people took notice. Soon there was a wave of interest and I was being watched. If I failed it would just be another great attempt but to simply finish would be one of greatness and well giving back to the community would be a demand.

The race day came and went. I finished easily but the price had been physically high; but now was the time to give back to the community and the telephone was ringing off the hook.

An article was printed in local newspapers, interviews on local radio station and yes, an article of the event soon appeared on a religious magazine called Guidepost.

Then schools began to call. "Can you find time to come and speak to my class about your journey and the race?" I couldn't turn them down and arrangements were made. I knew that simply talking about the race and training would be a good story but since 27 police departments backed me with money from their coffers, they now needed to be rewarded; so I came up with a shoot, don't shoot true story of an incident that I had survived. Now the students would hear from the Ironman and policeman, and be put in the shoes of a street cop working alone.

My first presentation was at a high school; it was actually two classes of students jammed into a room to hear me speak. I had arrived early between classes, met the teacher or teachers in some cases, then I moved to a chalk board at the front of the class room and drew out an apartment complex of four separate two story buildings with a court yard in the middle; and the four buildings to each side of the court yard, a square configuration of buildings. I made note to one special apartment on the bottom floor and its corner location to the front of the street. I then pulled down a filming screen to cover up my art work and waited for the arrival of the students. This would be fun.

As the students shuffled into the classroom, some stopped to talk to others and gave me a wary eye as they moved to an open seat; the late ones had to just stand and listen. After introductions I told them they would hear two stories today: one of the Ironman and another would involve them; they would be the officer and it would be up to them to make the decisions. I gave it a name, "shoot, don't shoot".

I started with the Ironman story and how I had qualified: some on my high school sports background; and then later a basic grassroots effort to get back into shape for a run at the world spectacle of swim, bike, and run.

"Now, you're the cop, its 0130 hrs in the morning and you're working alone, you get a call" I spoke. I told them it was 0130 hrs and the call was from a frantic woman in an apartment. "He just broke in and he's got a knife and fighting with my boyfriend" she screamed. The dispatcher relayed this information to "you", as I pointed to the class, and then the dispatcher said something else, "hurry, I can hear the fighting in the background over the phone, sounds bad," I replied "en route."

"How do you respond?" I asked the class, "0130 hrs, lights and siren?" I continued, and then I stopped, and started talking about the Ironman.

This had the desired effect; you could see it in their young faces that had become intense with the thought of going to such a violent call, alone. They were disappointed that I had stopped at a critical part of the story, yearning for more information.

I explained my training for the great race and regiment that I put myself thru on a daily basis. I saw a little reaction when I told them of the amount of miles I ran and bicycled every week, and a little more when they heard how far I would swim in the mornings. Then I really drove them into the ground; I spoke of my diet. They were a-swim in boredom.

I hesitated briefly then turned to the movie screen I had pulled down earlier to cover the drawings on the chalk board and slowly raised it. "Let's see hands of those of you that would be blaring your siren and lights at 0130 hrs going to this call," I asked of the crowd. I noticed lots of hesitation among them; fleeting glances, some fired their hands into the air, and others did not. It was about 50-50 by the time I finished egging out the answer.

I pointed to one of the hand raisers, "officer why were your lights and siren on considering the hour?" I quizzed along like a courtroom attorney.

"I needed to get there quick; people in danger" was her reply.

"Good answer, and you, young man, why did you choose not to turn on your lights and siren?" I asked.

"Considering the hour, traffic would be light and I wouldn't wake people up" he replied.

"Also good answer and both of you made valid points" I said. "I turned on my lights and siren, not because of traffic, didn't much care who I woke up; but I wanted the victim and more importantly the suspect to hear me coming. Victim might fight harder knowing help was almost there and the suspect, he is armed with a knife and I'm bringing a gun; so he definitely does want to meet me and hopefully he will leave," I stated.

"What happened when you got there?" a light airy voice from the other side of the room spoke up. I made a quick glance at her, then smiled and slowly turned away.

"Did I mention while training I ate no less than 12 pieces of fruit daily and carried a plastic bag full of fruit everywhere I went?" I stated.

I heard a collective moan from the crowd. I continued on talking of positive mental attitude; seeing success and never thinking of failure. Pretty standard thought process plus, currently, teasing them for the answers they were seeking. I moved the story to Hawaii and what it was like to acclimatize yourself, all the while recognizing the world champions training next to you. The students almost glared at me but remained polite, but I knew I was pushing their limits.

"When I arrived," I hesitated wanting them to wonder if I was still talking about arriving in Hawaii or the apartment, "the front door was open and a lady and man appeared in front of me. The man was covered with blood but not from any stab wounds, just head lacerations and he refused medical aid and said he would get himself fixed up. The two began to tell me what had happened. The suspect was known to them. It was the lady's old boyfriend and long since gone, she thought. Earlier that night he had shown up at the front door hoping to reconcile the relationship but learned of her new boyfriend. He had left the apartment upset and mad but showed no signs of violence. After going to bed they were awakened by the sounds of glass breaking in the kitchen and discovered "Author" had returned, smelled of liquor and had a large hunting knife. Very few words were spoken and suddenly Author went after the new boyfriend and tried to stab him. The boyfriend was able to grab the hand and arm that Author held the knife with, and the lady called the police. When Author heard the sirens he broke free, slashed one more time at the boyfriend, and jumped out the kitchen window and disappeared into the night. I took all needed info for a police report and then helped secure the kitchen window to keep Author out. I was afraid Author would return and assured the couple that I would park a couple blocks away, hidden and would not leave them till morning arrived. I made much fanfare as I said my goodbyes and even remarked, "I don't think he will be back" and then I left speeding away. If he were watching he might think he was safe and he would be bold enough to try again. I had no idea how bold he would be," I said to the class and slowly with a pause turned away from them.

I spoke as I turned back to face the students and said "I'll never forget it, helicopters flying above, TV cameras everywhere, ABC's Wide World of Sports doing spot interviews of the athletes prior to the start of the race." More groans from the students, but they knew I would finish the story, but their impatience was bubbling over. "There were about 1100 contestants from all over the world. I put faces to the names I had until then only read about in Sports Illustrated and Triathlete magazines that I consumed at an alarming rate. Dave Scott, winner of six Ironman races and current world record holder was now on the beach, the same one where I too stood."

I was at the door to the "meat" of the stories and the kids were showing interest in both by now.

"There was a silence before the cannon roared to life that sent all 1100 athletes plunging in the Pacific Ocean for 2.4 miles of swimming. I was a fast swimmer and soon I could not feel anyone climbing up my back and my stroke slowed. I wasn't leading, far from it, but nearer to the front than I thought I would be."

I continued telling the story, of my arrival back at the beach and how very pleased I was with my placement, top 100 and was moving to the 112 mile bicycle race, my strongest discipline, across lava flats climbing to the top of Mount Hawi. At the top of Mount Hawi we U turned and started the 56 mile journey back to where the marathon would start.

"I don't remember much about the ride back, it was hot and at one time on the downhill I glanced at my small speedometer and notice 66 mph displayed. There was a cliff and the beautiful blue Pacific Ocean to my right and walls of lava rock to my left; falling would be fatal," I remarked.

I was partially seated on the corner of the teacher's desk and stood and turned towards the door then stopped; as if to signal to the students, a changeup was coming.

"I remember sitting in my patrol car, staring into the dark, window rolled down and engine off; I had a feeling Author would come back," snapping their attention from one story to the other. I noticed several sit up and lean towards me, a sure sign they had been waiting for this moment.

"The radio came to life and the dispatcher informed me that Author had in fact returned," I continued. "He just tried to open the sliding door but the clank it made had gotten the occupants' attention and they were up barricading themselves in their bedroom. So I said to myself, 'Good, that will give me time to sneak into the complex'." I explained to the students that I had parked myself at the far end of the complex and I was now on foot quickly approaching Author.

"Let me see a sign of hands here. Who among you would have your gun out of the holster and in hand at this point?" I asked. A sea of hands went into the air but a few remained at their sides choosing not to have a gun out. I really wanted to ask them why but also did not want them to be embarrassed. "Good choice," I responded.

I went to my drawing on the chalk board and referred to it. I showed them my path: moving north along the front of the apartments and passing the front of the victim's apartment, then rounded the North corner of the complex as I slowly made my move to the rear of the victim's apartment, and Author.

"Let's see hands, how many of you have your gun out of your holster now?" I asked. It was unanimous, even one of the teachers had her hand high in the air. "Good choice," I remarked.

"I was almost to the back of the apartment and I stopped. I listen, nothing, not a sound."

"Ok officers, think about your next move, what are you going to do?" asking for hands.

A light airy voice from the back of the room said "I don't want to go around the corner," and the room erupted in laughter.

I told the girl "perfect comment and even better timing, but what do "you" do?" I looked at the entire class when I challenged them.

"Just go, run around the corner," he said.

"Okay, any other ideas?" I asked.

"I think I would peek around the corner, try to see him," another said.

"Here's what I did. I moved away from the wall, about five feet; I was afraid Author might be doing the same thing I was and if he was, I'd be in range of his knife." I pointed to the chalk board explaining my movements. "When I got to this point I did step around the corner exposing myself to the backyard, and Author. Author was also off the wall but twenty feet from me at the edge of the light from the parking lot. I didn't see a knife but had enough time to watch him raise a bow with loaded arrow, the hunting tipped type meant for killing. As the bow came up, the arrow was drawn back and before I could bring my firearm up to fire, the arrow was on its way. I only had time to duck."

The class and teachers were now riveted. "What now?" I asked.

Many said "shoot him."

"A show of hands, how many are shooting this guy?" A flurry of hands flew into the air, trap set and they jumped into it. "Why?" pointing to one of the students.

"He just tried to kill me," he claimed. Many agreed with him. I paused and took a look out the windows.

"As I began the marathon my legs felt like noodles," I said with a fiendish grin. I got booed.

"Come on tell us what happened" was pretty much the chant of the students. One teacher even showed signs of frustration.

I immediately jumped into their heads. "You know it, your wife, husband, father, mother, son, daughter and all your friends. They had read about it in the newspapers, watched it play out on the news, your name, your picture, the cop that killed an un-armed man," springing my trap.

You could have heard a mouse fart; it was so quiet. I got lots of confusing looks with questions demanding answers. "No way, he tried to kill you," one of them said.

Many agreed with him. I again stood from my perch on the teacher's desk; I reached down and grabbed a piece of notebook paper and rolled it up length wise. I held it in my left hand and told the kids "this is my bow." I then put the bow to my side and said "this is how Author looked after he shot at me, just a bow, not armed. Let's see a show of hands, how many of you are still going to shoot him?" I asked.

Not one hand, nothing, again silence. Finally a girl asked "how did it end?"

"I chased Author on foot till he left the apartment complex. I called for backup and if you shoot at a cop, other cops, many cops, will come. Author was tracked down by a tracking dog and spent many years in prison. The arrow had narrowly missed my right ear, good thing I ducked. The arrow had struck a tree behind me at eye level" I said filling in most of their questions. Shortly after this had occurred, the victims moved out of the apartment," I concluded my story.

The room was abuzz and time had almost run out when a male, clearly an athlete at the back of the room asked "and the race, how did you do?" "Six miles into the marathon I fell apart. I hadn't eaten enough and became dizzy. I had severe sun burns to my back and at the 20 mile mark my feet began to bleed. I slipped from 75th to 300 something but ran to the finish line" I replied, answering his questions. The buzzer announcing end of class went off and with a quick flurry of claps the kids left. Many nodded to me as they left, their approval of time well spent.

"You're quite the entertaining raconteur," the teacher said.

"It's easy when it's true," I responded.

"Trapping those kids is easy but you want to know the scary part?" I asked her.

"What?" she asked.

"The prosecutor asked me why I hadn't shot Author," I said. "And when I reminded him that Author was an unarmed man that would have made it an unjustifiable homicide, his response was, "wow, I didn't think about it like that.""

"So, did you think about it at the time?" she asked.

"No, I was just trying to get out of the way of the damn arrow; but after I realized he had missed, we just stood there, in the middle of the night staring at each other for a couple seconds. Him disbelieving he had missed me, and I disbelieving he had shot at me, and then it turned into a short track meet," I said.

I continued to be invited to speak at different schools, different ages, and even a couple of running clubs, but my favorite was the schools. The kids were riveted and drawn so deeply into the stories. After about a year the fever of my adventure wore off and someone else would be put into the spot light.

I did the Ironman again in 1987; my wife did it in 1988 and we both retired from racing soon thereafter. We told no one of our 1987 and 1988 campaigns except our families; we didn't want the attention.

Chapter 31

A.A.R.P.

I heard a sonar ping followed shortly by another one, a distinctive sound that only means one thing, my phone's ring tone; I was getting a call. Checking, caller ID says Kevin. It was his work phone so it was official and probably needed to ask a question of me, the now retired wily veteran sergeant. No such luck!

"Hey what you doing on the 14th and 15th of July?" he asked.

"What, is this a trick question or something? I'm retired, I do what I damn well please. What you want?" I fired off.

"I'm looking for an active shooter for a training scenario, you game?" he asked.

"If I get to shoot you, Pig, Rob, and a few other well deserving assholes then yes, I'm game," I said back.

"Good, I'll call couple days before those training date and give you the details, still making this up as I go," he mentioned.

"Ok, let me know," and our conversation ended.

Wonder what he is up to, I thought. He used to be a part of the metro SWAT team but had taken a break following his promotion to my spot as sergeant. I wondered if he had gotten back on the team and now they need a living, breathing target to shoot at and they had decided I'd be a good choice.

Back in the old days when we trained we pointed fingers or toy guns at each other to simulate shooting, but these day you actually used a firearm and shoot it out. The pistols looked like Glocks and the rifle looked like AR15s. Weapons had real parts from real Glocks and ARs but the trigger housing, barrels, and magazines were all modified to accept a 9 mm bullet that was tipped with colored wax wrapped in clear plastic and hurt like hell when it hit you anywhere, clothed or not. As the bullet impacts your skin, the plastic covering shatters and considering the speed at which it travels, cuts you. It's fun to dish it out and just the opposite if on the receiving end. Covering yourself with clothing sometimes helps but you still have a bump to rub when it's all over. The colored wax indicates where you got hit and who hit you, everyone uses a different color so when all is said and done, the shooter owns the mark; be it good or bad.

Several weeks had passed by when Kevin called again.

"Ok, here's the deal. This is going to be held at the Puyallup High School. The scenario will be a guy pissed off with his girlfriend, a student at the school. He shows up with a friend and both are armed and have taken hostages. You will be in room 305 holding hostages; your partner will be wandering the halls shooting people and the cops that show up," Kevin said.

"Who's my partner in crime?" I asked.

"Fritz," Kevin responded.

"Keeping this a family affair?" I asked, as Fritz is yet another nephew. "This is going to be the perfect shit storm, a fireman and a retired sergeant going to take on Puyallup P.D. and others, this is going to hurt," I bitched.

"You don't have to do this," Kevin said.

"You kidding? I'm curiously aroused by the thought of shooting it out with some of them assholes, I just hope all the right ones show," firing back.

"You get any death threats yet?" Kev asked.

"What you talking about?" I asked.

"The department found out that you were going to play shooter and couple of the smartasses thought it would be funny to call and threaten you," he explained.

"Well, not yet," I responded laughing.

Our conversation soon concluded and I began to collect some items I might need, like body armor, gloves, and eye protection. I was excited to see old friends and enemies and watch the kids that had followed me into my profession conduct business.

I arrived in the parking lot designated for participants and cops at 0600 hrs as instructed. To get onto the school property you and anything you have with you must be searched by correction officers for scene safety. Neither live ammo nor real weapons can be brought into the area with the exception of security personnel.

Soon I was chatting it up with old co-workers; some of those I never had gotten along with while working now seemed like old friends. Pig, Rob, and the remainder of the SIU team would be there the next day and they would be bringing an ass kicking with my name on it.

"Pistol or rifle, sergeant?" he asked.

"Well you need a pistol to fight with till you get to your rifle, so one of each will do the trick I believe," I responded.

"Don't know if we have enough for both," he responded.

"Skip it," Chance said, "He can use my personal stuff, pistol and rifle." Chance was a SWAT cop and would act as a "controller/instructor" today and thus not is in the fight. Besides, this was entry level stuff; Chance is far beyond that and was squad leader with metro SWAT. Chance was one of their big dogs. Before police work Chance was a member of Special Forces and part of the elite Delta force. During a training mission he and three other Delta force members were knocked from the side of a Boeing 747 during training at taking back an airplane that's under control of terrorists.

"At least I'll know it will be taken care of by someone that knows how the hell to use it," Chance said.

"Thanks Chance, much appreciated."

Small talk ensued and we agreed to talk more later. Then I spotted "the Terrier" across the parking lot. He too was eyeballing me and we began walking slowly towards each other as though we were gunfighters suddenly thrown into an itching showdown. Terrier was a shorter man but built like a fireplug. He was an Army Ranger before becoming a cop and had been and still is a member of metro SWAT. If you look up the word tough in Webster's dictionary there would be a picture of Terrier. He was strong and disciplined and took his work seriously and oh yeah, he has 16 kids, mostly adopted; but his house is a crazy place and how he and his wife don't go insane is beyond me.

Terrier and I have an odd relationship. All we do is insult each other, nothing more, strictly insults. It had been two years since I last seen him. Nothing changed, after shaking hands and a man hug the insults began. He targeted my age, and I his height.

Fritz finally showed up, an hour late. So fireman like, claiming that just prior to leaving he got a better offer from his wife, thus he was late. Cops are on time and if you're not it would be pointed out. Fritz didn't give a rat's ass and argued with all of them. Firemen and cops don't get along. Fritz would be a favorite target for the next two days. He had lots of desirable targets available and was a capable gun fighter. The best targets would be other family members. 'Men behaving badly' was the only rule and we had no problem shooting the crap out of each other.

At about 0800 Kevin came and got Fritz and I for a tour of the building and would lay out the scenario so we would understand our roles. The building inside was shaped like a large horseshoe with four stairwells and long halls connecting them. This would be Fritz's playground and he clearly was salivating over the prospects. On the first floor the entry doors led you into a large open room, 120 feet by 120 feet filled with lunch tables and tall ceilings. The walls were covered with championship banners from various sports the school participate in. Some of the banners had dated back to the 1950s. At one end of the room was a large smoke-making machine.

I noticed a pudgy sergeant dressed in khaki shorts, polo shirt, and white socks pulled geekishly high, finished off with white tennis shoes. Odd, he was a road sergeant and should be going through this training, but instead operating the smoke machine dressed as a European tourist. However, there was always tomorrow. I would make special effort to inflict some pain on him. The following day he showed up dressed exactly the same except he had a different polo shirt on. He operated a god damn smoke machine as his men went into battle!

When the machine was turned on, one could not see across the room. Fritz was definitely drooling. This is a run and gun dream, and Fritz would expose any and all weaknesses officers presented, and there would be many mistakes made.

We made our way to the third floor and room 305. One way in, one way out, no windows, basic kill box, mine. I would have 17 hostages in the room with me and a couple of controllers for review/teaching of the officers that came into the room. Fritz would have 20 plus hostages in the lunch room when the shooting would begin.

We returned outside to the gathering of officers and volunteers. There would be a short training session for officers to show them how to move about a large building looking to engage a mobile shooter and how to enter a room into an "L" shaped ambush and defeat a single shooter in a room full of hostages. That left time to burn for Fritz and I, and bullshit began. Fishing, kids, and anything else we wanted to talk about. We picked on a few of the volunteers, making them laugh. They were nervous, never been through something like this before. One of the volunteers was Kevin's wife. She was about as strong and independent as they come. Fritz and I agreed that shooting her in the butt would be a great idea and bounty of forty bucks was soon accumulated. When she caught us talking and laughing while looking at her, she sensed something was up. She confronted us.

"You two assholes, if either of you shoot me I'll kick the crap out of you in front of all your buddies."

She weighs maybe 110 pounds but somehow I actually believed she would beat the crap out of us. We continued to threaten her and she finally wandered off bitching and threatening us all the while.

"Crap. I think she will do it. Let's check with Kevin, see what he says before we do her. Get his thoughts," I said.

Finding Kevin, we ran our plan past him.

"Go for it, don't let fear and common sense get in your way," he said as he walked off with yet another problem to solve.

"Green light," I mentioned to Fritz.

"Yeah, I'm shooting her," he boasted.

"Yeah me too," I replied, talking tough and lying.

As it turned out neither one of us even dared shoot her, the price was too risky. I grabbed four boxes containing 50 rounds of shells in each. My color would be red, so anything hit with red I'd own. The cops would be shooting green, all green. I loaded up two magazines with 15 rounds each for the pistol and 25 rounds in the AR magazines, which I had two. The remainder of the ammo would be taken into the classroom for reloading between entries.

It was going to be a hot day in the Pacific Northwest so I wore tennis shoes, camo pants, and a sleeveless shirt covered by body armor. Most of the hits I would suffer would be center mass, my body armor would prevent me from even noticing the hits. I topped it off with a face shield, opting out of a helmet and face shield combo because of the heat of the day. Probably a mistake, and later I proved it.

As I entered the school I met my 17 volunteers, seated at various tables. They were a mixed bag of sex and races; some women, some students, and a couple older guys. I briefed them of my background and then of our scenario. Do any of you want to volunteer to be shot? Two of the high school kids threw their hands into the air and then a small older female simply said "sure".

"Does it hurt?" a female student asked.

"A little," I replied "but remember just being in that room gives you a good chance of getting hit. If you really want to up your odds of getting hit, stand next to me, almost guarantee it," I said laughing.

I led the yakkity bunch to the stairway and they followed me to room 305. They all found a place to sit.

"When the cops come through the door, better yet when you know they're outside the door crawl onto the floor. You will lessen your chances of getting hit," I instructed them.

We had some time to burn so the volunteers spent most of it talking. I spent it trying to make the room more difficult to move and shoot for the officers. I wanted a good training scenario for them.

Then the loud speaker barked to life, "We are about ready to start our first set, everyone to their positions."

By this time a handler/instructor from metro SWAT had found room 305. Young, tall, sharp kid, remembered him from my SWAT days but damned if I could not remember his name now. He had a police radio and I could monitor the officer's movements in the building, this would be a valuable assist.

His radio jumped to life, "shots fired at the high school," and then she said it again.

Numerous officers acknowledged the call and are en-route. Then the dispatcher said "there are reports of two suspects shooting and they have taken hostages."

By this time I began hearing voices of the officers saying they have "arrived" and was making entry into the building.

Then many voices came over the radio, some calm, some shouting and I could hear the rapid fire of weapons in the background. Fritz was doing his thing, raising hell. Fritz was running and gunning, and by the confusion over the radio he was completely confusing them. Reports he was here, no there, and where? Within a few minutes a radio report was put out, the shooter was down and in custody. Then radio reports that teams were heading to the second and third floor. We waited, and didn't have to wait long.

I grabbed one of the young men that wanted to be shot.

"Are you sure?" I quizzed him and he agreed.

I put the lad in the hall outside my door, had him kneel and interlock his hands to the top of his head. I wanted to see if the officers had been paying attention to training; if they stopped I could hold them off and try something clever like giving them three more hostages then I'd offer four and I would unload and drop my weapons and leave as the fourth hostage. I knew it wouldn't work because they knew me on sight, but it would give them a thought of the possibilities.

I could see officers tactically moving towards the closed fire doors. As the doors began to open I told them very loudly if they came through the doors the kid kneeling in front of them would be shot.

This had absolutely no effect. They came through the doors. I shot the kid and he did his best Oscar acting death, rather dramatic to say the least. I yanked my door shut and raced to the desk near the back of the classroom where ammo loaded magazines awaited.

"Everyone get down, they're not stopping," I ordered.

I quickly turned and faced the door. I brought my rifle up and waited. I could faintly hear them; they were stacking, preparing for the gun battle to start when the door cracked open.

The door did begin to open, slowly at first but it swung wildly open as I began shooting. As fast and as furious as I could, I squeezed off the red rounds. The first officer through was taking a terrible beating at the end of my rifle, he was moving left and forward. The second officer also met a horizontal rain of fire and he moved to the right. Officers 3, 4 and 5 were quickly into the room and they were finding their mark. Green round struck me all over, mostly around my weapon, hands, and of course body armor. There were a few that strayed, and those little bastards hurt when striking your forearms, legs, and wherever else there is meaty flesh.

It was over in seconds; my magazine emptied so I just fell to the floor to be pounced on. I'm sure they enjoyed this part.

I yelled "I'm an A.A.R.P. member," and to be nice.

At the end of the excitement there is usually an exchange of smartass remarks, this time would be no different.

"What's with the yelling A.A.R.P. while getting your ass kicked?" Pete asked.

"I'm an old guy, be nice," I replied.

It made for a good laugh and soon they were out of the room and awaiting their critic, the instructor. The instructor walked them through what they had done right, wrong, and offered different tactics to accomplish the mission. I checked myself and found a couple of bloody red impacts to my left forearm. I hadn't felt them hit but they clearly made themselves known to me now. The weapon had taken a few hits as did the body armor. This group had done a pretty good job; they had made good with the shots they took.

The remainder of the day followed the same path and by the end of the afternoon I had earned a few more bloody imprints on my shoulders and arm. The AR was covered in thick green wax. I was already thinking about the next day and my guys, SIU.

Special Investigation Unit: we bought and sold dope, bought stolen cars, bought anything illegal, and had even set up a fake store front as a pawn/chop shop. We worked many hours, and anything difficult. The people in the unit were the best on the department, all high rollers. They would no doubt enjoy bringing me pain.

There was no way in hell I was bringing my retired ass back into town the next day at 0600 hrs. *I'm retired,* I reminded myself; 0730 hrs or 0800 hrs is the best they're going to get. I arrived at 0815 hrs. Fritz arrived even later than that and didn't much give a damn. We compared wounds. We were a match, about the same. Even though he wore two long sleeve shirts, his arm wounds looked just like mine, he soon peeled down to a short sleeve T-shirt giving up on any protection other than the body armor.

I made my way to room 305 and there found my 17 hostages. After small talk we heard the announcement that would start the training in motion. I prepared. I slid a magazine into the AR and chambered the first round. I removed the magazine and replaced the round that now was chambered in the rifle. I wasn't about to go into this fight short even one bullet. The same pattern was followed with the Glock but this time I placed the Glock under the desk on a box. I had a plan. I knew they would come hard and fast throwing everything they had at me. They would expect it would be over quickly. They were correct; it would be and I'd go down when my AR emptied, but being true to SIU I would then grab the hidden Glock handgun and simply reappear and hopefully catch them clearing their weapons or reloading, not paying attention to me. I have a fully loaded Glock and would be within five feet of my group and I'd wreak damage.

Soon I heard over the police radio that shots had been fired at the high school and officers were responding. Then I heard they had arrived and were entering the building. Then nothing, not a peep.

"One down in custody," I heard over the radio from a voice I knew, Pig.

Are you kidding me, less than 30 seconds and they got Fritz?

"Puyallup, we are moving to the third floor" over the radio.

"What about the second floor?" I thought to myself.

Okay, now I got it figured out. They knew what room I was in, probably had studied the floor plans and knew exactly where I was, they were coming for me, that's all they gave a damn about. This was going to be wild and I would not disappoint them.

Within moments I could hear them and see faint boot shadows under the door. They were usually cat like but they are probably arguing over who got to go first through the door; bunch of assholes I thought to myself. The door didn't hesitate but wildly swung open. I was catching round after round. I returned fire as fast as I could pull the trigger and I was finding my mark, trying to spread the love so to speak. I think I felt every round hit me; even the windshield of my mask was covered in paint. My rifle emptied and I dropped below the desk and grabbed the hidden Glock. I hesitated one second then exploded back up and caught one of them in a reload and made him pay for his mistake. Rob however had not been fooled and began drilling me. We were practically muzzle to muzzle, shooting when the bullets stopped. Everyone was empty, everyone was laughing. I was covered in green paint, got the shit shot outta me. They too wore my paint but nothing like me.

The routine was replayed one more time only this time they had to check the second floor before they got to me. The second time around ended pretty much as the first; I got my ass kicked. We moved back outside and I found Fritz.

"Who is the big guy with all the tats?" Fritz asked.

"He is Big Kelly, an ex college football player; tough guy, why he hurt you?" I said, in a "poor baby" manner.

"Well, after I fell down and was supposedly dead he calmly walked up to me and pumped about 10 rounds into my ass. I got bullet wounds all over my butt," he complained.

"I told him you were a fireman; he doesn't like firemen," I said it with a menacing grin.

"Those guys had me cornered in no time and shot the crap out of me," Fritz still whining.

"Yep, they used to be my guys, best of the 311th" I told him.

"That big Spaniard over there walked by me as I was laying there and shot me in the top of my head, hurt like hell and then lifted his mask and smiled," Fritz still whining.

"That big Spaniard is my son in law, you know he has no fondness of firemen," I responded.

"I know but damn it I'm family!" Fritz' bitching continued.

I walked around and said my goodbyes to each of them individually. I was very proud of them and the way they conducted themselves. I felt that my family that lived in the area and attended these schools were well protected. I stood back and watched them pack their gear into their rigs, some did it comfortably as I had done so many times, and some ... well ... were more Pig about it, neat and orderly. I missed SIU, missed being their leader, missed being their sergeant, and all the adventures we had, but my time had come and gone. I wandered over to Pig and asked if he wanted some dinner and a beer or two.

"Sure," he answered, "just let me finish putting away my gear."

I just watched him tucking away his gear into well thought out locations inside his now fully marked police car. Pig had recently rotated out of SIU and was now back on patrol sharing his vast experience with kid cops that were working the streets. I envied him.

"Where shall we go?" Pig asked.

"Don't much care, some place quiet so we can talk," I responded.

"I'm going to drop my patrol car off at my house, pick me up; let's do Crockets," Pig stated.

"Works for me," I said and off we went.

We arrived at Crockets and found a spot close to the back door.

"I fought battles in this parking lot," I said.

"So have I," Pig responded.

We entered the restaurant and found a quiet spot that was tactically proper, giving us both views of the doors to the restaurant, a trait we have practiced for years. We ordered up a couple of beers and began talking about the day of training, those that did well and spoke of those that hadn't.

"I think I'll write a chapter in my book about it," I said to Pig.

"Really, what are you going to name it?" Pig asked.

"I think I'll call it A.A.R.P.," with a little grin as I said it.

"A.A.R.P., what kind of name is that: American Association of Retired Persons?" Pig asked.

"No, no my friend, A.A.R.P. today means **A**geing **A**sshole **R**eliving the **P**ast," saying it with the grin of a clever man.

I lifted my glass for a sip of cold beer as I watched Pig laugh.

"Perfect" he said. Pig then leaned forward and spoke quietly, "you remember that train car, the car hauling one, Sumner, the howling grunting people screwing on the top floor and how it mega phoned out of the ends of that damn trailer car?"

"O dark thirty I believe it was," I said laughing.

"How about that idiot that sliced cuts across his abdomen then claimed someone else did it?" Pig said.

"He did it more than once, correct?" I responded.

"Yeah, it was his girlfriend. She was somehow turned on by doing it, they'd get carried away with it and then need medical aid and tell us he was attacked," I continued.

"Yep, weird people for sure," Pig finished.

Our glasses were near empty. Pig then stated "do you remember that guy?" and I stopped him.

"Hold that thought, I'll be right back," I said.

I got up and trotted to the back door of my car. I rummaged around the back seat a bit and located a legal pad and pen. As I returned to the restaurant I was thinking to myself, 'I'm in a chapter writing mood and I had Pig in a drinking mood'. I'd force feed him a few more beers and his walls hiding more of these stories would fall temporarily and a wealth of material would be recorded. I entered, I walked by the bar maid, and asked for two more beers for our table. I was finally going to get Pig to open up, to help me remember the life and times of two small town cops. I slid into the booth, opened the pad, and quickly flipped through pages of notes and found a fresh page.

"As you were saying," I said looking at Pig.

He smiled and leaned forward and with low tone to his voice so not to be heard "Do you remember that guy, the one that ...."

I want to add that AARP is probably one of the finest organizations on the planet and if you are not a member I highly recommend you join.

Glossary of Terms

Adam Henry
Cop lingo for asshole.

AR
Assault Rifle

Banger
Flash bangs that when they explode create bright flash and enormous sound that stuns the suspects or suspect on the receiving end.

CQB
Close Quarters Battle

Hot pop
Police arrests the suspect(s) immediately after they buy or sell dope, cars or whatever.

Reversal or Reverse
Cops selling dope that always ends in a hot pop.

Walk
Suspect walks away and is not arrested after the deal.

414
Crazy person